# NIGERIA'S GOLDEN JUBILEE INDEPENDENCE ANNIVERSARY

## LEADERSHIP LIABILITY

A Clarion Call to Courageous, Compassionate and Wise Leadership

## SELECTED WRITINGS TO COMMEMORATE NIGERIA'S 50th INDEPENDENCE ANNIVERSARY

C. Kingston Ekeke, Ph.D.

Author House, MN, USA

Selected Articles and Essays on Nigeria's Return to Democratic Government (1999-2010)

T0171707

1

AuthorHouse™
1663 Liberty Drive
Bloomington, IN 47403
www.authorhouse.com
Phone: 1-800-839-8640

authorHOUSE®

First published by AuthorHouse    3/29/2011

ISBN: 978-1-4567-3327-8 (sc)
ISBN; 978-1-4567-3328-5 (e)

Library of Congress Control Number: 2011901876

Printed in the United States of America

This book is printed on acid-free paper.

# TABLE OF CONTENTS

# ACKNOWLEDGMENTS

I owe much gratitude to the men and women who battled for our nation's independence from the British rule.

I wish to thank Mr. Chuck Odili, publisher of Nigeriaworld through whom, I have published most of my writings and vision to the world.

I am grateful to the men and women who read my articles and found the courage to write me back to commend the article or disagree with me. Your constructive and objective criticism actually contributed to the success of this publication in book form.

I am forever grateful to my wife and children for their loving patience and their understanding. My unhallowed gratitude also goes to my wife, who finds time out of her busy and hectic schedule to proof read my articles and essays. She is my first critique and I always appreciate her constructive criticism. Although, she is not a professional secretary, she is always willing to proof read my lengthy articles. And to my amazing children, who always give me renewed strength and support, to them, I am eternally grateful.

My gratitude also goes to Adline Fuller Akparanta, a superb cousin, whose gesture of love has impacted my life greatly.

To Doris Glass Achinanya, for her selfless love. I also want to thank Evangelist Edith Chuta for her inspiration and encouragement.

To Christie Nwankwo, for her resourcefulness and support. I cherish each and every one of you dearly.

I am indebted to everyone whom I failed or forgot to mention in the acknowledgments. There are many Nigerians and non-Nigerians alike, who read my articles and write me generous comments and words of encouragement. I share your hopes, pains, anger and frustrations about Nigeria. I am very grateful for your advice, suggestions, ideas and encouragement.

And Finally, I am most thankful to the Heavenly Father, who gave me life, called me, anointed me, and gifted me with such passion for godly leadership, and who inspires me each day through His Word and by the person of the Holy Spirit to do the things I do.

This book reflects my personal thoughts and opinions and is my contribution to the debate on nationhood, development, leadership, and the progress of our nation. I have often stated that we must assume responsibility for our failures to lead wisely and compassionately. Let me add that we must assume responsibility for our destiny as well.

God bless Nigeria.

Rev. Dr. C. Kingston Ekeke<br>
Atlanta, Georgia<br>
October 2010

# FOREWORD

I was deeply humbled when my friend, Rev. Dr. C. Kingston Ekeke, asked me to write the forward of this book. I consider it a great honor and privilege to write the foreword of this collection of inspired writings put together in book form. Leadership Liability – A Call to Courageous, Compassionate, and Wise Leadership is truly a much needed book especially as our nation celebrates her jubilee independence this year.

Leadership liability – A Clarion Call to Courageous, Compassionate and Wise leadership is a collection of Rev. Dr. Ekeke's insightful, inspirational and prophetic essays, articles, and interviews on leadership being published in book form to commemorate Nigeria's Jubilee independence anniversary.

This book is titled "Leadership Liability," because it seeks to explain that true and genuine leadership is a divine duty. Dr. Ekeke writes that leading is a great sacrifice and service to humanity. It is a sacred task and it was originated and designed by God. Seeking to be a leader is an honorable ambition and a noble task. Leading is hard work and our nation is in desperate need for leaders who have the vision, character, courage, capacity, compassion, and wisdom to bring about peaceful solutions to the myriad problems facing the Nigerian people.

Nearly thirty years ago, the eminent scholar and International poet, Prof. Chinua Achebe in his famous treatise: The Trouble with Nigeria, writes, *"The trouble with Nigeria is simply and squarely a failure of leadership."*

Many concerned Nigerians as well as foreign observers have also attributed the pandemic poverty, diseases, corruption, and violence, ethical and moral decadence in our society as a result of bad leadership.

Leadership liability deals with the divine obligations that leaders owe to their people. It is also an inspiration of writings that list several nuggets for leading wisely, morally, courageously and compassionately.

Leadership liability is a call for moral and godly leadership. It teaches the secrets for godly leadership. Dr. Ekeke writes, "The greatest need of this century is developing authentic, courageous, compassionate and wise leaders that truly understand the divine obligations of leadership." Leadership liability lists and explains the responsibility of those elected, appointed or selected to lead and their divine duty and obligation to the people that chose them to lead.

In Leadership liability, Dr. Ekeke passionately addresses the religious, moral, social and leadership challenges impacting not just Nigeria but also its indirect impact on other African and Western nations. Genuine Leadership is the greatest need of our time. It will be perhaps the most important need of the 21$^{st}$ century. God kind of leadership is the only leadership that can lead our societies into a real and genuine change.

I have known Chima Kingston Ekeke since high school, and I have been blessed by his passion, intellect, devotion, and long life cry for compassionate and wise leadership, which is tremendously evident in his writings. Rev. Dr. Ekeke is a remarkable human being. His writings, articles, essays, interviews, and speeches have been a great inspiration for many and especially for me who knows him personally.

I have no doubt that leadership liability will not only be circulated globally, but that it will inspire and enlighten many to rethink the call to lead as a divine duty and enormous obligation. This book is a must read for many who care about our country – Nigeria. The reader will learn the biblical principles and wisdom for godly living and leadership. It is an unusual inspirational, insightful, and prophetic teaching on the subject of leadership. Leadership liability would be a timeless tool in your hand as a leader.

I am eternally grateful for the influence of his writings and the impact of his careful, consistent, faithful and diligent study on the subject of godly leadership. His writings have had tremendous influence in both my personal and professional lives. It is my fervent prayer that the Lord will continue to prosper his writing ministry as he continues to teach and challenge all of us to become better leaders. I pray that this book will draw many people into a close relationship with the Lord. I am truly privileged and deeply honored to be part of this great work. May all those who will read this book be filled with the vision of godly leadership. Amen.

Chief George Nwanguma, Ph.D.
Entrepreneur & Environmentalist
Katy, Texas

# PREFACE

It is a great honor for me to write the preface of Rev. Ekeke's latest book: Leadership Liability – A Clarion Call to Courageous, Compassionate and Wise leadership. As the founder and CEO of Nigeriaworld, I have had the unique opportunity of reading and publishing most of Dr. Ekeke's writings and articles. Rev. Ekeke has a deep passion for godly leadership and leadership liability addresses his heart on that subject.

Leadership Liability is a collection of writings, articles, papers, and speeches that Dr. Ekeke has given over the years put together in book form to commemorate Nigeria's golden jubilee independence anniversary.

In Leadership Liability, Dr. Ekeke argues that the greatest need of this century is not the need for stem cell scientists, more medical doctors, visionary MBA's, brilliant lawyers, caring educationists, technology and computer whiz kids, genuine religious gurus, hard-working farmers, transparent and honest accountants, heroic sport men and women or even charming and sensual entertainers but finding courageous, compassionate and wise leaders that truly understand the divine obligations of leadership. The greatest need of this century is not only finding oil and gas alternative, finding a cure for diseases such as cancer and AIDS but developing pure, true, genuine and authentic leaders. There are no doubt the professionals and careers mentioned above have made significant contribution to our society and continues to make. However, the greatest need of our society, according to Dr. Ekeke is finding courageous and compassionate people who are capable of bringing lasting solution to the myriad of leadership problems facing the peoples of this planet earth.

Africa is undergoing a terrible waste of human potential and therefore in desperate need of competent and visionary individuals to help bring relief and end the sufferings of millions of people. We live in a world, especially in the continent of Africa, where millions of people are faced with wrenching and insurmountable problems. Thousands are decimated each day due to lack of basic needs of livelihood. The plethora of problems facing our world especially the continent of Africa is not just economic, social, moral, environmental, or political issues but lack of courageous, compassionate and wise leaders.

Dr. Ekeke strongly believes that lack of authentic, wise, moral and visionary leadership is the primary cause for poverty and the travails of our nation. Nigeria does not lack men and women with natural abilities to lead; what is lacking is the failure to lead from godly perspective. Most of the leaders who made impact in our society have been those who led wisely, courageously and compassionately.

Dr. Joseph Nanven Garba in his brilliant book: Fractured History, Elite Shifts and Policy Changes in Nigeria, wrote, "Nigeria, to my mind, does not lack real men and women. The ingredients for creating a formidable nation exist. What is lacking is leadership with the political will and the selfless dedication to galvanize the entire nation." Good leaders exist inside and outside the shores of Nigeria. The missing ingredients are the political will, godly courage and selfless dedication, passion and divine strength to galvanize the Nigerian masses.

First, Dr. Ekeke believes that godly courage is one of the sterling ingredients of great leadership. No one can become a great leader without godly courage and divine strength. One of the great examples of biblical leaders with godly courage and divine strength is the biblical account of Israel's leader Joshua and how he faced a daunting task of

12

taking the nomadic troops of Israelites into battle against the fortified cities of Canaan. After the death of the great Jewish leader Moses, Joshua, his protégé was overwhelmed with the enormity of the task of taking more than three million Israelites into the fortified cities of Canaan, a land flowing with milk and honey. God commanded Joshua to be strong and courageous because he will lead the children of Israel into the land of Canaan.

God spoke to Joshua, "Be strong and courageous, because you will lead these people to inherit the land I swore to their forefathers to give them. Be strong and very courageous...Have I not commanded you? Be strong and courageous. Do not be terrified; do not be discouraged, for the LORD your God will be with you wherever you go" (Joshua 1:6, 9).

God promised to give the Israelites victory despite the overwhelming odds against them.

In Deuteronomy 31:7-8, "Moses summoned Joshua and said to him in the presence f all Israel, "Be strong and courageous, for you must go with this people into he land that the LORD swore to their fore-fathers to give them, and you must divide it among them as their inheritance. The LORD himself goes before you and will be with you; he will never leave you nor forsake you. Do not be afraid; do not be discouraged." Then Moses laid his hands on Joshua before all the assembly of Israel and before the High Priest Eleazer and commissioned Joshua as the LORD instructed.

According to Dr. Myles Munroe, "Courage is resistance to and mastery of fear, not the absence of fear." Leaders without this virtue will fail to make fair and right tough decisions" Former Senate President of Nigeria, Ken Nnamani said, "Courage is not absence of fear but to act."

Leaders without courage will fail to make fair and right decisions. Without courage and godly decisions, people will suffer and perish.

Second, Dr. Ekeke writes, that leading other people also requires enormous compassion. Enduring leadership, the kind that makes a positive, long-range difference, is always characterized by compassion. A compassionate leader cares about people. A compassionate leader seeks the greatest good for all people. True leaders must show compassion even when confronted with challenges. Showing compassion sometimes requires breaking the rules, often in ways that people don't understand. In Mark 1:41-42, "filled with compassion, Jesus reached out His hand and touched the leper. In Jesus' time, touching a man with leprosy violated Mosaic Law; according to the law, Jesus would be rendered ceremonially unclean, thus unable to pray at the temple. Jesus' desire to help a poor leper outweighed His obligation to the Law. Compassionate leaders care for those who need their help. A leader can only be effective when the needs of others are met. If anyone wants to be a great leader, he or she must be become a compassionate and servant leader. A leader must be humble and serve with humility, compassion and love. Jesus said, "If you command wisely, you will be obeyed cheerfully (Luke 22:26). If anyone wants to be successful as a leader, he or she must put other people first.

Many people admire a leader who demonstrates these qualities – love, grace, faithfulness, forbearance, and compassion Mahatma Gandhi, Martin Luther King Jr., Mother Teresa and Princess Lady Diana exhibited those virtues that made them exemplary human beings. Compassion is one of the great ingredients of courageous leadership. A leader who exhibits compassion will be loved and admired by millions around the world.

Third, Dr. Ekeke writes, that godly wisdom is an essential ingredient of pure and genuine leadership. King Solomon realized the need for godly wisdom for leadership despite his physical attributes and family heritage when he asked God for wisdom, knowledge and discerning heart to lead the people of Israel (1 Kings 3:7-9; 2 Chronicles 1:10-12. In First Kings 5:12, God gave Solomon wisdom just as he had promised him (In First Kings 5:12). He gave Solomon wisdom and very great insight, and a breath of understanding as measureless as the sand on the seashores. King Solomon's wisdom was greater than the wisdom of all the men of the East, and greater than all the wisdom of Egypt. During his reign as king every nation under the sun came to King Solomon for political, economic and strategic alliances (1 Kings 4:29-34). In the Book of Proverbs, which he authored, he wrote, "Wisdom is the principal thing; therefore get wisdom; and with all thy getting get understanding (Proverbs 4:7)." King Solomon makes it abundantly clear that godly wisdom is a very important ingredient of leadership as well as a key element for godly living. King Solomon applied godly wisdom to the economic and political benefits for his people; even though he failed to apply the same wisdom in his personal life.

Seeking to be a leader is an honorable ambition and a noble task. "If any sets his heart on being an overseer (leader), he desires a noble task (1Timothy 3:1)."However, it requires wisdom, character, integrity, prayer, perseverance, passion, shared vision and strategy in order to lead others. Leadership is a divine and a sacred duty and our society is desperately in need for courageous and strong leaders. Leadership is hard work that requires divine strength, godly wisdom and great courage that can only be given by God. Leading involves great sacrifice and selfless service to the people. Jesus Christ, the greatest leader of all time made this powerful statement, "whoever wants to become great leader among must be your servant, and whoever wants to be first (leader) must be your servant just as the Son of Man did not come to be served, but to give his life as a ransom" (Matthew 20:26-28). Jesus profoundly made it clear that if one desires to serve in any position of authority and power that one must be willing to serve, be a slave and ready to die. This is what genuine, pure and godly leadership is all about.

Leadership Liability –a clarion call to courageous, compassionate and wise leadership addresses the divine duty and obligations of leaders. In Leadership liability, Dr. Ekeke passionately addresses the religious, moral, social and leadership challenges impacting not just Nigeria but also its indirect impact on other African and Western nations. Leadership liability is a call for moral and godly leadership. It teaches the secrets of godly leadership.

Mr. Chuck Odili
Founder, CEO & Publisher
Nigeriaworld Online
USA

# NIGERIA@50 – HISTORY

## BRIEF HISTORY AND AMALGMATION AS A NATION

It is an established fact that Nigeria is a creation of the British Empire during the 19th century. When the Europeans especially the British, French and Portuguese invaded the continent of Africa in search of slaves and mineral resources during the later the 19th century, the kingdoms of Oyo, Bornu, Hausa, Benin, Bonny, Jukun, Idah, Aro and Ibo-land in the Western Coastline of Africa lived in peace and traded among themselves. These peoples and kingdoms had existed hundreds of years even before the coming of the Europeans. The peoples of these kingdoms and empires had deep political, social, religious, tribal and linguistic differences. By the later part of 1890's when the British invaded and conquered these kingdoms, they created a monstrous nation for their political and economic interest and power rivalry with the French. And so, the peoples of Hausa, Fulani, Kanuri, Ibo, Yoruba, Kalabari, and Ijaw were forced to live together without a well-defined set of core values that addressed national unity, patriotism and parameters to discourage social, cultural, religious and linguistic differences between the peoples of this new nation. Flora Shaw, the wife of Lord Lugard, Nigeria's second governor general who suggested the name Nigeria for these variant groups of kingdoms and territories around the Niger over which Britain had established a Protectorate.

Then Britain imposed a system government and administration popularly know as "indirect Rule" in which the local affairs were largely left in the hands of Nigerian traditional rulers such as the Emirs, Obas and Chiefs while the national affairs were completely controlled by the British officials. The political structure was also intended to preserver the tribal distinctions in her new found colonial empire.

While the North accepted the Indirect Rule without problems, some local leaders from the South, who had managed to receive some education through British established missionary schools in Nigeria, began to challenge the British system of Indirect Rule. Some years later, a good number of Southern leaders including some Northern leaders aspired to share in the national government, which was the exclusive preserve of the British. Those elected to the congress were all British officials and the nationalists thought that the national administration did not represent the Nigerian masses and therefore protested against the British government to revise the 1922 constitution to include Nigerians in the Legislative Council. And so nationalist leaders such as such as Dr. Nnamdi Azikiwe, Chief Obafemi Awolowo, Alhaji Abubakar Tafawa Belwa, Alhaji Ahmadu Bello, Ernest Ikoli, H. O. Davis, Chief S. L. Akintola, Dr. M. I. Okpara, Solanke, and Eyo Ita among many others wisely challenged British style of government which was established for the people of Nigeria and most of Africa then.

Through their struggle and pressure against the British colonial rule, Nigeria's independence was granted due to the activities of people like Dr. Nnamdi Azikiwe, Chief Obafemi Awolowo and Ahmadu Bello, who were the pioneers of the nationalist grievances against the British system of indirect rule. Nigeria received her independence from Britain in October 1, 1960, and became a Republic in 1963 under a British Parliamentary system of Government. However, Sir James Robertson became the first Governor-General of the Independent federation of Nigeria. While Alhaji Hon. Sir Ahmadu Bello, Sarduna of Sokoto, premier of Northern Nigeria and President-General of the Northern Nigeria People's Congress, Dr. Nnamdi Azikiwe, the national president of N.C.N.C, was elected President of the Senate. Chief S. L. Akintola became the Premier of Western Nigeria and Deputy Leader of the Action Group, Dr. M. I. Okpara, Premier of Eastern Nigeria, and Chief Obafemi Awolowo, Leader of the Opposition and Leader of the Action Group.

The nationalist leaders established the parliamentary system of government, in which Sir Abubakar Tafawa Belwa became the first Prime Minister of Nigeria and Dr. Nnamdi Azkike, the first indigenous governor general of Nigeria. That arrangement did not last before tribal politics and religious sentiments led to the truncation of the parliamentary system. The first Nigerian military coup was planned and in 1965, Sir Abubaka Tafawa Belwa was assassinated. Major Agui Ironsi became the military head of State. Within six months, he was assassinated by a group of Northern military boys, who revenged against the killing of Sir Abubaka Tafawa Belewa. The activities led to the horrendous pogrom against innocent easterners living in the Northern states in which over 300,000 Ibos were massacred. The events of that turbulent period 1965-9167 led to the political crisis, tribal and religious violence that led to unforgettable genocidal civil war of 1967-70 that decimated more than three million lives and left so much bitterness, anger and hatred among the peoples of Nigeria.

Before the civil war, Nigeria had established three regional government regions – North, West and Eastern regions.

After the war, General Gowon became the head of State of Nigeria. In the 1970's with the oil price at all time high, oil coming primarily from Eastern region, yet General Gowon through his finance minister, Chief Abafemi Awolowo, introduced monetary policies that were purely punitive and spiteful treatment of the so-called enemies of the Nigerian state, that kept the majority of the people from the Eastern region people poorer than they were during the civil war. Nine years of spite and punitive rule against the people of Biafra despite the end of War Slogan, "No Victor NO Vanquished", and the military peacefully ousted him, but the short-lived administration of General Murtala Mohammed paved the way for General Obasanjo to head the government. Despite the excess external reserves and more than $25 billion oil revenue during that time, General Obasanjo surprisingly introduced austerity measures and prudent fiscal measures which had severe effects on millions of people from the Eastern region. Poverty, pandemic diseases including quasiokor and other health hazards of the war era became rampant and afflicted many Ndi-igbo especially the children and elderly.


## DETAILED HISTORY

In 1890, British reporter Flora Shaw, wife of Lord Frederick Lugard, suggested that the country be named "Nigeria" after the Niger River.

1914: The Northern and Southern Protectorates were amalgamated to form Nigeria. Colonial officer Frederick Lugard became the governor-general.

1914 – 1922: Nigeria was presided over by a Governor-General. In 1922, as part of the constitution of the time, the British introduced the principle of direct election into the Legislative council.

1951: The British decided to grant Nigeria internal self-rule, following an agitation led by the NCNC, Dr Azikiwe's political party. A new constitution elevated the provinces to regional status. The National Council of Nigeria and the Cameroons (NCNC) had control of the Eastern Region government, the Northern Peoples Congress (NPC) had control of the Northern Region, and the Action Group (AG) had control of the Western Region.

1954: The position of Governor was created in the three regions (North, West and East) on the adoption of federalism.

1957: The Eastern and Western Regions attained self-governing status.

1958: Nigerian Armed Forces transferred to Federal control. The Nigerian Navy was born.

1959: Northern Peoples Congress (NPC) and Niger Delta Congress (NDC) formed an alliance to contest parliamentary elections. The Northern Region attained self-governing status. The new Nigerian currency, the Pound, was introduced

October 1, 1960: Nigeria obtained its independence... First Republic of Nigeria under a British parliamentary system Abubakar Tafawa Balewa was elected Prime Minister. Dr. Nnamdi Azikiwe became Nigeria's first indigenous Governor General.

1960-1966: Nigeria was admitted to the United Nations as the 99th member.

February 11-12, 1961: After a plebiscite, the Northern Cameroon, which before then was administered separately within Nigeria, voted to join Nigeria. But Southern Cameroon became part of francophone Cameroon.

June 1, 1961: Northern Cameroon became Sardauna Province of Nigeria, the thirteenth province of Northern Nigeria as the country's map assumed a new shape.

October 1, 1961: Southern Cameroon ceased to be a part of Nigeria.

1962: Following a split in the leadership of the AG that led to a crisis in the Western Region, a state of emergency was declared in the region, and the federal government invoked its emergency powers to administer the region directly. Consequently the AG was toppled as regional power. Awolowo, its leader, and other AG leaders, were convicted of treasonable felony. Awolowo's former deputy and premier of the Western Region formed a new party--the Nigerian National Democratic Party (NNDP)--that took over the government. Meanwhile, the federal coalition government acted on the agitation of minority non-Yoruba groups for a separate state to be excised from the Western Region

1963: Nigeria shed the bulk of its political affinity with the British colonial power to become a Republic. Nnamdi Azikiwe became the first President. Obafemi Awolowo leader of the Action Group (AG) became leader of the opposition. The regional premiers were Ahmadu Bello (Northern Region, NPC), Samuel Akintola (Western Region, AG), Michael Okpara (Eastern Region, NCNC).

Dennis Osadebey (NCNC) became premier of the Midwestern Region just created out of the old Western region.

1964: Prime Minister Balewa's Northern Peoples Congress (NPC) aligned with a faction of the Action Group (AG) led by Chief Ladoke Akintola, the Nigerian National Democratic Party (NNDP), to form the Nigerian National Alliance (NNA) in readiness for the elections. At the same time, the main Action Group led by Chief Obafemi Awolowo formed an alliance with the United Middle-Belt Congress (UMBC) and Alhaji Aminu Kano's Northern Elements Progressive Union (NEPU) and Borno Youth Movement to form the United Progressive Grand Alliance (UPGA).

November 1965: Violence erupted in the western region, and criticism of the political ruling class created unease in the new republic.

January 15, 1966: Some junior officers of the Nigerian army, mostly majors overthrew the government in a coup d'état. The officers, most of Igbo tribe, assassinated Balewa in Lagos, Akintola in Ibadan, and Bello in Kaduna, as well as some senior northern officers. The coup leaders pledged to establish a strong and efficient government committed to a progressive program and eventually to new elections. They vowed to stop the post-electoral violence and stamp out corruption that they said was rife in the civilian administration. General Johnson T. Aguiyi-Ironsi, the most senior military officer, and incidentally an easterner, who stepped in to restore order, became the head of state.

May 29, 1966: Massive rioting started in the major towns of Northern Nigeria and attacks the Igbos and other easterners to avenge the death of many senior northerners in the coup.

July 29, 1966: A group of Northern officers and men stormed the Western Region's governor's residence in Ibadan where General Aguiyi Ironsi was staying with his host, Lt. Col Adekunle Fajuyi. Both the head of state and governor are killed.

August 1, 1966: Lt. Col Yakubu Gowon a fairly junior officer from the north became the new head of state.

January 4, 1967: Gowon moved to split the existing 4 regions of Nigeria into 12 states. However, the military governor of the Eastern Region (Colonel Chukwuemeka Odumegwu Ojukwu) refused to accept the division of the Eastern Region, and declared the Eastern Region an independent republic called Biafra.

This led to a civil war between Biafra and the remainder of Nigeria. The

May 30, 1967: Lt Col Ojukwu, governor of the east, declared the Eastern region the Republic of Biafra.

In June 1967, Nigeria's military leaders travelled to Aburi in Ghana to find a solution to problems facing the country and to avert an imminent military clash between the north and the east.

July 6, 1967: First shots were fired heralding a 30-month war between the Federal government and the Republic of Biafra. The war officially started and continued until Biafra surrendered on January 15, 1970 and over 2 million people perished and another one million severally injured.

January 15, 1970: The civil war ended and reconstruction and rehabilitation begin.

April 2, 1971: Nigeria joined the Organization of Petroleum Exporting Countries (OPEC).

1974: General Gowon said he could not keep his earlier promise to return power to a democratically elected government in 1976. He announced an indefinite postponement of a programme of transition to civil rule.

October 1975: Gowon was overthrown in a coup, on the anniversary of his ninth year in office. Brigadier (later General) Murtala Mohammed, the new head of state promised a 1979 restoration of democracy.

1976: The federal government adhering to the recommendations of a panel earlier set up to advice it approves the creation of a new Federal Capital Territory, Abuja, away from Lagos. In 1976, Nigeria was further broken down into 19 states, and plans to move the capital to Abuja were in the works.

February 13, 1976: Murtala Mohammed was killed in the traffic on his way to work.

February 14, 1976: General Murtala Mohammed is succeeded by General Olusegun Obasanjo who pledged to pursue his predecessor's transition programme.

1979: Nigeria approved a new constitution.

October 1, 1979: General Obasanjo handed over to Alhaji Shehu Shagari as first elected executive President and the first politician to govern Nigeria since 1966. Five parties had competed for the presidency, and Shagari of the

National Party of Nigeria (NPN) was declared the winner. The other parties were: Unity Party of Nigeria (UPN), National People's Party (UPN), Great Nigeria People's Party (GNPP), and People's Redemption Party (PRP)

1983: The conduct of the general elections was criticized by opposing parties and the media. Violent erupted in some parts of the west.

September 1983: Alhaji Shehu Shagari was re-elected president of Nigeria in August-September 1983.

December 31, 198: Following a coup d'état, the military returned to power. Major-General Muhammad Buhari was named head of state.

August 27, 1985: Buhari was overthrown in a palace coup. The army chief, General Ibrahim Babangida took over power.

1986: The seat of government was officially moved from Lagos to Abuja

1987: 2 more states were created.

1991: 9 more states were created, making it 30 states at the time. Also in 1991, Abuja was formed as a new (more central) section of the country, and the capital of Nigeria was officially moved from Lagos to Abuja.

June 12, 1993 after several postponements by the military administration, presidential elections were held. Businessman and newspaper mogul Moshood Abiola of the SDP took unexpected lead in early returns.

June 23, 1993: Babangida on national television offered his reasons for annulling the results of the Presidential election. At least 100 people were killed in riots in the southwest, Abiola's home area.

August 26, 1993: Under severe opposition and pressure, Babangida resigned as military president and appointed an interim government headed by Chief Ernest A. Shonekan.

In 1993, over 300,000 Ogoni marched peacefully to demand a share in oil revenues. They had formed an organization called MOSOP (Movement for the Survival of Ogoni People). The group was led by Ken Saro-Wiwa.

November 17, 1993: General Sani Abacha, defence minister in the interim government and most senior officer, seized power from Shonekan, abolishes the constitution. Also in November of 1993, the military government led by Abacha began terrorizing Ogoniland with arrests, rapes, executions, burnings and lootings.

May 1994: Saro-Wiwa was abducted from his home and jailed along with other MOSOP leaders and charged with the murder of four Ogoni leaders.

1994: Abiola, who had escaped abroad after the annulment, returned and proclaimed himself president. He was arrested and charged with treason.

July 1995: Former head of state, Obasanjo was sentenced to 25 years in prison by a secret military tribunal for alleged participation in an attempt (widely believed to have been fictional) to overthrow the government.

October 31, 1995, the military government tried Ken Saro Wiwa and other 8 people, and found them guilty of the murder of the 4 Ogoni people. The sentence immediately drew national and international outcry

November 10, 1991: Saro-Wiwa and the 8 others were executed anyway. Their execution resulted in more international outcry, a lot of which Nigeria was almost immediately suspended from the Commonwealth.

May 1996: Nnamdi Azikiwe, Nigeria's first president, died. Nigerians mourned the great Zik of Africa.

June 8, 1998: General Abacha died suddenly and mysteriously. The official cause of death: heart attack. Nigerians swarmed the streets rejoicing.

June 9, 1998: Gen. Abdulsalaam Abubakar was named Nigeria's eighth military ruler. He promised to restore civilian rule promptly. Abubakar took his place as the interim president

July 1998: A month after General Abacha's death the United Nations General-Secretary Kofi Annan arrived in Nigeria to conclude deals for the release of Chief Abiola.

July 7, 1998: Chief Abiola died in detention of a heart disease, a week after Annan's visit, before he could be released in a general amnesty for political prisoners. Rioting in Lagos led to over 100 deaths.

July 20, 1998: Abubakar promised to relinquish power on May 29, 1999.

February 15, 1999: Former military ruler Obasanjo won the presidential nomination of the Peoples Democratic Party (PDP).

May 1999: A new Constitution was adopted. It was based on the 1979 Constitution.

May 29, 1999: Former Military Head of State, Olusegun Obasanjo, was sworn in as Nigeria's First democratically elected civilian President in the 4th republic.

May 2003: President Olusegun Obasanjo was re-elected in an election that was heavily rigged. General Muhammad Buhari who ran under ANPP challenged the election result and took President Obasanjo and his party PDP to court.

2003-2007: During President Obasanjo's second term, corruption of government officials was the order of the day. 31 out 36 governors in his administration were charged with money laundering and impropriety by EFCC. Former Governor of Bayelsa State, Diepreye Alamieyeseigha was arrested in London, England. He escaped from his house arrest dressed like a woman to deceive the British authorities. Corruption and impunity reached all time high.

May 2007: Umaru Musa Yar'Adua won the 2007 elections, which was deemed the worst rigged elections in the history of Nigeria. He was sworn as Nigeria's second democratically elected civilian President in the 4th republic.

November 2009: Umaru Musa Yar'Adua was flown to King Faisal Specialist Hospital and Research Centre in Jeddah, Saudi Arabia, for acute pericarditis illness – a debilitating auto–immune disease, known as Churg Strauss Syndrome, where he stayed for 3 months. And First Lady, Hajia Turai Yar'Adua, and company of present's men lied to the nation about the president's sickness.

29

February 24, 2010: Umaru Musa Yar'Adua was smuggled back to Nigeria on Wednesday February 24th morning under cover of darkness, a move described by a diplomatic source as a desperate gamble by his wife and her cabal to hold on to power.

March 2010: Vice President Good luck Jonathan, a 52-year-old biologist from Bayelsa State in Niger Delta became acting president.

May 5, 2010: President Muar Musa Yar'Adua dies.

May 7, 2010: Acting President Goodluck Jonathan was sworn third president in the 4th republic and the 13th head of the Federal Republic of Nigeria.

## LIST OF NIGERIAN RULERS PRIOR AND AFTER INDEPENDENCE

| | | | |
|---|---|---|---|
| | | | |
| Sir Lord Frederick Lugard | Colonial | 1914 - 1919 | Governor General |
| | | | |
| Sir Bernard Bourdillon | Colonial | 1635 - 1943 | Governor General |
| | | | |

| Sir John Macpherson | Colonial | 1948 - 1955 | Governor General |
|---|---|---|---|
| | | | |
| Sir James Roberson | Colonial | 1955 - 1960 | Governor General |
| | | | |
| Benjamin Nnamdi Azikiwe | Civilian | 1 Oct 1960 - 16 Jan 1963 | President of the Republic |
| | | | |
| Alhaji Abubakar Tafawa Balewa | Civilian | 30 Aug 1960 - 15 Jan 1966 | Prime Minister |
| | | | |
| Johnson Thomas Umurakwe Aguiyi-Ironsi | Military | 16 Jan 1966 - 29 Jul 1966 | Head of the Military Government |
| | | | |
| Yakubu Gowon | Military | 1 Aug 1966 - 29 Jul 1975 | Head of the Military Government |
| | | | |
| Murtala Ramat Muhammed | Military | 29 Jul 1975 - 13 Feb 1976 | Head of the Military Government |

| | | | |
|---|---|---|---|
| Olusegun Obasanjo | Military | 14 Feb 1976 - 1 Oct 1979 | Head of the Military Government |
| Alhaji Shehu Usman Aliyu Shagari | Civilian | 1 Oct 1979 - 31 Dec 1983 | President of the Republic |
| Muhammadu Buhari | Military | 31 Dec 1983 - 27 Aug 1985 | Head of the Federal Military Government |
| Ibrahim Badamasi Babangida | Military | 27 Aug 1985 - 4 Jan 1993 | Chairman of the Armed Forces Ruling Council<br><br>Chairman of the National Defence and Security Council |
| Ernest Adekunle Oladeinde Shonekan | Civilian | 26 Aug 1993 - 17 Nov 1993 | Head of the Interim National Government |

| | | | |
|---|---|---|---|
| Sani Abacha | Military | 17 Nov 1993 - 8 Jun 1998 | Chairman of the Provisional Ruling Council |
| | | | |
| Abdulsalam Abubakar | Military | 9 Jun 1998 - 29 May 1999 | Chairman of the Provisional Ruling Council |
| | | | |
| Olusegun Obasanjo | Civilian | 29 May 1999 – May 2007 | President of the Republic |
| Umaru Musa Yar'Adua | Civilian | May 2007 – May 5, 2010 | President of the Republic |
| Goodluck Jonathan | Civilian | May 7, 2010 - | President of the Republic |

(Compiled from Online Nigeria, Motherland Nigeria, and other sources – *Emphasis added*)

# RETURN TO DEMOCRATIC GOVERNMENT

## A GODLY APPEAL TO PRESIDENT OLUSEGUN OBASANJO AND HIS LEADERSHIP TEAM

The recent democratic elections in Nigeria, Africa's most populous nation, and the overwhelming success of PDP in both the state and federal levels has been a theme of much discussion around the world especially among Nigerians more than any other election in the history of Nigeria. The situation became even more intriguing with the nomination of Chief Adolphus Wabara, my kinsman as the senate president despite his contested election result as Abia South Senator by his opponent Elder Chinyere Dan Imo who recently withdrew all his litigations after waging a fierce battle earlier on during the nomination of Chief Wabara to the Senate presidency.

Frankly speaking, this past democratic elections is not fun to write about. First of all, there were enormous fraudulent activities as evidenced by many lawsuits currently awaiting adjudication in the tribunal. Even international observers also reported quite a number of fraudulent election malpractices and activities at the polling stations. In one case, the election results of one party alone surpassed the total number of registered voters in that region. But the most despicable distressing truth of this election is the inefficiency of INEC officers to organize and conduct successful elections in Nigeria. The INEC as a government agency needs to be reorganized or abolished with a competent agency of men and women of character and integrity.

However, despite the fraudulent activities and inefficiency of the INEC officers, democratic government must be encouraged in the Nigeria. Yes it was not a perfect democratic election but there was clear evidence that Nigerians voted based on the vision, integrity and character of the candidates. The voting record and statistics clearly demonstrate that Nigerian voters were making right choices in choosing their candidates. Secondly, despite the accusations of election fraud and many lawsuits still hanging against many candidates who claimed to have won the elections by showing illegal winning certificates issued by unqualified and sometimes unknown INEC officers, Mr. Obasanjo was successfully and peacefully sworn in as the second time president elect of Nigeria. I am of the opinion that this is a huge success for the nascent democratic government in Nigeria as well as for entire African continent.

Again, many Nigerians are asking these questions, how did Mr. Obasanjo work his way to become PDP presidential candidate in 1999? How did he rise to become Nigerian president for second time consecutively in this democratic dispensation of Nigeria political history? How did he bargain his way with Major General Ibrahim Babangida while in jail to become the leader of the PDP, a party that was formed and organized by former Vice President Alex Ekwueme? A few days ago, a dear friend of mine sent an email with this statement, "Mr. Obasanjo is one of the luckiest people on the face of this earth." Another friend quibbled to me this weekend while discussing the political situation of things at home, I quote, "how could Mr. Obasanjo the bad guy win this election again"?

These questions are worth asking. However no one is asking the question why did God allow such events to happen the way it is unfolding presently in Nigeria? I do not want to digress here, but I have also asked why does God often choose unlikely people to become such influential leaders of our time? For instance President George W. Bush of the United States has obviously risen from nowhere to become one of the influential leaders of our time. Even though he was the son of ex President of the United States, George Bush and ex-governor of the state of Texas, he was not considered to be one of the Republican strong candidates or even to make a strong presidency. But it did not take much time especially during the events of September eleven and his subsequent fight against AL Quada and countries that harbor terrorists to proof to all of us of his strong-willed character and moral values. His act of bravery in fighting such a huge and invisible war against AL Quada and terrorism has been a remarkable and immense political success for him, his Republican party and the United States of America in general.

An old adage says there is no smoke without fire. The election result of President W. Bush especially in the state of Florida was fiercely contested but despite it all, he was successfully inaugurated the 42nd president of the United President in 2001. Nothing happens without a reason. There are absolutely divine purposes and plans for very event and circumstances whether good or bad that happen in our lives. Some political analysts have argued that if Al Gore had worn the 2001 United States presidential elections, probably the war against Al Quada would have never been fought. Even many Church and charismatic religious leaders enumerate the moral contributions that the presidency of Mr. George W. Bush has brought to our world. I want to suffice here to make this point that, God will always use whatever happens in our lives and world to bring glory and honor to His Holy name. God is sovereign and masterfully controls everything that happens in our lives as well as in the nations.

For President Obasanjo and Senate leader, Chief Adophus Wabara, what will be your fight for Nigeria? No one can fully understand how Mr. Obasanjo through unexplainable circumstances got released from prison to become now second time elect president of Nigeria. The same goes for Chief Adolphus Wabara, an Ndoki man from the minority group of Ukwa and most ignored and neglected area in the governance of the state despite our rich cultural heritage and natural resources has risen to become the Senate president and the third citizen of Nigeria. His election to Senate presidency is absolutely something unthinkable for an Ndoki / Ukwa people. We are absolutely thrilled and happy for his success because that will open the door for the bright minds of Ndoki and Ukwa people to dream again for their share in the political system and landscape of Nigeria for which we have been ignored for so long.

I have had the privilege to meet Mr. Olusegun Obasanjo on a few occasions especially during his official and pleasure trips to the United States. At first glance during a forum organized on his behalf by the department of Business and International Economics at Georgia State University, I was very embarrassed and disappointed with his demeanor. He did not have the charisma and communication skills to be Nigeria's spokesperson in the world. He spoke arrogantly and unintelligently. He lacked insight, understanding, passion and wisdom. At another forum where he was invited to speak, he answered a question fielded to him by a humble and educated Nigerian lady "to go to hell." His response clearly demonstrated his insensitivity, lack of diplomatic courtesies and presidential etiquettes. Hoverer, despite of all his shortcomings, God chose him to be the leader of Nigeria at this time of our political history. How could a seemingly unlikely person like Obasanjo exert such overwhelming influence among the most educated people and bright minds in Nigeria including those in PDP? How did he manipulate and bargain with everyone to become the party leader and subsequently successfully win the presidential elections now for the second term?

The answer to those questions can only be found in the Word of God. The Apostle Peter writes, "Humble yourselves under the mighty hand of God, that He may exalt you in due time" (1 Peter 5:6). In the book of Judges 7:16-25, the Bible clearly teaches how God often chose unlikely people to becomes leaders in order to carry out His divine plan and purposes on earth and to bring honor and glory to His Holy name.

Perhaps while Mr. Olusegun Obasanjo was in prison, he read the Holy Book, the Bible cover to cover and deepened his spiritual walk with God through His Son Jesus Christ. To proof his heightened spiritual relationship with God, Mr. Obasanjo gave his daughter in marriage to a British Baptist minister. Among all the world leaders, Mr. Obansajo is one of the few presidents who frequently quotes the Scriptures and boasts in the Lord about the favors that God has poured upon his life. Mr. Obasanjo was also the first if not the only military head of state that voluntarily and successfully transitioned Nigeria with all of its ethnic complexities and religious problems to a democratic elected president of Shehu Shagari in our first republic in 1979. This was unheard of anywhere in world especially among African leaders. The entire world applauded his bravery and democratic insight and that earned him the name "Father of African Democracy"

That nascent democracy which Mr. Olusegun Obasanjo, then major General and head of State gave birth to did not survive because suddenly the second republic elected civilian government under again the leadership of Shehu Shagari was brutally stopped and ripped apart through a bloodless coup by the dubious and greedy military generals under the leadership of then Major General Buhari and other military juntas accusing the president elect and his party NPN of rigging the elections. Again darkness fell over Nigeria for another twenty years. From that time until four years ago, Nigerian people suffered not just untold economic crisis of our time but worst of all, psychological, emotional, mental torture and social apathy until in 1999 when through divine providence and intervention of God, Mr. Obasanjo was elected the fourth Republic democratic president of Nigeria.

Mr. President, may I say that, you are actually reaping the democracy dividends, which you gave birth to in 1978. When you coined this phrase in 1999, you did not perhaps understand its divine and deep root meaning and implications. Recently while reading some of the speeches and statements you made during your inauguration ceremony, I was impressed by the constant mention of God's name and Scripture quotes. For instance, in one of your statements at a press conference in Abuja, you made the following remarks: God has a reason for binding the country together in spite of a 30-month civil war. "The Lord is gracious, compassionate, loving and, have course, merciful. He has been kind to this nation. After the election, they said there would be bloodbath. I thank God that they have been proved wrong. God has a purpose for this country." Also at the national thanks-giving and dedication service held in Abuja to round off the 2003 presidential inauguration ceremonies, you said, I quote, I've often said that if there is any man who should spend all his life to thank God. I'm the only man. "I've been to prison and there were vows that Basorun MKO Abiola, Maj-General Shehu Musa Yar'Adua and Obasanjo would never come out of the prison alive. But as it turned out, two of these vows were fulfilled but one was not. If anything was in spite of me, it was God. God decided to shine His Light on us."

Your speeches and statements are biblically sound, impressive, captivating, humble, and compassionate. You sound like a father to all Nigerians. God has surely shined His light and poured His grace and mercy upon you. But you must remember that the favor of God comes with responsibilities also. I believe that you are not calling the name of God in vain when you make these public statements and speeches because one of the severest laws of the Old Testament is that God's name should not be taken in vain (Exodus 20:7, Deuteronomy 5:11). I also believe that you are a genuine Christian who loves God and wants to do well.

You must realize that your second time win as president of Nigeria did not happen without a reason. The Bible clearly teaches that God reproves leaders for our sakes so that we may live a quiet and peaceful life in all godliness and honesty. Obviously, we did not see such peaceful times during your last four years, but Nigeria as a nation did not disintegrate in spite of all the economic, social, religious and ethnic upheavals of the last four years. Without doubt your second time presidency has much more divine purpose. God has allowed you to win again in spite all the inefficiencies of our system for a greater plan and purposes for Nigeria.

You must know that God is sovereign and that there is nothing that happens in our world that takes Him by surprise. Whatever is happening now has been preordained before time began by God. Remember, God before eternity and time decided that His only begotten Son Jesus Christ would be born of a woman on earth and to be crucified by the Romans so that through His life, ministry, death and resurrection, we can be reconciled to God Almighty. That was a bigger gain for God.

My primary objective here is not to inform you of Christian history or to relive the sad events and deprivation of the Nigeria masses of their God given rights, privileges, opportunities and blessing, but to make a godly appeal to you and your team of leaders. Your presidency is not your own making but a clear divine intervention by God. God has called and elevated you to be a godly leader over the affairs of our people in order to deliver the Nigeria masses from the satanic and demonic oppression of the past regimes. The Nigerian people have suffered all kinds of abuse and satanic oppression that have afflicted the nation for over twenty years - such social issues such as corruption, safety, order, security, ethnic and religious hatred.

Even Nigerians living overseas also indirectly suffer incalculable physical, mental and social oppression due brutal and corrupt regimes of the past governments. We are oppressed everywhere we are found in the world. Host countries look at us as criminals and corrupt people. Foreign state agencies and task forces are specially setup to monitor the activities of Nigerians overseas. We do not have the rights, privileges and protection of our government any where in world. Despite some scattered individual successes of Nigerians abroad, the few criminals among our people have basically shattered the image of Nigerians overseas.

Today, the psyche of every typical Nigerian is either experiencing some kind of desperation or seriously damaged. This is an area I believe that God is calling you as the leader and father of all Nigerians at this time to work on in order to bring some healing, comfort and hope to all of us again. I am not just talking about economics, which is also a very important element in our nation building, but I am specifically talking about establishing the plan, strategy and infrastructure that will restore order and security back to our nation. I think that your greatest task as the president of Nigeria will be to restore order, security, hope and the opportunities for all Nigerians to dream again

I believe with all my heart that God has called you and elevated you to establish the structure and implement the strategy to move our nation and our people to the Promised Land. The natural and human resources exist for you to execute the tasks that God has called you to do. Nigeria as a nation does not lack the will power and the strength to rebuild if you and your team will do the right things. We are resilient people.

You must be willing to learn to trust and depend upon God rather than men around you. God will honor you if you show character, integrity, faith and dependence upon God in discharging your duties as the president. You must also be a man of great vision and mission. As a leader in this contemporary time, you must be willing to mobilize, motivate and inspire Nigerians everywhere to achieve, succeed and reach the fullest potential that God has deposited in all of us.

You must make sure that people under your influence and authority hope again; live sensibly, peacefully and responsibly. Your primary job will be to inspire your team to work for Nigeria and not for their states, tribal folks and families. The situation of the people and the nation as a whole, demands for you to show strong character and integrity in all your undertakings. To be successful, you must surround yourself with men and women of character and strong moral values. In many of your inauguration speeches and statements, you also talked about providing quality leadership by using the most caliber men and women in your cabinet. You talked about appointment criteria that will be based on ability, integrity, competence, shared vision and character. You also said I quote, "The performance of all ministers who will have target will be carefully monitored and assessed to ensure effective implementation of policies in their respective ministries."The present structure of the presidency will be critically reviewed to include a monitoring unit that will follow up and report on the effective implementation of policy decisions."

It is my prayer and many Nigerians as well that you do what you say and promise. Otherwise history will judge you as well as God. You must not listen to the voice of men and women around but only to the voice of God. You must work for the betterment of Nigeria and its masses. We Nigerians have suffered a lot in the midst of plenty. God has not brought you so far for you to disappoint Him. God has divinely orchestrated the plan for you to be over the affairs of Nigeria for divine purposes. Do not fear what men can do you but only fear what God can do to you. Remember, you will certainly make an account to God how and what you did with the privileges and opportunities that God gave to you as the president and leader of Nigeria. The great Israelite leader, Moses could not enter into the Promised Land because he failed to carry out one simple instruction from God. God is always tough with those placed in leadership. They face the severest consequences.

In conclusion, I encourage you Mr. President to lead with integrity and character. To lead with a vision that is embraced by all Nigerians, to focus on a mission that will provide a sense of momentum, to rekindle the passion and patriotism that will inspire all Nigerians to make impossibilities possible again, to establish the structure and implement the strategy that will shape the nations future and most importantly I encourage you to work to establish a value system irrespective of religious beliefs that will shape our daily routines, drive our lives, dictate every decision and determine our life's priorities. In so doing, you will not only contribute to the nation building but will create peaceful environment for good change with great opportunities for all Nigerians to live peacefully and responsibly in order to fulfill the potential that God has deposited inside each and every one of us. Anything else will be ungodly, unnatural, and satanic leadership.

## VICIOUS CIRCLE: WILL THE NEXT GOVERNMENT FINALLY RESURRECT NIGERIA?

In a few days, Christians all over this world will celebrate Easter, which is historically the remembrance of Christ's resurrection from death. Theologically, his resurrection marked the beginning of His exaltation as Lord and Savior in the heavenly throne. Morally, Christ resurrection is the means by which God provided salvation and forgiveness for the sins of mankind. In raising Jesus from the dead, God proclaimed Him to be the divinely appointed leader by which mankind is indeed reconciled to God and made righteous with all heavenly privileges such as grace, mercy, access, peace, hope, love, power and prosperity. Socially, economically and politically, Christ resurrection reminds of the divine purpose that Jesus came to save mankind from the penalty of sin and power of poverty and to offer us abundant life (Hebrews 2:15; 1 John 3:8; John 10:10).

Christ resurrection reminds that the blood of Jesus was shed for our freedom and that freedom means more than infirmities, sickness and disease. Christ freedom empowers us to be free from the shackles of slavery and all kinds of bondages and injustices. Christ resurrection empowers us to live life full of joy, love, peace, purpose and abundance.

If God forgave mankind and freed us from the slavery of sin, sickness and power of poverty and graciously empowered us to lead a life of abundance, I must ask then why most Nigerians are still enslaved economically and politically? Why are the people of Nigeria still trapped in the vicious circle of economic injustice and political bondage? Why is the most populous and richest nation in the continent of Africa still enslaved and pillaged by an army of old and incompetent cronies? Who will deliver Nigeria from this economic bondage and political corruption? Will Yardua's government finally resurrect Nigeria from this economic and political death coffin? I doubt it but I must remain optimistic.

As the nation prepares to vote in a few days, the political playground does not exhibit any sign that we are heading for a free, fair and credible election. President Obasanjo has vowed that the election is 'do or die for him'. He told the mammoth crowd in Aba last month that he would not hand over to crooks and criminals. In fact the 70-year-old president is out more campaigning for the two young PDP presidential candidates than he did during his time. I did not see him campaign so vigorous when he was running for president in 1999 and 2003. President Obasanjo has also ordered sophisticated automatic weapons and election uniform for the police. The Inspector-General of Police, Mr. Sunday Ehindero said recently that his team would deal mercilessly with anyone caught causing trouble during the elections. I am not here to analyze Obasanjo's gesture or the police boss comment, however, I just know that this is unprecedented in our nation's history. The president and PDP cronies are just out to win the elections by all means. To further assist PDP in its quest to retain power, INEC's chairman Prof. Maurice Iwu and EFFC boss, Mallam Nuhu Ribadu are working tirelessly to undermine the rulings of the nations' courts.

This month's election will determine whether Nigerians are ready to vote consciously in order to break-off from the vicious circle of incompetent and inefficient rulers that have hijacked the affairs of the nation since 30 years ago. Or if we will still be trapped in the same vicious circle of inept and visionless political leaders who are incapable of moving Nigeria forward and restoring her dignity in the comity of nations. Honestly, I do not harbor any prejudice against Governor Yar'dua but Nigeria of today does not need a president who is weak and unwise. As a matter of fact, I am beginning to admire the man because of his recent pledge to be a servant leader who will serve with fear of God. He has also been visiting some religious gurus for prayers. In fact his attitude shows humility and signs of someone who wants to genuinely serve the people. However, Governors Yar'dua and Jonathan do not have the same temperament, strength, boldness and courage like president Obasanjo. Even though both men may have leadership style different from the president, Nigeria needs a strong, courageous and fearless president like Obasanjo.

Surrounding a president with technocrats, bureaucrats and advisers may not even get the job done. Most of the tasks of the president are decision-making and most of the time; the president makes decision not the technocrats, bureaucrats and even the advisers. Today's political leaders do not know how to delegate even in decision-making.

President George W. Bush surrounded himself with the best advisers ever, yet more half of them have left his administration. Why, because none of their advices were even considered since 2000. Also our president surrounded himself with some of the brightest men and women in our country, and yet most of the president's impudent decisions have been made without due process. Even though these so-called technocrats achieved notable accomplishments especially in the area of fiscal and banking reform, economic reform, foreign debt repayment, and fight against bribery and corruption in public service, yet these achievements have not provided basic life needs such as clean water, electricity, good roads and employment. Rather looting of state and national treasury has been so rampant in this democratic dispensation than any other. Perhaps it's more pronounced and visible because of the bold actions of EFFC chairman Nuhu Ribadu. Despite the fact that his commission's job has been selective, Nigerians are proud anyway of his courage and determination so far to fish out the crooks, cronies, criminals and mere office holders who have hampered Nigeria's progress for so long.

There is no doubt that Obasanjo's government has opened up Nigeria's coffin. However, he did not wake or resurrect the dead Nigeria lying in it. His achievements are noteworthy and commendable. However, the question this writer is asking is this: will Yar'dua and Goodluck be able to resurrect Nigeria from death? Nigeria has been dead for too long and it's time, we elect people who are strong, courageous and credible to move our nation forward. If both men win the presidential elections would they perform more than president Obasanjo accomplished for Nigeria? If the answer is no, Nigeria would have to look elsewhere for visionary men and women who have the tenacity, courage and capacity to do more than president Obasanjo has done.

Chief Olusegun Obasanjo has the tendency and history to enthrone incapable people into leadership position after his term. In 1978, after his robust not exceptional military government, he handed over to the first democratic elected president of Alhaji Shehu Shagari, a primary school teacher who was then handpicked by the king makers to lead Nigeria. Shehu Shari's government was so corrupt that the military guys patiently waited for the end of first term to take over the affairs of governance from the inept and visionless government of Shehu Shagari. That period led to the dictatorial military government of Buhari, IBB, and Abacha and now the demo-crazy of Olusegun Obasanjo. Again, at the end of his two terms, he is making the same very mistake to hand over to Governor Yar'dua, who until one month before the PDP primaries was not even considered a candidate. So much has been written about the man, his selection and his health. However, the question I am passionately asking is: will Yardua's government finally move Nigeria forward. Does Governor Yar'dua have the strength, capacity, courage and boldness to deal with the diverse issues that confront our nation today? Let me encapsulate few of these major domestic issues.

1. **Unity of Nigeria**: A national and federal government controlled comprehensive package is urgently needed to resolve the legitimate yearnings of the Niger Delta militants. Also militant leaders currently held in federal prisons should be released. The federal government should engage in a serious and sincere dialogue with Alhaji Dokubo, Chief Uwazuruike, Mr. Ledum Mitee and other militant leaders.
2. **Crime and Security of Life**: State and local police should be created and police officers empowered through training and good pay to monitor our neighborhoods in order to restore order and tranquility in our communities.
3. **Constitutional Amendment**: The constitutional amendment is long overdue. Nigerian lawmakers must come together to develop a constitution that addresses the diversity and multi-cultural norms in our society in order to correct the injustices as enshrined in the current constitution of Nigeria.
4. **Religious Bigotry and Violence**: Nigeria is a secular society with freedom to associate, assemble and worship. Innocent people should not be killed for professing their faith in any part of Nigeria. Religious intolerance, ignorance and hatred must be eradicated through fearless religious laws and sincere policies.
5. **Job Creation**: Our youths are jobless and hopeless. Job creation is not entirely the main task of the government, however, with appropriate laws, policies and good enforcement, industries and businesses can be empowered to create jobs.

President Bill Clinton created over 30 million jobs in eight years through labor laws and wise policies.

6. **Health Care Crisis**: Nigeria is epileptic here and will honestly need to woo Nigerian healthcare professional living and working in USA and Europe to come home and help with the situation otherwise, we will continue to fly to America or Europe to treat catarrh and ligament in the knee. A poor person will have to die for a commonly treatable disease or sickness. This area must be urgently addressed.

7. **Power Sufficiency**: The inability of Nigeria to provide power and electricity to every home in Nigeria is a shameful thing. We have all the right ingredients and resources to have constant power supply and power sufficiency. Experts in generating electricity must assist to address this shameful situation.

8. **Clean Water**: Access to pipe-borne clean water for all Nigerians is a right and privilege for livelihood. 80% of our body is made of water. If we don't drink clean and pure water, it is just a matter of time before our bodies get sick. Nigeria is surrounded by water and there should be no reason why we can tap, drain, filter and purify water for human consumption. South Korea and other countries are doing that today.

9. **Good Road**: Without good road, transportation of goods and services would not be easy. Commerce and business are hindered due to lack of good roads. Billions have been contracted for road construction and yet our roads are death traps and heaven for armed robbers.

10. **Bribery and Corruption**: The next government must continue to work with Mallam Nuhu Ribadu to completely eradicate the cankerworm that has

crippled our progress for so long. To further facilitate this work, the next government should create local and state EFFC offices and appoint credible people to lead corruption charges against any public official no matter the person. Those in private businesses and beefcake activities should also be monitored.

11. **National Reconciliation**: Could it be that Nigerians have not yet forgiven one another of its past. The end of war slogan 'No Victor No Vanquished' was good statement but was never sincerely implemented. There is no doubt that the variant groups of people that make up Nigeria have profound political, social, cultural, religious, tribal and linguistic differences. The next government must begin a process of reconciliation with a well-defined set of core values that addresses national unity; promote patriotism and set parameters to embrace every Nigerian as equal citizens.

12. **Moral and Social Decadence**: The government do not legislate moral and social code. However, it is time the government regulates proliferation of churches to curb dubious and satanic ministries that are out there destroying people's lives in name of God. I receive more 419 letters from religious leaders and organizations than from secular ones. Laws can be put into place to regulate authenticity and proper conduct. Also it is time that Nigeria enacts laws to punish people who abuse children, rape young girls and traffic human organs.

13. **Environment**: Thousands of Nigerians die each year from diseases caused by environmental hazard and pollution. Nigerian environmental experts are urgently needed to assist the next government introduce laws and policies to control continued and severe damage to our environment

These are just few issues; there are other domestic issues including regional and international problems.

It's true that Governor Yar'dua is not the only candidate running for president in April 21st. There are other candidates, but he's most favored to win. Even though I have written this article with the impression that he will be the next president however, I believe any thing can happen in this election. Nevertheless, the caliber of people running against Yar'dua may not be better. Personally I have written off Atiku as potential president of Nigeria because of his disloyalty to his boss, even though the president never earned his loyalty. Secondly, vice-president Atiku sounds very ambitious. He also appears to be chronically corrupt. Buhari was a brutal dictator during his military government in 1984. I don't know if he has really changed now. I am not sure if he would be able to lead Nigeria as a civilian president. Would he be able to take pressures, challenges criticism etc without resorting to decrees and brutal laws? For Prof. Pat Utomi, he sounds intellectual as far as leadership is concerned but I don't know if he has the experience, fortitude and character to preside over a complex society like Nigeria.

Rev. Chris Okotie is eloquent and admirable for waking up the religious leaders that they are not only called to lead in the four square walls of their churches but to lead outside the church as well. Jesus Christ led in the public squares. Whenever, he withdrew with his apostles to an inn or upper room, it was time to plan and strategize how to carry on with their public ministry. If today's spiritual leaders do not get involve in shaping the nations laws, the ungodly people in government will continue to make laws and policies that impact negatively on the people. If religious people shy away from politics and public office, they have failed in what God called them to do. However, one thing I have against Rev Okotie is for lying on two different occasions. In 1999 and 2003, he publicly announced that God spoke to him that he would be Nigeria's president. If God spoke, it should be so no matter what. The Reverend lied twice against God.

I have restrained my self from writing about the charismatic and outspoken governor of Abia State for personal reasons. Actually, I have at least ten unpublished articles on his leadership and uncontrolled utterances. There is not a doubt that Governor Orji Kalu has been an outstanding critic of president Obasanjo and against his former party leadership. He possesses the charisma, eloquence, boldness, strength and courage to speak out against evil and injustices in the system. However, what did he do as Governor in his state? Though he complained that Abia State receives meager revenue from federal government because of his fallout with the president, nevertheless, what can he show for the meager revenue he was receiving? Today, the city of Aba, one of the major industrial cities of Nigeria and perhaps the only one in Abia State is an eye sore. How can he aspire to lead Nigeria when he could not transform Aba, the only major industrial city in the state? Moreover, who will live with him in ASO Rock, his invisible wife or his first lady mother? I admire certain leadership qualities in him but I do not think that he possesses the wisdom and integrity to lead Nigeria. His adoption by Ohanaeze and Igbo World Congress (WIC) as the consensus presidential candidate for Ndi-igbo sadly reveals the truth that there is leadership vacuum in Igbo-land. Not that there are no credible Igbo leaders, but they may not have the kind of cash, strength, courage and boldness that Governor Orji Kalu possesses.

Nigeria as a nation has all the right ingredients to create a peaceful, purposeful and prosperous society but our greatest problem I think is finding that divinely anointed and supernatural leader who is strong and courageous enough to deal with the ugly system of our nation. Personally, I do not care really who becomes the next president of Nigeria. What I care for is whether that person has what it takes to truly empower all Nigerians to compete with other nations. The only thing hindering Nigeria from being among the first class nations is incompetent leadership. I have been reading about South Korea recently and it is amazing to me how a country with less than 20 million people and without any tangible natural resources is able to transform their country into a first class society. Today, the USA and EU are having talks with the South Koreans about their telecommunication technology, which is first class in the world. Koreans work harder than any nation in the world except Japan. They own and operate 80% of so-called Chinese's restaurants worldwide. Their business acumen and technical skills are unprecedented. Their success has been attributed to government laws and policies that promoted patriotism, hard work and level plain field for all South Koreans to succeed. It's time Nigeria search for a leader who is truly competent and compassionate to deal squarely and sincerely with the problems that have hindered Nigeria from assuming its rightful position among the richest nations in the world. Nigeria is in dire need of visionary leadership, bold, strong, and honest leaders who are not afraid to say enough is enough, let's us get the system corrected. The Nigerian people have been denied for too long because of our ugly past and incompetent leaders.

This week as we celebrate Easter and prayerfully prepare to cast our votes in a few days, let us remember that Christ died and resurrected so that we might have life and have it more abundantly. God has blessed the planet earth beyond comprehension and has given mankind the intelligence and ability to tap into the limitless resources that abound on planet earth. Let us celebrate Christ's resurrection with full recognition that it is time to unite in order to accomplish our common aspirations and desires. Let's celebrate this Easter knowing that together we can accomplish our common purpose and destiny. Let us celebrate Christ's resurrection knowing that we have been forgiven and freed from the shackles of injustice, power of sin, and penalty of death and empowered to have a lovely, joyful, peaceful, and prosperous life. Let us vote this week with that mindset.

Wishing all of you a great Easter and May God grant you the power of Christ resurrection and the blessings of courageous leadership.

## 2007 ELECTION APRIL FOOL – PDP OUTSMARTS THE OPPOSITION

Since the chairman of INEC, Prof. Maurice Iwu declared Yar'udua winner of the presidential election, there has been a deluge of writings, articles, comments, videos and so forth on the just concluded state and national elections in Nigeria. Many Nigerians and most of the international observers called the April elections a sham and mockery of democracy. The opposition parties have called for an outright cancellation and a re-run asking the Senate president to form an interim national government. Mass protests are being planned at home and abroad to disrupt the handover ceremony on May 29th. In a nutshell, most Nigerians are baffled, traumatized and even disgusted about the entire April election.

Personally, I have spoken with several people – Nigerians and non-Nigerians around the world, and the feeling is almost the same. Some think that Nigeria is a failed endeavor. I have also participated in panel discussions especially on NIGERIA This WEEK for BlackTelevision.com where most of the panelists and experts on Nigerian political affairs felt slightly different. I have also received a number of emails from friends and colleagues soliciting for my comments about the just concluded elections. Frankly speaking, I remain very humbled to those who seek my opinion especially on political issues of our day. I have often told them that I am not a politician, but as a public theologian and spiritual leader, I am very concerned about the social, economic, moral, and leadership challenges we face today in our society. And for that particular reason, I try to remain engaged by writing and off course through my speaking engagements to bring insight, awareness and consciousness on how bad policies do hamper progress and negatively impart people's lives and destiny.

What I will like to do in this article is to bring to my readers and general public some of my comments on major issues of the concluded elections and perhaps add to it the list of things I believe Yar'udua /Jonathan government should focus on if they genuinely want to make impact in peoples' lives.

Before I begin, I must establish the following facts / assumptions about the April election

1. The April 2007 election was a sham and a mockery of democracy
2. It was massively rigged perhaps more by PDP
3. Violence and killings marred the elections, which is rather unfortunate
4. The Nigerian voters acted very courageously in the face of intimidation and harassment
5. The INEC and its chairman worked for PDP
6. The EFCC and its chairman worked for the incumbency
7. The Police and armed forces protected PDP candidates and their votes
8. The courts and tribunals delayed in their decisions prior to the elections
9. The opposition parties aided PDP to win the elections

In addition to the above, I also want to establish a couple of historical facts.

First that Nigeria is bequeathed with a culture of government that is biased, corrupt and immoral. It is a system that undermines people's interest but favors a few elite. The style of government that the colonial masters bequeathed to us was formulated to shut out true, credible and visionary leaders but rather designed to enthrone weak, incompetent and visionless rulers into position of power and authority. The inability of visionaries like Dr. Nnamdi Azikiwe, Chief Obafemi Awolowo and others to lead Nigeria during their own era is a perfect example. Our current system of government does not recognize nor reward honesty, character, integrity, talents, skills or potentials but rather it recognizes and rewards dishonesty, violence, crooks, cronies, criminals and visionless people. In a nutshell, we are victims of a biased and bad colonial system of government.

Second, Nigerians are also victims of their own envy, jealousy, greed, corruption, rage, anger, bitterness and hatred of one another. I need not to write more sentences here. The civil war, tribal sentiments, religious, cultural and linguistic differences are just a few examples.

Third, God gave mankind a system of government known as theocracy, in which leaders – secular and spiritual are divinely chosen or selected while people give their approval. God instituted government so that we can have order, security and peace in the society (Romans 13). Maintenance of order and protecting the citizens were the original main functions of government. Theocracy is a flawless system because God chose the leaders through prophetic announcements, visions and dreams. However, as mankind became smarter and even wiser than God, they created their own systems namely: democracy, socialism, communism etc. These systems of government are simply superficial and limited. The late Ronald Reagan during his presidency called the Russian politburo an evil empire. The Russians also thought the same about democracy. In fact our new friends, the Chinese thought that democracy is demo-crazy. In short, these systems are organized by human wisdom, which is often driven by greed, ego, selfish and personal interest.

**Comments on April 2007 Election and Results:**

**The 2007 April Election**

According to my evaluation, the 2007 election was successful. Was the election free of rigging, free of violence, fair and credible? No. No one can deny the fact that the April election was a sham. For me, it was an April fool, perhaps the biggest April fool of our nation's history. But we have to understand that it was a successful election for the simple reason that this is the first time in Nigeria's history, there will be smooth democratic transition from one civilian government to another. It has never happened in the history of our country without the interruption especially by the military rulers. It seems to me that the jinx (nemesis) of military ruler-ship is broken forever in

59

our country. And so for me, that is a huge success. I do not have any ill feeling toward the courageous men and women who choose the military but they should remain in the calling that they chose. Their primary duty is that of defense of our country. I do also think that they should not be barred for political participation either. But they have to re-align their mindset to democratic process and freedom of civil societies rather than use of decrees and arm weapons. Moreover, there are many areas in which the military personnel can pursue their leadership aspirations.

**Election Results**

Many have questioned the legitimacy of the results especially the presidency in which Chairman Maurice Iwu declared Yar'udua winner with 70% of the electoral votes. For sure there is some skepticism there. Presidential elections were conducted on Saturday April 21$^{st}$ and by Monday April 23$^{rd}$; chairman Iwu gave Yar'udua /Jonathan a landslide victory of a whooping 70%. Personally, I do not believe that INEC had the capacity, resources and manpower to collate and count all the votes from 36 states of the federation. May be the actual presidential result was based on the eleven states as some have written. If Yar'udua /Jonathan were leading in those eleven states, Chairman Iwu may have projected Yar'udua winner based on the results of the eleven states. He may have also based his projections on the fact that a week earlier, PDP won 29 out 36 governor seats in the federation. I believe in a genuine democratic process, there was no way ANPP or PPA or AC with their handful governors and members of the national assembly would run the country successfully when PDP won majority of the state governors and national house of assembly. We have to be realistic here.

I am also concerned because all the political strategists for the opposition parties never saw the results coming. On the Atlanta based program: NIGERIA This WEEK for BlackTelevision.com, Dr. Femi Ajayi dedicated several episodes on April 2007 elections. On those shows, the panelists and experts on Nigeria's political affairs painstakingly and precisely dissected the voter's registration exercise, census, EFFC, INEC, PTDF, candidates, historical tendencies and with common sense prophesized that PDP will clear the elections. The panelists were not religious or spiritual gurus except me yet; the men and women on that program precisely prognosticated the results. We suggested to the opposition parties on what to do to give PDP a good fight but apparently, they never listened or ignored us.

**Voting, Rigging and Violence**

I have always maintained that the April 2007 election was rigged during the voter's registration and national counting exercise in which Kano was counted as having more people than Lagos and Baysela more than Abia. We must understand that the national census a very important exercise for national planning and development. And even here, we are not realistic. One of the ways we can move forward as a nation is to rectify the injustices and imbalance in our society and promote fairness, equity and prosperity across the board. The 2007 April election was also rigged during the voting exercise. Otherwise why would certain individuals go to voting camps with guns and knives to kill people, carting and snatching of away ballot boxes? In some local areas, the voters were intimidated, humiliated and threatened to be shot when they did not allow strangers to snatch away ballot boxes. The police and armed forces aided the major riggers in the April election. However, the most immoral situation is when innocent Nigerians trying to exercise their basic constitutional rights are killed or murdered in cold blood by hooligans and power seeking cabals. Ours is a culture of corruption and power drunk murderers who are lazy, unskilled, incapacitated and visionless human beings. A lot of democratic education is urgently needed to restore hope and dignity to mankind's best system of government. What we saw last month is a mockery and those who have written to compare what happened in Nigeria last April to what is obtainable in the United States, India or elsewhere are very mistaken. Here in the United States, voters are highly civilized and educated. Their voting right is a very powerful tool. And they know how to use to achieve political or leadership change. Our people need a lot of training, learning, development if they must continue this democratic system which is without doubt mankind best system of government.

**The Opposition**

The opposition also parties aided PDP in winning the April 2007 elections. The AC, ANPP, PPA and other mushrooms parties had ample time to work together to give PDP a good fight but they failed because of personal ego and selfish interest. Their leaders lacked foresight and wisdom. How could they remain as small and insignificant as they were and expect to defeat PDP? Forming strong alliances and collaboration is a key leadership skill and the leaders of the opposition parties lack keen insight in this area. The outcome of this election would have changed if AC, ANPP and others had formed an alliance and collaborated in the April elections. Now, they have the audacity to organize mass protest and resort to tribunals. Why do they want to collaborate now for mass protest? They should apologize to Nigerians for their failure because of selfish and personal compromise. They should apologize to Nigerians for their egoistic mannerisms instead of disgracing themselves by mass protesting and going to the tribunal. If they had worked together to produce credible candidates and put their men on the ground to checkmate any rigging, perhaps the election results would be different. Even few days before the state elections, they still could not broker any strong alliance because of their egoistic and selfish desires. Moreover, these parties lacked political strategists and negotiators. They should apologize to the Nigerian people and learn from their mistake

**International Observers**

I read a number of comments released by international observers including African groups. They reported what they saw, which were mostly in the big cities and towns. Unfortunately, the cases of rigging, missing ballot boxes, manipulations, intimidations, violence and killings were worse in the villages and small towns. They are right; however, elections cannot be cancelled because the international observers say it was fraudulent. Our nation's supreme court will have to make that decision. If that will be the case, we will have to spend billions of Naira that were supposedly spent by INEC again. In addition, if preventative measures are not taken, more people will die again. And the worst scenario, the winners now may resort to militancy and sectional violence against the government if they loose. My take, let us just learn from this and begin now to put policies, strategies and disciplinary measures in place to prevent it happening again four years from now.

## INEC and Chairman Maurice Iwu

President Obasanjo hired the chairman of INEC, Prof. Maurice Iwu and assigned him a duty. That duty was clearly to make sure PDP wins in April 2007 elections. The chairman obediently and pragmatically accomplished his assigned task. Why wouldn't the party in power win the April elections when the opposing parties never did anything to show seriousness? PDP is the party in power, the biggest party in the continent with vast resources, manpower, and structure and systems in place. Most of the opposition parties do not even have wards and offices in many states. PDP has in all the states of the federation. How would forty something political parties work independently and hope to win April elections? PDP also showed some wisdom when they completely left campaigning and spending money in the states in which AC and ANPP have strongholds. The chairman saw these things and knew that most of the opposition party leaders were a joke. How would AC or ANPP or PPA win the presidency when they had no organizational strategy, resources and adequate planning to execute the elections?

If we are serious in Nigeria, we should have no more than two strong political parties. That is the only way we can minimize the public spectacle and shame we have now and thereby enhance and practice good democracy.

## EFFC and Chairman Nuhu Ribadu

Mallam Nuhu Ribadu has been courageous in his fight against corrupt leaders. However, we have to remember that he was appointed to that position by president Obasanjo. The president later used him to tackle the enemies of PDP. The senators, governors and VP who failed to win re-election or even run for other offices are good examples of how EFFC was used to hamper and stop their success. There is not doubt that the EFCC and INEC were used to win the April 2007 elections for PDP.

## The Courts and the Tribunals

The nation's judges and magistrates appear to be doing a good job in this democratic dispensation however, bribery and corruption still run rampant. Most of the judges are politically motivated and are generally influenced by the executive. Some of the court decisions have been very confusing and late coming. Most of them were not enforced. The appeals and high courts in many cases gave contradictory adjudications. Even the nations highest court, the Supreme Court also acted very untimely especially on the case of whether VP should stand for presidential elections or not. If the decision was made on time rather than two days before the presidential elections, perhaps the manipulation by INEC officials and monumental rigging would have been minimized. The courts and tribunals aided in this sham election. I hope they understand that as the third arm of the government, their role is that of sustainability of democracy and balance of power between the executive, legislative and judiciary. The judiciary must work for democratic justice and betterment of the people and country rather than for a few selfish cabals.

**The Religious Leaders and False Prophets**

Some church pastors, self acclaimed prophets and religious leaders are an embarrassment to Nigeria. I cannot begin to name the prophecies, satanic comments and pronouncements that have been delivered by many of them and yet none of them came true. I was so mad that I have to respond to one Prophet Dr. Olagunroye Faleyimu, who claimed that God told him that Buhari will win the presidency. Even another false Chaplin claimed that Governor Orji kalu will win the presidency. How short sighted and myopic can these false prophets be. Are these self acclaimed prophets stupid or crazy? May God have mercy on them! Up till date, the leader of Fresh Party, Pastor Chris Okotie still believes that when all is said and done, he will be crowned the president. Yet, he does not want to march; he does not want t go to court. He thinks that God will give him the mantle without working for it. They have lied against God, abused his Word for their selfish greed and manipulated gullible people using their satanic influence and powers. I have no sympathy for ignorant Christian people anymore. They are just gullible and don't want to study to show themselves approved to God.

## Ndi-Igbo

The Igbo nation is in a precarious leadership dilemma. I believe that there is a crisis of leadership among Ndi-igbo today. I also believe that the leadership mess in Nigeria today is largely due to lack of leadership in Igbo-land. Otherwise how would someone explain all the agitation and buzz for Igbo presidency by Ohaneze and United States based Igbo World Congress and yet, no credible candidate stood for presidential elections in April 2007? The Igbo's must purge themselves and their egoistic leadership attitude. The popular saying "Igbo Enwegh Eze" must be stopped and eradicated. We must recognize our sons and daughters who are gifted with genuine leadership skills such as character, integrity, honest, trust, courage, compassion and vision. It is time we reject superficiality and traitors who parade themselves as Igbo leaders. We need credible and courageous men and women to herald the affairs of Igbo nation otherwise, our future and survival in nascent democratic Nigeria is at risk and uncertain. I admire the courage of Chief Odimegwu Ojukwu, who stood against the irrationality and murderous mayhem against the Igbo's that led to the civil war. But there comes a time when a leader realizes that his usefulness is no longer in the leading role but that of mentoring, training and developing young leaders. Chief Ojukwu and many Igbo leaders have failed woefully in this very important leadership succession. He would have rightly remained as mentor rather the mess and shame he has brought upon himself since he returned to Nigeria. Today, even young leaders like Chief Chekwas Okorie are throwing stones at him. What a shame Igbo leaders!

### President Obasanjo's Legacy

President Obasanjo wisely protected his life, leadership succession and legacy. No one in his shoes would do otherwise. First, he obeyed the gentleman's agreement to give back the presidency to the North. If he had done otherwise, the Northern would have come after him when he leaves office. Now, no one can touch him. He is as free as a fly in the present Nigeria. Second, among all the candidates that competed in the PDP primaries, Yar'udua met and satisfied all the all the criteria OBJ was looking for. He is from the North; he is the young brother of his very dear military and political friend. He is shrewd, honest, has integrity and can be trusted. Yar'udua will be loyal to president Obasanjo period. So, he met all the criteria and that's why the president backed him in a "do or die" election in order to protect his life and secure his leadership legacy.

### President Yar'udua and Vice President Jonathan's Cabinet

One of the signs of leadership that would be great is the make up of the cabinet. A leader demonstrates wisdom by the kind of structure and organization of his or her team. I hope that Yar'udua will not succumb to pressures coming from these incompetent Nigeria office seekers who have no real job but to play politics. These men and women do not realize that playing politics is not a job. Most of the politicians in the West are doing it part time or temporarily. After a defeat, they go back to their business, teaching, or community development. It is only in Africa and most third world countries that people think that politics is a job.

Again, most of the people who engage in politics are individuals who have excelled in their previous careers or businesses. Some do not even take salary. Arnold Schwarzenegger, Governor of California is an example. He was compelled by law to accept a dollar for year salary to comply with Internal Revenue Service and other work related laws and policies in the country. The Georgia State legislatives work part time. Most of them are successful lawyers, educators and business men and women. Nigeria needs a rethinking in this area. What we have today in our society is an enormous waste of resource to maintain the fragrant and arrogant lifestyles of these incompetent politicians while the society and majority of Nigerians perish with their skills, talents and potentials.

It baffles me that some Nigerians are running after president elect for ministerial and political appointments. That's a shame. Capable individuals do not solicit for political appointments. It is given to them based on their qualification, character, competency and perhaps past public and private accomplishments. Those Nigerians who are soliciting for political appointments do not have the capacity to head any ministry or office. In fact, they are incompetent because a competent person will not be chasing anyone for office appointment. This is exactly what President OBJ tried to do with Due Process by cleaning out incompetence and visionless directors and ministers who have lead wastefully all these years. Yar'udua must begin now to show some wisdom in the way he chooses his team. For sure, he can retain some of OBJ's folks who performed brilliantly but should not be compelled to retain those incompetent and visionless cronies around OBJ who ill advised him during his tenure. Yar'udua's leadership team will reveal his wisdom, focus and direction of his government.

**What Nigerians expect from Yar'udua and Jonathan Government**

Many writers in this forum have given similar list. I have in the past. Also on NIERIA This WEEK, this subject has been discussed exhaustively. In fact we were even joined by a newspaper publisher from Nigeria. The show will air sometime this month. However, let me once again list them without much explanation. They are self explanatory.

1. Order & unity of Nigeria - Niger Delta Militancy, MASSOB and others.
2. Security of life – Police reform, good pay and empowerment. The openly 20 Naira bribe at checkpoints must stop now.
3. Eradicate bribery & corruption in our society
4. 1999 Constitutional Amendment to address some of the injustices such as resource allocation, economic and political power sharing in the multi-ethic society like Nigeria.
5. State of Emergency to restore educational glory of Nigeria again. None of the Nigerian universities is listed among the best colleges and universities in the world. This is shameful. We are producing half-baked graduates who are not able to compete in international labor market. There is need for specialized and skilled training in technology, medicine and engineering.
6. The diversification of the economy& job creation
7. Healthcare – Build hospitals and clinics in every state and major cities in the country

8. Power and rural electrification
9. Construction and repairs of roads for easy and safe transportation of people, goods and services
10. Infrastructure and Social Services – The less fortunate Nigerians must be assisted
11. National reconciliation ministry to address the cultural, religious and tribal sentiments that hinder qualified Nigerians and hamper realistic growth. There is a need for a genuine healing and reconciliation among all the ethnic and variant groups that make up Nigeria.
12. National value system – Institute basic core values that recognizes all as equal citizens of Nigeria. Setup laws and policies to curb and minimize immorality and social decadence.
13. Environment – More than half of diseases and sickness in Nigeria are environment driven, poverty and lack of medical care not juju or voodoo.
14. Enact and reform the current electoral act law to eliminate god-fathers and money bag politicians from the system. No unskilled or jobless individual should be allowed to run for office. State and national assembly should be on part-time basis except the senators.

In conclusion, I believe we should give Yar'udua /Jonathan a chance to lead the nation. The opposition failed the Nigerian people. Mass protest would not resolve the acrimony and rectify the biased system that we inherited. Yar'udua government must address these anomalies. He must gather all leaders, concerned citizens and public intellectuals to have a discussion on how to move Nigeria forward as a nation. Failure to do would be detrimental to the unity of Nigeria. I think people of good will agree that we need to move on. Mrs. Clinton, the US democratic frontline candidate has expressed her dissatisfaction with Nigeria's April 2007 election. However, she wisely called on the opposition to address their concerns in the court and seek ways to avoid this from happening again.

Yar'udua has pledged to form a unity government to embrace the opposition leaders in his cabinet. He knew that election was not fair; he knew it was manipulated but he is willing to work with everyone to make sure this does not happen again. Most Nigerians are angry, frustrated, discouraged and unhappy. But let's remember our young ones who just want to be fed and taken care of. Let's us eschew bitterness, envy, jealousy and egoistic attitude for the sake of the country. We have all been victimized, traumatized and trapped in a borrowed system without the needed education and economic empowerment to support it. Our youths are hopeless and most of them have been turned into political thugs rather than leaders of tomorrow. Go to foreign embassies and see the lineup and desperation of many of these young people to leave Nigeria for good. Our young girls, mothers of tomorrow have been turned into professional prostitutes in Europe. Our elderly ones are dying like chicken every day in the villages. Many Nigerians are now relocating to South Africa, others to Ghana and some to the Middle East. These are shameful signs that Nigerian leaders need to wake up. Enough is enough. Let's think about posterity not personal prosperity.

## ADOPTING TWO-PARTY STRUCTURE FOR BUILDING STRONG AND STABLE DEMOCRACY

## NIGERIA'S FIRST MADAM SPEAKER – A TRAGIC LEADERSHIP LESSON

I'm hesitant to criticize women in leadership for the simple reason that women are generally more compassionate leaders than their male counterpart. Additionally, a number of women in our world have distinguished themselves whether we are talking about running a country, a corporation or a charity. Not too long ago, we can remember Margaret Thatcher, the iron lady of Britain, late Golden Mier of Israel, Benazir Bhutto, former prime minister of Pakistan, late Mother Teresa of India, Martti Ahtisaari of Finland, Mary Robinson of Ireland, German Chancellor Angela Merkel, Oprah Winfrey, the iconic TV host of America's highest rated "The Oprah Winfrey Show", and currently the founder and president of a $40M Oprah Winfrey Leadership Academy for Girls in South Africa, Nancy Pelosi, first female Speaker of the United States Congress, Dr. Condoleezza Rice, the 66th and first black woman appointed to the United States Secretary of State, Senator (Mrs.) Hilary Clinton, possible first female president of United States not to mention the African super ladies like Ellen Johnson-Sirleaf , current president of Liberia, Dame Virgy Etiaba, ex-Governor of Anambra

State and the first female governor in Nigeria, Dr. (Mrs.) Cecilia Ibru, Managing Director/CEO of Oceanic Bank International Bank Plc and the only woman on the Board of Directors, Dr. (Mrs.) Ndi Okereke-Onyiuke, OON, Director-General, the Nigerian Stock Exchange, Dr. (Mrs.) Dora Akunyili, Nigeria's Drug Czar, Mrs. Oby Ezekwesili, former education minister, madam due process and now VP World bank for Africa and off course the indomitable Dr. (Mrs.) Ngozi Okonjo-Iweala, Managing Director, World Bank. These women depict the virtues and essential leadership qualities of biblical superwomen like Esther, Ruth, Deborah and host of other women who led their people and conquered nations.

And so, when the members of House of Representatives selected Chief (Mrs.) Patricia Olubunmi Etteh last June to become Nigeria's first ever female speaker, most of us received the news with elation as well as with some reservation. The joy was based on the fact that Nigeria's democracy is growing. Nigeria is thinking outside the box and coming of age to elect a woman as speaker. In fact I even dreamed the day, we would see Nigeria's first woman president especially at a time when Nigerian women are occupying leadership roles in global stage. The other aspect of my joy was based on the fact I mentioned earlier that women tend to be more compassionate than men in their leadership duties. They would not normally abuse public funds and squander resources unlike their male counterparts. Nevertheless, I also had reservation especially when I read that Madam Etteh used to be a hair dresser and do not have any sound and credible educational qualification. In addition, she was selected as speaker due to the political wrangling and maneuvering of her political godfather, ex-president Obasanjo. At that time, I knew that Nigeria is in for another bumpy ride in this legislative dispensation. Obviously, my fears and reservation have proven to be true. Nigeria's first female speaker has turned out to be a shame of a nation and a disappointment to millions of women around the world. Her elevation to such an enviable leadership position was a tragic mistake. We should not have elevated a woman who was unprepared morally and who lacked self-discipline and wise counsel.

So, when Mrs. Etteh finally resigned last week amid a monumental scandal of N628 million she approved without due process to renovate her official residence and that of her deputy, Alhaji Babangida Nguroje, it proved the simple truth that when people are elevated to such position of leadership without preparation and discipline, such leader will eventually fail. Examples of such failures abound in our society even within our National Assembly. However, Mrs. Etteh resignation as the speaker did not come easy. Most of you who followed the wrangling and debacle will agree with me that it was a wasted three months in which the so-called honorable members of our hallowed House argued, debated, and even exchanged fists fight. Mrs. Etteh faltered judgment and her blunt refusal to resign led to catastrophic consequences and sudden death of one of their colleagues at the floor of the House. Dr. Aminu Safana, one of the ardent supporters of the embattled speaker succumbed and died of a heart attack during one of the fist fights at the floor of the House. It was also a shameful and unfortunate circumstance in which Hon. Safana died. The men and women at the House could not offer him help.

Even a CPR would have resuscitated him while a non-existent emergency ambulance arrives amid bad road and terrible traffic jam. What a nation! I would strongly encourage the new speaker to hire some nurses and medical practitioners and station them at the House to assist in such medical emergencies.

Nevertheless, the scandal divided the house. The integrity group called for Mrs. Etteh resignation but she insisted she was innocent. A panel headed by Hon. David Idoko was setup to probe the award of N628 million. Rightly, the Idoko panel found her guilty. She has violated the rule of law in awarding the contract and therefore failed in her dereliction of constitutional duty. She was asked to step aside yet Nigeria's first madam Speaker did not think it was wise and honorably thing to do. The civil society, writers, journalists and even the Nigerian masses voiced out their frustration in the matter and publicly asked her to go yet she insisted in order to save her speaker-ship and position of authority. The labor union threatened with a strike to protest at the door of the House yet our admirable Madam speaker remained deceived by her ardent supporters and off courses her almighty party, PDP. Their ill advice and evil influence turned her into an unspeakable vile woman. She turned into an enigma and became Nigeria's nightmare. Even with the death of one of her ardent supporters, Dr. Safana, she did not recant or repent. What a Jezebel spirit!

However, in all this, our servant leader president felt not to intervene in the legislative process. I am yet to understand this political correctness of President Yar'udua who claimed to be a stickler to due process , rule of law and transparency, yet one of his principal leaders approves a sum of N628 million to renovate a house without due process, and the president felt his hands are tied to intervene. What's it that tied the hands of the president from even advising the speaker to do the right thing. The president was not asked to intervene in the legislative matters if our failed constitution hindered him from doing so. But at least, he could have privately, boldly and courageously as a stickler to rule of law and due process asked the embattled speaker to quit. Again, this is a classic case to stimulate serious discussion on the 1988 constitution, which was by the way given to us by Nigeria's worst brutal dictator. How is it possible that in the 21$^{st}$ century, with all the brains, intellectuals and bright people we have in and outside of Nigeria, that we continue to govern our nation using late General Abacha's biased constitution? The national assembly must as a matter of urgency reform our polity starting with this half baked constitution of the federal republic of Nigeria. Today, all the ex-governors who served under ex-president Obasanjo who were clearly indicted for looting of state treasury and money laundering overseas are still walking and talking freely in Nigeria. None of them is imprisoned yet because of this nonsense immunity in the constitution. When will this country get serious about the business of governance and transparent leadership? The world is watching at a nation that claims to be the giant and recently the heart of Africa and yet our leaders are such a national and international embarrassment.

At a time when Nigerians are cleaning their image abroad and dazzling the world, yet at home, our leaders are a laughing stock. Just in the last few months, Nigerian women are taking over global leadership at the Apex bank. Mrs. Oby Ezekwesili is now the VP of World bank for Africa region while Mrs. (Dr). Ngozi-Okonjo Iweala has been appointed MD of World Bank. Last June, the world was stunned as Mr. Rotimi Adebari, became elected as the first black mayor in Ireland while the Junior Eagles dazzled the world winning the under 21 world cup by beating Brazil, Argentina and Germany respectively. Mr. Samuel Okon Peter brings the World Heavyweight Boxing title to Nigerian (WBC) and an 8 - year old Nigerian baby wins world teen beauty pageant. As usual, the international poet and pride of Africa, Dr. Achebe wins the highest US prize on Literature and Nigerian scholars and scientists dazzle Howard, Oxford universities in England and USA respectively. Yet, at home, we let half baked and undisciplined people to continue to direct and govern the affairs of our nation. It is a known fact that intellectuals in most cases do not engage in politics because of the brutality of the game of politics. However, many intellectuals and bright people aside from leading in academic universities have also forcefully engaged in industries, businesses and certain aspects of governance. It is because of the foolishness of our leaders and their colonial mentality that a frail James Watson could make such insane comments about people of color and black race in general. Dr. James Watson forgot to understand that the zenith of power that the U.S. enjoys today were primarily attained due to the hard work, labor and intellectual minds of many people of color that were brought or who came to this free new land since its discovery.

Nigeria's first female speaker and her deputy tended her resignation blaming the press for their failure. Their reasons for resignation again restate their hardened heart and unrepentant spirit. It clearly demonstrates a "smelling revelation of a Jezebel spirit." Sources claimed that ex-president OBJ, PDP Chairman Ahmadu Ali, and PDP leadership may have asked her to resign to avoid being impeached. Moreover, the labor union was prepared to shut things down at the House. The attitude of Mrs. Etteh clearly reveals her legislative inexperience and lack of self-discipline. She exposed her lust for power, folly of pride and poor leadership skills. She was not prepared to lead such a hallowed House. Since the House was constituted nearly six months, the honorable members have not passed any single law. Rather, all they had done was to share committee positions, pay themselves car, house and furniture allowances. Then the honorable and admirable speaker took a birthday bash to the United States where she lavished tax payer's money.

Mrs. Etteh was unprepared. Lack of preparation and self-discipline will always lead to poor leadership. I have often said and written widely that preparation is such a neglected aspect of leadership especially in our country. Effective leadership requires physical, emotional, spiritual and moral preparation in addition to educational and professional qualification. Without adequate training and mentorship, leadership will suffer and be painful. This is exactly what we experienced with our first ever female speaker. She lacked the wisdom, discernment and moral attitude to lead the House of Representatives. In a country where more than 80% of the population earns less than a dollar a day and where millions live under broken huts and thatched houses, Mrs. Etteh should have know that before approving N628 million to renovate her official residence. Who does she think she is? She is a disappointment to millions of women who looked up to her to enact laws and legislations that will provide jobs for their children and save their young ones from the shackles of injustice, hopelessness, joblessness and economic slavery. She is a humiliation to millions of women who looked to her for a compassionate leadership, where most men have failed. Mrs. Etteh is a tragic mistake because she was a product of a nation where the game of politics is still driven by greed, envy, jealousy, corruption, use of threat and innuendos to achieve political power, superficial authority, bad influence and temporal material gain. In a nutshell, Mrs. Etteh is a global embarrassment at a time when Nigerian women are going places according to Patience Akpan-Obong in her recent article. She exposed her in-experience and poor organizational skills. I hope that our society would not hold this tragic leadership experience against other possible talented and visionary women in our society. Undoubtedly, it would be difficult to trust women with such sensitive leadership positions so soon in Nigeria.

**Lessons Learned**

1. There is still hope for Nigeria's democracy. Nigeria's democracy will evolve.
2. There are still men and women of character, honor and integrity in the House
3. When all Nigerians are united to speak with one voice – morally, powerfully, courageously, there is no evil, we cannot overcome – Third Term Agenda and Mrs. Etteh.

4. People should not be elevated to a position of authority when they are not prepared and qualified professional and educationally.
5. People without fortitude of character and discipline should not be placed in such powerful leadership positions.
6. Without self-discipline and accountability, there is no leadership.
7. Bad leaders always remain rigid and inflexible, insisting upon their own dictates regardless of the situation.
8. Personal and positional power will succumb and fail when people rise up against immorality and abuse of public office.
9. Sometimes, we fail to realize and recognize the true source of our success, elevation and power.
10. God is the true source of power and authority. He elevates, sustains and demotes when we remove our eyes from Him and depend on our abilities, power, connections and influence.

## Advice to the incoming Speaker, Hon Dimeji Sabur Bankole

First of all, I congratulate Hon. Dimeji Sabur Bankole for his selection as new speaker of the House. You are an educated and talented young man. Your selection as speaker is without doubt a leadership shift to a younger generation. I'm amazed that educated, bright and young visionaries like you are in the House, while uneducated, undisciplined and hairdressers are selected as speakers. I know that you are still celebrating, thanking God and obviously still in euphoria for your selection as speaker; however, this is not the time to suddenly realize you never knew you will be flying presidential jet. This is a time to roll down your sleeves and get down with the business of the House. You have a huge task before you. You must not fail; otherwise all the young people of our country will be disappointed in you just like the millions of women in Nigeria today. You must learn from this tragic mistake. A good leader will always learn from past mistake and I do hope that you learn from this tragic leadership mistake. You must develop the moral character and fortitude to lead the House. You must work very hard to restore dignity to the House. You must restore confidence to millions of Nigerians who have lost hope in their elected officials. You must be a wise young man who is skilled in management and conflict resolution. You must work hard to reconcile the aggrieved groups within the House and restore the lost confidence in our elected officials. It is my prayer that future leaders will learn from this mistake and correct the abuse and recklessness in the public service. Leaders are elected to serve, protect and teach followers how to live better lives. Leaders are not elected, appointed or selected to exploit their followers. God despises leaders who exploit others. Wise leaders always learn from failure. I hope Mrs. Etteh learns a lesson from her failure and political demise and that the new speaker will do everything within his power to avoid such mistakes.

God bless Nigeria.

# NAIRA POLICY SUSPENSION – A MISGUIDED LEADERSHIP DECISION

*The hastily suspension of the Strategic Agenda for Naira by the President without any careful thought and serious consideration of the new policy is unwise and misguided leadership decision –*
*Dr. C. K. Ekeke*

According to the Book of Proverbs Chapter 23, Good leaders make wise decisions. In my recently published book: Leadership Wisdom – Inspirational Insights for Supernatural Leadership, I wrote these words on page 28, "Most of leadership activity is about making decisions. A wise leader must depend on God and wise advisers when making tough decisions. Life changing decisions must not be made based on human intellect and rationalization alone but must be made with complete reliance on God." In a nutshell, wise leaders make good decisions.

The Strategic Agenda for Naira (SAN), which was announced by the Central Bank of Nigeria (CBN) Governor, Professor Chukwuma Soludo some weeks ago generated a lot of discussion and dialogue among Nigerians at home and abroad. While many Nigerians – experts on economic matters and novices as well are still discussing, learning and enjoying this special area of economics discipline known as monetary economics, the office of the presidency suddenly announced the suspension of the policy for lack of due process and other unnecessary reasons which will be reviewed in this article.

Why did the president who claimed to be a servant leader abruptly suspend a policy that could well add value to our economy and thereby improve the lives of so many suffering Nigerian people? The CBN Governor, Prof. Soludo brilliantly explained the microeconomic as well as the macroeconomic benefits of SAN. Some economic experts and public policy experts also articulated the socioeconomic merits of the new Naira policy. Why would the office of the president and his economic team not take sometime to review the policy rather than such a hastily manner in which the Naira re-denomination policy was suspended. Prof. Soludo's Naira re-denomination or decimalization policy according to my estimation is a much-needed monetary policy that will not only liberalize our battered currency but also reverse the scandalous Structural Adjustment Programme (SAP) – the devaluation of Naira by General Babangida in the 1980's. And lest I forget, including the visionless monetary policy of another autocratic and tyrannical ruler, General Sani Abacha in which the Naira was officially pegged against the US dollar and other Western currencies. The suspension of new Naira policy by President Yar'Adua is sad and unfortunate. It's rather regrettable that President Yar'Adua suspended such a great policy that will benefit the country's economy just for lack of due process. I think that the Minister of Finance, Dr. Shamsudeen Usman and the Attorney General of the Federation and Minister of Justice, Mr. Mike Aondoakaa are misguiding the president in this situation. This is just politics which is bad for the common masses while promoting the egoistic and unbridled powers of those involved in the tussle. I hope the president will rethink his decision otherwise; he's just flip-flopping and double speaking unlike who he claimed to be.

By the way, economic reforms and monetary policies are not new to Nigerians. We Nigerians have been through a lot of them since we became independent from our former colonial masters. Despite the civil war era monetary policies that were purely punitive and spiteful treatment of the so-called enemies of the Nigerian state, our leaders have always foisted on us borrowed economic and monetary policies that kept the majority of the Nigerian people poorer than they were before. For instance in the early 1970's when oil prices were at all time high, General Gowon was in power, he boasted that Nigeria had so much external reserves. When the military peacefully ousted him, the short-lived administration of General Murtala Mohammed paved the way for Obasanjo to head the government. Despite the excess external reserves and more than $25 billion oil revenue during that time, General Obasanjo surprisingly introduced austerity measures and prudent fiscal measures which had severe effects on millions of Nigerians. Poverty, pandemic diseases including quasiokor and other health hazards of the war era became rampant and afflicted many Nigerians especially the children and elderly.

However, Obasanjo cowardly managed to finish his three-year term, which ushered in the first democratic elected government of Shehu Shagari in 1979. In October that year President Shagari and his administration quickly discarded the austerity measures instituted by outgoing Obasanjo's regime. Shehu Shagari's government introduced corruption and greed that are elevated in our society today. Corruption rose to all time high and his governors and senior government officials looted the national treasury and laundered money just like Obasanjo's governors of few months ago. Many rose from rags to riches while those without any representation in government malnourished and starved to death.

The inept government of Shehu Shagari with the monumental corruption among his cabinet led General Buhari to oust him in a bloodless palace coup. General Buhari re-introduced the stringent fiscal responsibility and instituted war against indiscipline and corruption in the country. However, his fiscal policies did not survive due to another palace coup that brought in yet another general, this time, the so-called Maradonna of Nigerian politics, General Ibrahim Babangida. General Babangida introduced perhaps the most popular economic and monetary policy known as Structural Adjustment Programme (SAP). I could not forget SAP because not only did the policy devalue our currency and made life extremely difficult for many students of average parents studying overseas to remit their tuition, but I wrote a paper on the scandalous economic and monetary policy in one of my finance classes discussing the merits and demerits of SAP.

SAP, which was later known as "Suffer and Perish" had devastating effects on the economy and severe consequences on millions of Nigerians worldwide. According to Babangida's economic team and their Western friends at World Bank and IMF - the writers of the economic package, SAP would restructure the economy and achieve a realistic exchange rate for Naira. Rather than achieve the economic benefits promised by General Babangida and his protégées, SAP created a comatose economy with wrenching problems - severe inflation, massive unemployment, declining foreign reserves, huge balance of payments and a valueless Naira. General Babangida celebrated corruption, enthroned the new super rich while millions of Nigerians suffered. Up till today, General IBB and his cronies have not accounted for the 1990's oil windfall and the billions that were made in oil revenues. In fact the era of IBB led to the beginning of the moral decadence and purposeless society that we have today. The depth of corruption and degradation led to moral decline, ethical and spiritual decadence at all levels in our society. Where is the moral conscience of our leaders? I think our leaders have crisis of conscience and are morally bankrupt.

Well, to make to this article readable, I will not waste much of my time on another visionless ruler by the name of General Sani Abacha. He ruled for five years and did not even understand what the nation's economy is all about. He disbanded SAP programme and introduced a monetary policy that began the official pegging of the Naira against dollar and other industrialized currencies. During Abacha's era, the official rate of Naira rose to nearly 200 Naira for a dollar. He destroyed the Naira and basically rubbished the Nigerian economy, which actually elevated greed, bribery, and corruption and enthroned most of the crooks, cronies and pathetic individuals we have today as leaders in our nation. The billions he looted out of the country are still being located around the world and can never be completely recuperated. He was perhaps the worst Nigeria has had. And thank God, the law of nemesis caught up with in his sadist and adulterous life style.

How would anyone then compare the economic reforms and monetary policies briefly described above with the current visionary policy of Prof. Soludo, which is by the way the second phase of the NEEDS economic reform of the party in power? As I said earlier, Prof. Soludo has brilliantly articulated the benefits of his policy and it is the responsibility of the President and his economic team to review the policy for its merits and demerits, technicalities and implementation etc, as well its implication on the economy, on the people, inflation, trade (import & export), prices of goods and services etc. If the policy needs to be amended anywhere, the CBN folks can be then be briefed about it. For the President and his misguided advisers to disown the Naira policy for lack of due process is an indication of unpreparedness and lack of focus as the leader of a complex country like Nigeria.

In a simple and layman's economic language, the Strategic Agenda for naira (SAN) as announced by the CBN governor will remove the last two zeros from the Naira. For example, a 100 naira will become 1 Naira and 500 Naira will become 5 Naira. Even though I do not believe such intervention in monetary matters is the best way to achieve economic growth, however, many countries including the industrialized nations sometimes do use government intervention to save declining currency and help their economy. The CBN monetary policy arrangement was supposed to liberalize our currency and position Nigeria with the gains in banking and financial sectors to be the financial center of Africa. Without doubt the microeconomic, macroeconomic and socioeconomic benefits far outweigh what we have had in the past.

For sure, we do know that the Naira policy was not designed to achieve any realistic exchange with dollar. That will not happen with an unproductive economy and dilapidated infrastructure. Moreover, the United States economy is 1000 times stronger than Nigeria's economy. Even South Africa that is often cited has an economy that is 100 times stronger than ours while that of Ghana is 6 times stronger than Nigeria economy according to World Economic Forecasting magazine. So, this policy is not designed to achieve any favorable exchange rate with US dollar. That is not its main thrust, rather it is designed to reverse the scandalous monetary policies of Babangida and Abacha era, which basically rubbished the country's currency and created the unbridled greed, corruption, ethical, moral and spiritual decadence in our society today. If President Yar'Adua wants to protect some interest groups it means then that he is no longer the servant leader he's claiming to be. I think that this policy will be a big test for his presidency and perhaps demonstrate how he cares for the generality of Nigerians irrespective of their ethnic, religious, linguistic, cultural and class background.

The reasons given for the suspension and rejection of Prof. Soludo's Naira re-denomination policy do not hold water. I do agree that the CBN governor should have briefed the president and his economic team before his public announcement; however, there is speculation that the Attorney General of the Federation and Minister of Justice, Mr. Mike Aondoakaa and the Minister of Finance, Dr. Shamsudeen Usman would have frustrated it. However, other reason that the economy is not in hyperinflation is irrelevant and in-fact senseless statement. Babangida's monetary policy - the devaluation of Naira, was implemented when the Nigerian economy was in hyperinflation, then his economic team and their IMF friends argued that devaluation would cure the hyperinflation and restructure the economy. Now we do not have any hyperinflation, it means that if Babangida and his IMF monetary gurus were right, a non-hyperinflation economy like ours today would need Prof. Soludo's policy - the re-valuation of Naira in order to consolidate on the economic gains already taking place in economy.

Another reason according to the president that adopting the re-denomination of the Naira policy would have amounted to "applying surgery on a patient that is not sick" does not hold any water either. In fact our economy does need an urgent surgery. What we have today despite the economic reforms of president Obasanjo is an unproductive, jobless, distressful and hopeless economy with dilapidated infrastructures. If there is anything to do is now to rehabilitate the oppressive and repressive economy. President Yar'Adua promised that he will continue President Obasanjo's economic reform, admitted recently that Nigerians are going through hell and promised to create 40 million jobs within 10 years, lower interest rates, reduce inflation and achieve realistic exchange rate for Naira, yet he does not want to support CBN monetary policy which is the second phase of PDP economic agenda.

Inasmuch as the CBN governor may have sounded with some air of pride and arrogance in this matter, for a highly educated young man at his current position, it is hard to avoid. However, the guy has performed and has proven that his ideas can work. In this matter, I believe he should not have overlooked the presidency knowing fully well that President Yar'Adua is big on due process and rule of law unlike his predecessor, who abused every law and power beneath ASO Rock. I also agree to an extent some of the comments made by many writers on this forum. If the 500 and 100 Naira notes were just introduced last year amounting to billions of expenses, why would the CBN governor want to disband those high notes for 20 Naira as the highest currency in the new policy? I think that the new Naira policy should include 50 and 100 notes. Nigerians don't want to appear or sound poor. Those who have billions in the bank do not want to wake up one morning and hear that they have only millions or those who have millions now, do not want to be told that they have only thousands. It is a psychological thing.

However, I do disagree with our respected economist and scholar, Prof. Aluko and others who alleged that the World Bank, IMF and other Western powers are using the CBN governor. Even though the World Bank was the first to hail the new Naira policy and pledged their support, the Nigerian Government officials did not brief them about it. They only read it in the papers according to the Director of the World Bank in Nigeria, Ms. Sotirova Galina. Rather, it is the CBN governor who has been an ardent and forceful supporter of African autonomy in the management of its banking, financial and monetary matters. I believe Prof.

Soludo formulated this policy with his team and they mean well for the nation's economy.

I do not also believe that the Naira policy was designed to derail Yar'Adua's government as some have alleged. The people who will derail Yar'Adua's government are those he has surrounded himself with like Justice Michael Aondoakaa, Finance Minister, Dr. Shamsudeen Usman and others who have suddenly become the Fani Kayode's and Uba's of OBJ era. It is the enemies of the Nigerian people who will "do or die" to sabotage the efforts of Prof. Soludo and his colleagues at CBN.

As I have written before, President Yar'Adua is yet to demonstrate that he is truly a servant leader he claimed to be because a servant leader gives serious considerations to matters and always endeavor to make wise decisions. Decision-making is a fundamental responsibility of leaders. Harry S. Truman, the thirty-third President of the United States of America has been called a great leader because he had the ability to decide and was willing to accept the consequences of his decisions. The Nigerian people need the assurance that their president is capable of making wise decisions. As the leader of this great and complex country, President Yar'Adua and Vice President Goodluck Jonathan need wise and godly advisers' not selfish and egoistic individuals who are rattling around them for their selfish interest.

Leadership decisions are not made hastily, casually, flippantly or untimely either. Life changing decisions must be made with careful thought because as Peter Drucker wrote in his book - The Effective Executive, "Every decision is like a surgery. It is an intervention into a system and therefore carries with it the risk of shock." And that's why leaders must be prayerful and seek God's wisdom in making decisions. Leaders must also be students of history, which will guide them in making good decisions. Great leaders make decisions and stand by it. A Servant makes decisions and stand by his or her decisions. President Yar'Adua must cultivate the fortitude to stand by his decisions and accept whatever merits or consequences of his decisions. He must look to God and trusted advisers in running the affairs of this great, giant and heart of Africa – called Nigeria. Servant leaders are also aware that one day they will stand before God and give an account to Him.

## TWO-PARTY SYSTEM – A VITAL INGREDIENT OF POLITICAL AND ELECTORAL REFORM

*I believe that two-party system should be a critical element in the political and electoral reform for developing Nigeria's political culture, for enhancing our system of government and for building a strong democratic nation – Dr. C. K. Ekeke*

About two weeks ago, the House of Representatives voted down two-party system, which was proposed by the Minority Leader, Hon Ali Ndume, which suggested limiting to only two political parties to be registered for 2011 elections. Even though, the two-party amendment was not among the forty amendments that were proposed to improve the 1999 Nigerian constitution, however, most of us have been writing since the beginning of our 4th

93

Republic and return to democratic presidential system, which was modeled from the United States of America, to adopt a two party structure and perhaps allow few independent political candidatures and political parties.

I am acutely aware of my limitations and skimpy knowledge on the subject of political science and game of politics because I am not a politician or a student of political science. But as a public theologian and passionate student of leadership, I decided to take on this subject matter for the simple reason that it has persisted for so long in my mind. This piece is perhaps an attempt to awaken our able political science scholars, politicians, law makers, and those enlightened minds on the subject of political science and art of governance to rethink Nigeria's current political culture and figure out how our nation can tailor and construct its political systems that are capable of producing credible candidates, knowledgeable electorates, build strong democratic values, and able to yield the expected dividends of democracy.

Historically, Nigeria has had various systems of government – unitary, parliamentary, military and now democratic presidential system, yet without any political peace or progress. It was the erudite scholar and Nigeria's former permanent representative to UN, Dr. Joseph Nanyen Garba, in his book, Fractured History , who said "In our thirty-four years of nationhood, we have made an unprecedented turnaround; going from a nation of hope, strength, abundance, economic prosperity and high aspirations to a nation which has become the embodiment of a degenerate society."

Since independence, Nigeria has been governed by a group of selfish, greedy, egoistic, visionless, malicious, mischievous and treacherous political and military rulers. Despite the enormous human potential and abundant natural resources Nigeria is endowed with, she has not enjoyed any genuine political peace and national prosperity. Instead, the country has been ruled and governed by military and political tyrants that denied the masses basic governmental provisions such as security, order, peace and basic necessities of livelihood and also denied the people the yearnings of every human being, which is the inalienable right to life, justice and pursuit of happiness.

For nearly fifty years now, what we've had in Nigeria is a military dictatorship and political tyrants that oppressed the poor and minority members of the Nigerian state. The promises of these various governments have been a dismal failure. They have not kept their promises or dealt with wrenching problems facing the people and nation but floundered and left the Nigerian masses worse than when they were under the British colonial regime. In a nutshell, Nigeria's ruling class with their borrowed systems of government have failed to fulfill its obligations to the nation and to the people.

And so, with the return to democratic system of government in 1999, people felt relieved but since then Nigeria has not had any credible and fair elections or seen any substantial dividends of democracy. The INEC has not been able to organize any fair and free elections. The 1999 and 2003 elections were marred with massive rigging, ballot stealing, violence, killings, political thuggery, and all sorts of court actions against political opponents. The 2007 election was worse. It was just a sham and mockery of democratic elections. The INEC did not have the capacity, resources, and manpower to collate and count all the votes from 36 states of the Federation and yet declared the late Musa Yar'Adua as president elect. What we have seen since the last ten years or so has been sort of a perilous political environment of the worst kind.

One of the key reasons among many for this political muddle is because of Nigeria's weak political culture. In 2003, about fifty political parties were registered by INEC for general elections and about twenty-five candidates for presidential election. Even though democracy is a system of number, it does not mean that every Dick and Harry will have to form a political association and run for office. In fact, as at today, there are about fifty-seven political parties in Nigeria and about 47 candidates are nursing ambition to run for the office of the president. I read recently where 1,200 candidates are running for PDP chairmanship in Cross River State. This is absolutely a joke and mockery of democratic system of government.

It is for this reason that most of us have been writing and speaking out for years about the need for our nation to truly model the United States style of democracy of two party system even though our electorates and nation's infrastructure may not be at par with the U.S. I still think that two-party system should be a critical element in the constitutional amendment because it will help to develop

Nigeria's political culture, enhance our system of government, and build a strong democratic nation.

There are those on the opposing side who think otherwise. I strongly believe that electoral reform will never work effectively no matter who the President appoints as INEC leader without political reform. And the key to electoral reform is limiting to only two-party systems for general elections such as the House of Representative, Senate, Governors and Presidency. The INEC officials must be trained and provided with vast resources, manpower and systems in place in order to conduct free and fair election. In fact the electronic voting system suggested by Senator Ayo Arise of Ekiti State should be a viable solution if the Nigerian State truly wants to have a genuine, fair and credible election.

Most people I talk to including politicians and regular Nigerians from all walks of life believe that two-party system will actually help to restrain some of the cultural, social and political ills in our society – such as ethnicity, tribalism, religious intolerance, corruption, bad leadership, etc. Today, Nigeria is grouped into six-geopolitical entities. The political wrangling and debate over the zone that will produce the next presidency – the so-called zonal or rotational presidency may be reduced and with time permanently eliminated if Nigeria adopts two political parties that are broad based and with shared vision and political will to transform not just one region of the country but the entire nation. The zoning arrangement in PDP today will not exist if there was another strong opposition party. Names such as - Peoples Republican Party (PRP) or

Nigerian Republican Party (NRP) have been suggested that can be formed with broad based structure, ideals, and visions that are embraced by all the ethnicity and tribes within Nigeria with credible and visionary people, who have great aspirations to transform not just one region of the country but the entire nation.

Today, PDP is the only broad based Nigerian party and that is why every one is joining the party. But it will be a sad day if Nigeria happens to become a one party state. General Abacha tried it in the 1990's and failed. I think that the leaders of ANPP, AC, APGA, PPA, CPC, PMP, PDM, and other mushroom political parties for the interest of our nation must set aside their egoistic and selfish desires, power greed and come together to form a strong alliance with a refined vision that is embraced by all so that it can present itself as a credible opposition party to PDP in 2011. In a country of nearly 250 ethnic groups and 57 political parties will further divide the nation and create a national dilemma and political nightmare. Since democracy is a system of numbers, there will be no hope for any party that does not have a broad based national influence or possibility of winning any national elections or even within state level will be a mirage.

I'm afraid to say that what we have currently in Nigeria is a democratic totalitarian statecraft in which power is concentrated in the center and if the other political parties do not find common ground to come together as one strong opposition party against PDP, Nigeria may be heading toward a one party state, which is a very dangerous thing and may lead to denial of the individual rights, limitation of freedom of speech, abuses of equal rights and privileges.

Off course, one party system is no longer democracy but communism. More so, even with one major party in power for nearly eleven years now, there is no way internal democracy can be enhanced without strong opposition. Our political culture will never be strong because of political persecutions, violence, killings, thuggery and political godfathers. Nigerians may be forced to embrace programs that are overly policing against popular will and against the interest of the poor masses. There will be no social, economic and political justice at the council, state and national levels. There will be a sort of political impenitent and impunity which will be lethal damage to peace, unity, progress, and well-being of most Nigerian people.

But two-party arrangement with strict party Code of Conduct with criteria such as leadership as service, patriotism, integrity, ethno-neutral, religious tolerance, shared vision, transparency-driven, knowledge-driven, good virtue, basic education, and character can discourage a lot of unskilled and unprepared people from running for political office. Such party ideals will discourage those crops of Nigerians that are superficial, cryptic, inept, greedy, corrupt, unqualified, arrogant and incompetent, whose stock in trade is to steal, embezzle, diminish and rubbish the potential of Nigerian people and society.

It is so sad that the House of Representatives did not give the two-party amendment any serious consideration in their constitutional amendment exercise. The constitution ought to be a document designed to protect the unity of the country and its citizen from tyranny. It ought to be a document that defines the rights of her citizens and not just assigning duties to them. Even in the Western culture, with particular reference to the United States of America, the constitution is revised from time to time otherwise the constitution falls captive to the anachronistic views of long-gone generations. If any constitutional amendment does not acknowledge shortcomings and in our case - establish a well-defined set of core values that addresses national unity, patriotism and parameters to discourage ethnicity, tribalism and religious intolerance among the peoples of a diverse and complex nation like Nigeria, then we are just wasting our time as one indivisible nation. We cannot move forward as a nation and fulfill our common purpose and destiny if ethnicity, tribalism and injustice are not addressed in our country. We truly need a national identity that harbors ethnicity and discourages tribal identity.

Today, what we have in Nigeria is a culture of government that is biased, corrupt and immoral. It is a system that undermines people's needs but favors a few elite. The style of democracy that we practice in Nigeria today is designed to discourage true, credible and visionary leaders but rather designed to enthrone weak, incompetent, visionless and ruthless rulers into position of power and authority. Our current system of government does not recognize nor reward honesty, character, integrity, talents, skills or potentials but rather recognizes and rewards dishonesty, violence, crooks, cronies, criminals and visionless people. In a nutshell, we are victims of a biased and slave mentality system of government. The Bible clearly teaches that government is instituted so that people may have order, security and peace in the society (Romans 13). That has not been the case in Nigeria and for Nigerians. Additionally, Nigerians are also victims of their own envy, jealousy, greed, corruption, rage, anger, bitterness and hatred of one another. The civil war, tribal sentiments, religious, cultural and linguistic differences are just a few examples that continue to divide the nation into various ethno groups.

If we are serious about building strong democracy and enhancing our political culture, we must reverse the culture of cultic political associations that we currently have today. Today, our political culture is a culture of impunity, money worshippers, egotism, greed, avarice, envy, hatred, jealousy, immorality, idolatry, atrocities, ignorance, darkness and death. Political rituals, divination, astrology, sorcery, witchcraft, magic, and all manners of evil and satanic manipulation have become the order of the day in today's Nigeria political landscape. No one can be nominated to even a state commissioner without entering into some sort of cultic and ritualistic worship. Because of this idolatrous democratic system, qualified and well meaning individuals have removed themselves from such satanic worship and refused to participate into something that will defy their conscience and true worship of God.

Sadly enough, what we have today is a political culture of corruption, greed, arrogance, violence and killings because being elected to political office have become the surest and easiest way to amass wealth. We must change the trend and reverse the political mentality in order to encourage intellectuals and other talented individuals to join politics so that we can truly transform our nation. Until we restructure our political systems and the electoral reform which is in the mouth of millions, we will not see any fair, free and credible elections, no matter who the President or an independent body appoints as INEC chairman. I believe without a doubt that two-party structure will help to enhance Nigeria's political culture and eradicate the political callousness in our nation today.

## THE ROLE OF RELIGIOUS LEADERS IN DEMOCRATIC ELECTION AND GOVERNMENT

## THE ROLE OF RELIGIOUS LEADERS

---

*When the righteous rule the people rejoice, when the wicked rule, the people suffer (Proverbs 29:2)*

*"If you are not electing religious people, then in essence, you are going to legislate sin." - By Katherine Harris, who ran for Senate as a Republican in Florida?*

One of the key legacies of great leadership is the joyful transfer of power and authority to trustworthy, honest and ethical individual. From biblical days until present, great leaders have always personally prepared successors or persons they believe have the courage and capacity to lead. In the Holy Scriptures, we read how Moses mentored Joshua and before his death, formally presented Joshua to the people and publicly charged him to be strong and courageous (Deuteronomy 31:1-8). His personal preparation and public recognition of his successor made the leadership transition smooth and unambiguous. In chapter 34 verses 9 of the same book, we read that Joshua the son of Nun was filled with the spirit of wisdom because Moses had laid his hands on him, so the Israelites listened to him and did what the LORD had commanded Moses.

President Obasanjo has in the past joyfully transitioned power as military head of state to a democratic elected president of Alhaji Shehu Shagari in 1978/79. That singular act of leadership, which is unusual for most African leaders, earned him respect and honor among the leaders of the world. As he prepares to leave office in May 2007, his leadership legacy especially his presidency cannot be laudable without a smooth transition to a president that Nigerians will accept and trust. I mean President Obasanjo owes Nigerians smooth and fair elections in 2007 and a guarantee that the next tenant at ASO ROCK will be a person of integrity, character and vision. Nigerians want a president who would continue the bold and courageous reform and fight against the cankerworm that has hindered us for a long time. This to my estimation would be perhaps the greatest achievement of Obasanjo's presidency. For those who would be called to write his leadership legacy, the smooth transition in 2007 would truly be a great chapter to write about. President Obasanjo is destined to become an icon and great leader if he can carefully and wisely transition power to a man or woman who will continue the democratic reform that he has initiated.

To achieve this kind of peaceful transfer of power, everyone must be involved including the leaders of our great religious institutions. Their role in the social, political and economic issues of our day should not be ignored or denied. In addition to praying for the government which is a divine mandate from God so that we can have peace and order (Romans 13), religious leaders must also be actively involved in running the affairs of the nation. Katherine Harris, US representative who ran for Senate as a Republican in Florida, said something recently during one of her campaign meetings that caught my attention. She said, "If you are not electing Christians, then in essence, you are going to legislate sin." Even though I do not subscribe to her political insights especially after the validation of the presidential votes in 2001 when she was Florida secretary of State, but she is right this time. If religious people do not get involve in the political life of the nation, then unrighteous laws will be made which will impact negatively upon the lives and destiny of the people. Rather than stay inactive and powerless, complain and criticize, religious leaders should get in involve in national politics otherwise the unrighteous decisions that are being made will impact them and their children negatively. A single decision that was made in White House four years ago has destroyed the lives of nearly 100,000 people, displaced millions and cost American tax payers over 700 billion dollars so far. This is an example of how bad policies, laws and decisions that are made by leaders can change destinies of people's lives and history of humanity.

Christian and religious leaders must not also shy away from public service because of the myth and call for separation of Church and State. People who make this kind of statement or sometimes ask preachers and Christian leaders to remain in the pulpit are ignorant and mistaken. First, we have to understand that God is interested in all nations, "for the kingdom is the Lord's and He is governor among the nations (Psalm 22:28). God has answers for the political and leadership direction of every nation, tribe, tongue, kindred and people. He will not do anything without first revealing it to His servants and prophets (Amos 3:7). Second, there are categories of preachers and religious leaders. All of us may be called but the calling is different. God's call does not only limit you to be an ambassador of good news but also to engage in the social, economic and political issues that affect His people. You are not only called to be a pastor, priest, and prophet but to be a patriotic citizen. Patriotism and politics are inseparable.

Moses was not only called to be a priest but a prophet and politician. He was not only the spiritual leader of the people but a great lawyer and politician. He wrote the law, which formed the foundation of much civil and criminal law in many countries today. He was used by God to bring the children of Israel out Egyptian captivity, bondage and slavery. Samuel was a priest, Judge and King of Israel at the same time. Even in our recent times, we have seen the social, civil, economic and political activities of past and present religious leaders such as Rev. Martin Luther King, Archbishop Desmond Tutu, Rev. Jesse Jackson, and Rev. Al Sharpton and many others. Part of being God's servant, minister, ambassador or general is a call to divine duty and many times it involves fighting for people on issues that impact their lives negatively. For instance, I consider myself a public theologian and part of my divine obligation is to engage in shaping public policies, decisions and laws that would have positive impact on God's people.

Third, you cannot separate the church from the state. It is like separating the church from the church or the family from the state. These are inseparable and indivisible. God established the institutions of family, government

106

(Theocracy) and church to work together in order to establish His good and divine purposes on planet earth. While the family is the first and most important as well as the foundation of any society, the church being the last is also very important in its function as the custodian of the divine truth. The government is the second institution in order of divine plan and act as an organism for peace and order on planet earth. These three unique institutions were designed to work together in order to bring about God's divine purposes on planet earthly kingdom. They are organism not social clubs, which some people have made them to be today. The only difference between the church and state is the type of people that make them up. And that is where we need to make some changes and bring more religious and genuine Christian people into the government

Christians and religious leaders who shy away from politics are also ignorant because they have not understood the central message of Christ pertaining to the kingdom of God. In fact they sin for failure to teach and practice the primary purpose for which Jesus died which is to redeem and reclaim the Kingdom of God from Satan. The truth is that Jesus died for the entire world; He died for the kingdom of God. The theology of kingdom agenda and social justice are so clear in the teachings of Jesus. Christ spent three and half years illustrating the truth of the kingdom when He went throughout the Galilee teaching in their Synagogues, preaching the good news of the kingdom, and healing every disease and sickness among the people (Matthew 4:23). Jesus used everyday story and parables to illustrate the spiritual condition that will prevail on the earth within the visible manifestation of the kingdom of heaven. Jesus spoke of the present and future kingdom, the physical (earthly) and spiritual (heavenly) kingdom. The kingdom He spoke primarily carries the idea of God coming into the world to assert His power, glory and rights against Satan's dominion. The kingdom of God is the rule of heaven on earth. It is the reign, rule and restoration of God's creation. The kingdom that Jesus spoke of is the destruction of Satan's rule, reign and dominion. The earthly kingdom therefore is a religious-political theocracy. It is God's direct rule and reign over His creation in order to stop the violence being meted against it now. It is the release of power, presence and provision of God over His earthly kingdom. It is a kingdom of righteousness, peace, joy and order.

I am not a strong advocate of theocratic system of government because it will not work in our current world where sin, disobedience, wickedness and immorality are rampant. It did not work with the children of Israel. They rejected God's leadership through Prophet Samuel when they asked for a king to be like other nations (1 Sam 8). Moreover, we live in a pluralistic, multi-cultural and religious society nowadays with monotheistic, dualistic, polytheistic and atheistic beliefs about God. It would be extremely a nightmare to introduce theocracy. However the wisdom of theocratic government will prevail with time especially at the return of Christ to planet earth. For now, it is the responsibility Christians and believers to seek the manifestations of God's purpose on earth. Jesus prayed, 'Our Father in heaven, hallowed be your name, your kingdom come, your will be done on earth as it is in heaven (Matthew 6:10.). Religious leaders and their adherents must seek unceasingly God's kingdom in all manifestations, hungering and thirsting for God's presence and power among our government leaders and especially in the family because the family is the bedrock and foundation of society. The kingdom of God cannot be achieved by those who seldom pray or compromise with the world. It can only be achieved when men and women think and act like Moses, Joseph, Nathan, Elijah, Daniel, Peter, John, Stephen, Paul, Deborah, Ruth, Esther, and Martin Luther King etc.

One of my mentors, Dr. Mike Murdock used to say all the time that, "the person of Jesus will take you to heaven but his principles will give you riches, wealth, joy and peace." Believing in the name of Jesus will guarantee you entrance into His heavenly kingdom. However calling His name will not give you riches and wealth. It is only by putting into practice his teachings and principles that will guarantee you true riches, wealth and prosperity. Mr. Mike's statement validates the mentality of most Christians and church leaders today. While the people of the world are applying Jesus teachings and principles to create big businesses and dominate world economy, religious and church folks are socializing and having petty parties. Rather than getting involve in the management of God's earthly kingdom resources, they are complaining, criticizing and waiting on God to rain dollars on them without working for it. Basically, our religious leaders are teaching and preaching their flocks to death while they are going through the back door to ask for money from corrupt politicians and from big businesses.

One of the great apologists of Christian faith, Dr. Hank
Hanegraaf wrote few years back, that Christianity is in
crisis. He is right. What we have in the church today is
spiritual capitalism. Despite the monumental challenges
that face our planet earth, religious leaders have remained
powerless and inactive while people perish everyday.
Rather what we hear and read all the time are unimaginable
scandalous and shameful activities of the so-called
religious leaders. Most of the successful ones are in fierce
competition of building million dollar buildings and
temples where the presence of God is absent. Satan
himself inhabits most of those buildings. Where there is
presence and glory of God, there should be His power and
His power will destroy sin, wickedness, witchcraft and all
manners evil. But what we have today in most of our
churches is religious teachings that are totally inconsistent
with the Word of God. What we have today is pragmatic
psychological philosophies and metaphysical powers to
attaining success or solving spiritual problems rather than a
sound exposition of God's Word. Religious hypocrisy,
rituals, divination, astrology, sorcery, witchcraft, magic,
and all manners of evil and satanic worship abound among
the people. Greed, hatred, corruption, idolatry, jealousy and
envy continue to be rampant among our people yet we have
Evangelists, Bishops, Priests, Pastors and Prophets who
claim to speak for God. They claim to be God ambassadors
and representative of Christ on planet earth and yet the very
people that God has entrusted into their leadership are
dying and perishing in darkness and ignorance. Church
leaders must restore their confidence, trust and credibility.
Christianity must restore its credibility.

Nigerian religious leaders must work together to ensure that Christians, Moslems and paganisms become partners in this 21$^{st}$ century rather than enemies in solving the social, economic and political obstacles facing our nation. They must work together to hold our government leaders accountable to the promises and principles of fairness, justice and equity. They must get involved in shaping public policies, laws and decisions that hinder God's people from fulfilling their God-given purposes on planet earth. Our religious leaders must work together to educate their followers about tolerance and peaceful cohabitation? As human beings we do not grow in isolation rather we grow, develop and mature as people in the context of love, relationship and fellowship. And until we learn the cardinal principle of Islam and Christianity, which is forgivingness and reconciliation, we will never live in peace. Without genuine forgiveness and reconciliation, there cannot be unity and peace. Another cardinal truth of Christianity and Islam is love and without love, we cannot have genuine relationship. Relationship is the most vital aspect of life. Relationship is in fact the greatest human asset. Character, courage, love and relationship are the greatest assets of every major faith in the world.

King Solomon, one of the wisest leader and king wrote this about 5,000 years ago, "when the righteous rule, the people rejoice; but when the wicked rule, the people groan (Proverbs 29:2). God established government to bring about peace and order as well as to create opportunities for His human creation to discover and fulfill their God given desires and dreams through those who are placed in position of power and authority. Many people who occupy leadership positions today in government seem not to comprehend this divine duty of leadership. They appear to forget that the greatest task of the leader is to inspire, motivate and to help those under their influence to become all they can be. They do not understand that the primary goal of leadership is to inspire people to live rightly and to enable them to accomplish their God-given purpose and mission on earth. This is why religious and righteous people must get involve in social, economic and political issues that directly or indirectly impact God's people. Earlier this year, I read how the president of Swaziland wanted to marry more wives. He then organized a contest of about 20,000 very young girls to walk through his enormous palace bear naked in order to choose the most beautiful one to marry. This and many more are the kind of stories about the unrighteous people who are over the affairs of many nations in our world today while religious folks stay on the side, watch, complain, criticize and do nothing about it

The Apostle Paul wrote to the saints at Ephesus saying, "for we are God's workmanship created in Christ to do good works, which God prepared in advance for us to do (Ephesians 2:10). God works on the fulfillment of His purposes planet earth through us. God's emphasis is not really the church but His earthly kingdom. Christ loved the church but he died for the world – God's kingdom. The church is just the custodian of that truth. The church is the canal or instrument of the kingdom of God. A prevailing church will bring about the kingdom of God on earth. Jesus called us the salt and light of the world (Matthew 5:13-18). He said, let your light shine before men, that they may see your good deeds and praise your Father in heaven (Matthew 13:16).

Jesus was kingdom minded. As religious leaders, let us seek the same mind of Jesus. I have always wondered what would have been Jesus leadership style if he were still walking among us today. Jesus said, "This into my Father's glory, that you bear much fruit, showing yourselves to be my disciples (John 15:8). Jesus wants us to be the salt and light of this world. He wants us to be God's workmanship and He wants us to bear much fruit. We cannot become the salt, the light and God's workmanship and bear much fruit without complete dependency upon the Holy Spirit. The Holy Spirit is the one who will teach us, enlighten us, empower us and strengthen us to carry out God's plan and purposes on planet earth. God's agenda is more than winning people to Jesus. It involves managing his earthly resources so that His people can live peacefully, joyfully, happily, orderly and purposefully. And this is the function of the government and without the help and assistance of the religious leaders and institutions, God's agenda for earthly kingdom will not materialize and Jesus will not return any time soon.


## THE ROLE OF FATHERS – FATHERLY WISDOM, INFLUENCE AND LEADERSHIP

---

*Fathering is a divine obligation and the greatest responsibility of man -- Dr. C.K. Ekeke*

On Sunday, June 17th, 2007, millions of children, friends and family members would celebrate Father's Day. Modern Father's Day celebration began in the early 20th century. It was established to complement Mother's Day, which began in 1830's. Both events were designed to celebrate, cherish and honor parenting, which is a divine duty and mandate (Exodus 20:12). Even though Father's Day is a secular holiday, the first modern Father's Day was celebrated as a church service at Williams Memorial Methodist Episcopal Church South, Fairmont, West Virginia on July 1908. Since then both of these events are celebrated around the world in a variety of dates and ways.

Today in the United States, Father's and Mother's Day celebrations are huge commercial sales period. Even though Father's Day celebration is not noisy as Mother's Day celebration, that notwithstanding the malls, stores and shops across the nation are already inundated with electronic gadgets, sleek handsets, designer sport wears, cars, books, and special gateways targeted for father's day gift. Many families are absolutely going crazy in their shopping spree to find that perfect gift for the dads.

Last Saturday evening, I took my kids to borders bookstore located inside the mall in my area. For over half an hour I drove around the mall area in scorching sun searching for a place to park. Finally I found a parking place almost quarter of a mile away from the main entrance into the mall. Inside borders, there was no empty seat to sit. At the mall, I also noticed that people walked up and down like ants. Beside the entrance to the mall was a large gathering of people listening to life musicians playing rock and country music. Moments later, I heard the lead singer announce that there is free beer and hotdogs asking guests and visitors to relax, enjoy themselves because it would be a long night. Curiously I asked a standby what was going on. He told me that a beer place hired the musicians to play this weekend and next for father's day celebration and that they will be offering free beer and hotdogs to dads for two weekends as a way to promote their business in the area.

For a moment, I thought about the social, moral and health consequences of eating so many hotdogs and drinking many cans of cold beer that afternoon. The promotional strategy may sound logical to them and advantageous in the long run because for many men and drunkards, it would a cool place to hang out. It is near the mall where many beautiful bodies pass through. On the other hand, I thought about how we are obsessed with food and having fun in this country while most of humanity is degenerated into violence, poverty, disease and death.

However, the fundamental concern that occupied my mind throughout that day was whether Father's Day celebration is supposed to be a time of eating, dancing, drinking and receiving gifts. I wondered whether today's dad fully comprehend the divine obligations of fatherhood? Do fathers of this generation understand the purpose of fatherhood? Are fathers of today courageously passing the touch of manhood and fatherhood to their children? Are we teaching our children godly wisdom, positively influencing and shaping their behavior and character in order to prepare them for a tough life and leadership in this crazy world? What type of leadership legacy are we passing on to them?

If truth may be told, many of you will agree with me that our planet earth is in a desperate need of courageous and compassionate leaders. In fact our world is in a dire need of prophets like Dr. Martin Luther King; spiritual leaders like Pope John Paul II and Mahatma Gandhi; scientists and thinkers like Albert Einstein, visionaries like Ronald Reagan and Margaret Thatcher; war heroes like Winston Churchill and Charles De Gaulle, charismatic and compassionate leaders like Mother Theresa, Princess Diana, and Bill Clinton and iconic leaders like Nelson Mandela. We need a generation of young men and women who think, write and speak like some of the leaders mentioned above. They were not just great fathers and mothers, but their thinking, writing, actions and leadership inspired and empowered millions to positive action which made significant impact and contributed immensely to world peace and prosperity during their time.

Our generation for now lacks leaders of such magnitude. What we have today are weak and compromised leadership. For Africa, it is even worse. Most of what we have in Africa today are visionless and incapable men as leaders. A look at the continent reveals shocking atrocities of religious and tribal conflict, moral decadence, political instability, corrupt rulers, violence, poverty, disease, and death. From Senegal to Sierra Leone, Nigeria to Sudan, Eritrea to Ethiopia, Uganda to Somalia, Tanzania to Congo, Mozambique and others, all you see is conflict, militancy and corrupt rulers. Transparency International and other credible financial crime agencies have reported that African ruler have stolen from the continent trillions of U.S. dollars since the last 45 years. These monetary assets are stashed away unfortunately in foreign accounts of the rich Western countries.

THISDAY on June 12, 2007 reported that the Economic and Financial Crimes Commission (EFCC) has recovered assets of some of the former state chief executives worth over N100bn This monumental amount of monetary asset does not include hard currency that was looted out of the country since 1999 in addition to hundreds of mansions and properties owed by these rulers overseas. This is a sad commentary on a continent that gave the world its first civilization in the 3rd century. Seventeen hundred years later, Africans talk, act and behave like uncivilized people. Ours is a culture of corruption, violence, diseases, and death. Today, African leaders and their people have become a global embarrassment and disgrace to mankind. And yet, the irony is that Africa is the richest continent on planet earth with its vast natural and talented human resources. The African continent is desperately in need of economic revival and political emancipation.

Africa is doomed if courageous African men and women, boy and girl and well wishers of Africa do not stand up against this satanic destruction and inhumanity to the people of Africa. The World Health Organization (WHO) reported recently that more than 30 million children and 20 million women are infected with HIV in Africa. About 13,000 children die daily in Africa. Treatable diseases such as meningitis, malaria, polio, tuberculosis are on the rise due to lack of clean water and public health care facilities. Instead of building hospitals and clinics, African rulers and wealthy people fly overseas for minor treatments like ear and eye infection and minor surgeries like knee ligament and crowns. There is something definitely wrong with African leaders.

Part of this blame I will also portion to African fathers. The reason why we have corrupt leaders in Africa is because African fathers have not fathered their sons and daughters properly. Before the coming of colonial masters, fatherhood in Africa was an honor and a cherished duty. African fathers taught their children character, courage, integrity, honest, love and fear of God. Today they have relegated that duty and responsibility to the children themselves. Today, our children are raising themselves in front of a TV set, or by their peers or Western culture and influence, while the dad is busy chasing illicit wealth, position, power and sex. No wonder, we have today these weak, corrupt and visionless rulers as leaders in our rich and blessed continent; men and women who are not patriotic, lacking self esteem and pride in the continent of their birth. This ugly and satanic influence on the continent of Africa can never be corrected if today's fathers ignore and neglect to teaching their children godly wisdom and shaping their behavior and character in a positive manner. These children will be leaders of tomorrow and if they are not properly and positively influenced in the virtues of life and morality, the future of Africa is doomed forever.

Here are five things (godly wisdom, character, integrity, honesty, service and prayer) I believe fathers of today can begin now to teach their children in order to prepare them to reclaim redeem, restore and emancipate Africa and her people from economic slavery, social decadence, religious violence and political instability. If they inculcate their children these basic and foundational things, Africa will rise up again and stand among the comity of nations in less than no time. I am very hopeful and optimistic that our children are the ones who will have the courage to say enough is enough, let us reclaim our father-land from these satanic rulers who have destroyed millions of lives, wasted enormous natural and human potential because of greed and lack of vision.

The first thing that African fathers can begin now to do in order to prepare their young ones for leadership is to teach them godly wisdom. One of the treasured gifts a child can receive from his or her father is godly wisdom. Young people will face challenges and enticement to sin in their early life. They will face peer pressure from their friends. And most of them will succumb to sinful pleasures in order to belong to their social group. However, if fathers will take the time to teach their children the Word of God and help them to develop close relationship with their creator, they will develop the capacity to resist such temptations when it comes knowing that compromise with evil and sinful pleasures will lead to heartache, distress, calamity, destruction and death.

King Solomon wrote these words 6500 years ago, "wisdom is supreme; therefore get wisdom. Though it cost all you have, get understanding" (Proverbs 4:7). Wisdom is one of the most important treasures of life. It is the spiritual capacity to see, evaluate and conduct life from God's point of view. Godly wisdom involves making right choices and doing what is right according to God's will and ways by the leading of the Holy Spirit. Wisdom is more precious than rubies and nothing you desire can compare with her and how much to get wisdom than gold: to choose understanding rather silver (Proverbs 8:11).

Fathers must treasure wisdom far more than silver, gold and precious jewels. They must also teach godly wisdom to their children. King Solomon did not only spend time writing about the wisdom that God gave to him, he taught his children to embrace wisdom, warned them against rejecting wisdom, against enticement to sin, against adultery, against folly, riches, possessions and material things. King Solomon warned all of us against those things that God detest such as pride, lying tongues, haughty eyes, hands that shed innocent blood, a heart that devises wicked schemes, feet that is quick to rush into evil false witness and a man who stirs dissension among brothers. King Solomon wrote that riches, possessions and materials things are all vanity. And he encouraged his children to embrace wisdom, stating the moral, economic and political benefits of wisdom such as peace, favor, wealth, happiness, justice, power, safety, protection, blessing, and prosperity. In a nutshell, wisdom is supreme. Apart from prayer, wisdom is the most treasured ingredient of leadership. No father or leader can lead effectively and efficiently without godly wisdom. Godly wisdom is the ability and capacity to live and lead wisely, morally, courageously and compassionately. And that is what the young ones need

120

more than anything else from their dads not money or material possessions.

The second thing fathers can teach their children is character. The Bible teaches that a good name is more desirable than great riches; to be esteemed is better than silver or gold (Proverbs 22:1). Character equates to good name, credibility and reputation. Character is one of the special attributes of having a great life and successful leadership. No one can be great without a consistent genuine and credible character. Those aspiring to become great fathers and leaders must have Christ-like mind and exhibit godly character. They must endeavor to control their behavior and weaknesses through dependence upon the Holy Spirit. The Bible teaches the qualities that constitute godly character are faith, goodness, knowledge self-control, perseverance, goodliness, brotherly kindness and love (Galatians 5:22). These godly virtues are lacking in people today and especially in our leaders. Today's fathers must do a better job to teach their children these essential virtues, which constitute godly character.

Godly character is also very important to the life of a leader. A person may have impressive skills, talents, and personality but without character. Godly character is not developed overnight. Teaching and building godly character takes time and requires a teachable spirit and mindset. It involves acquisition of godly wisdom, which I talked above. Deuteronomy 5:23-33 and Proverbs 2:1-11, teach us the discipline for developing godly character as well as the rewards of such discipline. I encourage fathers of this generation to reflect on those qualities for teaching and developing godly character. God expects us to cultivate them and teach them to our children. As we learn and cultivate these virtues, God will fill or minds and hearts with wisdom, our character will become solid and people will delight in us. When we build godly character, we partake in the divine nature of God and vain things such as stealing, corruption, envy, bitterness, and greed etc will become ineffective and unproductive in our lives. Without this quality of character and positive attitude, there cannot be effective fathers and leaders.

The third virtue that fathers can impress upon their children is integrity. The Bible teaches that the integrity of the upright guides them, but the unfaithful are destroyed by their duplicity (Proverbs 11:3). Integrity is doing what you promised you would do. Integrity can be good or bad. Godly integrity is true ethical behavior, genuine morality and consistent honesty. Godly Integrity is one of the greatest characteristics of wise and godly leadership. Genuine fathers and leaders must cultivate godly integrity. Integrity means honesty, trust, good morals, sound ethical values and courageous character. Integrity and honesty are the most valued and admired traits in a leader. People value honesty and integrity in a leader more than vision and competence. Millions will follow a leader who has godly integrity and can be trusted. Fathers will save our land and culture by teaching their children the value of integrity and honesty.

The fourth influence and leadership skill that fathers can teach their children is service. Jesus Christ, the greatest leader who ever lived said these words to His disciples,

"For even the Son of Man did not come to be served, but to serve, and to give his life as a ransom for many" (Mark 10:45). Leadership is about service and service is the essence of life. There cannot be successful leadership without service and stewardship. Today's leaders want to be served rather than serve. Either they were not taught that to lead is to serve or they just ignore the most essential task of a leader.

However, there cannot be selfless service without patriotism. Service is driven by patriotism and patriotism is driven by well-defined set of core values that shape the lives and especially those who are called to lead. Core values are constant and passionate beliefs that drive people lives, business decisions or nation's priorities. Core values determine and shape daily actions of people, business or government leaders. They are hidden motivations that dictate every decision and determine life's priorities. Without core values or code of conduct, people, families, businesses and even nations will have a broken focus? Dr. Mike Murdock, one of the great wisdom teachers of our contemporary time said, "The passion of our daily routine is the hidden secret for our success, people fail because of broken focus." Daily routines are core values or value systems that drive and determine life's success. Daily routines determine and shape our daily actions.

The same is true of a nation. Today, our nation's value system is dominated by a lust for power, sex and material possessions. Our leaders cruelly destroyed the moral value system of integrity, character, honesty and patriotism. Core values ask the question, why do I do what I do? Developing national core values and the passion for why we do what we do will be the secret to our nations success. Well-defined strong national core values will not only contribute to our nation's success but also will also inspire people to reach their fullest potential, embrace good change, communicate what is important and enhance credible leadership. Without a strong national value system no individual, business enterprise or even nations will be very successful. There has to be patriotic values and passionate actions that determine and drive our nation's priorities. And our children must be taught the power and rewards of patriotism and selfless service to our nation.

The last thing and certainly not the least that fathers must teach their children in order to prepare them for great life and leadership is prayer. In fact without prayer, none of the four virtues mentioned above will work. Prayer is the greatest ingredient of purposeful life and leadership. Prayer is a divine communication with God. It is the first act and true mark of a wise and fatherly leadership. Prayer must be the first priority of any father or leader who wants to achieve greatness. It is the key to successful leadership. Without persistent and passionate prayer life, no father can lead effectively.

For instance, Jesus the model leader did not do anything while on planet earth without praying to the heavenly father - while on earth, Jesus often looked for time to be alone with God in prayer especially during times of critical decision making (Luke 5:16). And His time alone with God produced tremendous results. Jesus had a lifestyle of prayer. Jesus said, "Man shall not live by bread alone, but by every word that proceeds from the mouth of God" (Matt. 4:4). Jesus taught and talked about prayer and meditation on the Word of God as the only essential ingredients for spiritual life of man on planet earth.

Time alone with God is essential to the spiritual well being of everyone who aspires to lead. Prayer is the key to effective living and leadership. It is a necessary ingredient for tough times and difficult challenges that we will face in life. These times of prayer will strengthen and sustain us - perhaps more than any other help and assistance we may receive from our families and friends. A lifestyle of prayer prepares us to teach and lead others through difficult times and challenges in their own life.

As fathers and leaders, we must make prayer the first act and true mark of our lives. Prayer is the key to dynamic faith, strength, power, success, victory, great life and successful leadership. It is a noble act and a divine habit that must be cultivated in our lives. Cultivating the lifestyle of fervent prayer and teaching your children the act of divine communication with the heavenly Father will prepare them for a great life and courageous leadership. The late William R. Bright, founder of the Campus Crusade for Christ said this on winning the Nobel Prize for Religion, "I believe that biblical prayer is the most enriching and energizing of all the Christian discipline and can accomplish more for the Glory of God and ensure blessing upon the people of the earth more than anything else we can do." I believe that. Jesus, Moses, Daniel, Joseph, Apostle Paul and many modern great leaders achieved greatness because of their fervent and persistent prayer lifestyle.

In conclusion, I challenge all of us who are fathers and who care for our country to cultivate this lifestyle of prayer and make effort to teach it to our kids. When our children learn and master the act of communicating with God, the blessings of God will pour down upon our beloved land, Africa. Let us also teach them how to lead with integrity and character; how to lead with honesty; how to serve and lead in prayer with a vision that is embraced by all; with focus on a mission that will provide a sense of momentum, rekindle the passion and patriotism that will inspire all Africans to make impossibilities possible again, to establish the structure and implement the strategies that will shape the continent's future. Mostly importantly I encourage you fathers today to teach your children moral values irrespective of religious beliefs that will shape their daily routines, drive their lives, dictate every decision and determine their life's priorities. In so doing, we will create peaceful environment for good change with great opportunities for all Africans to live peacefully and responsibly in order to fulfill the potential that God has deposited inside each and every one of us. If we fail to teach our children these basic essential virtues, we have failed as fathers, our honor and dignity of fatherhood will be rubbish before humanity and Almighty God.

# GOVERNMENT CORRUPTION – A NATIONAL TRAGEDY

## THE SCOURGE OF BRIBERY AND CORRUPTION - A CALL FOR COURAGEOUS LEADERS

*Courage is not absence of fear but to act – Senator Ken Nnanmani*

*Corruption is a decay of ethical, moral and societal value system –Dr. C. K. Ekeke*

In the last few months or so, there is hardly any day you logon the Internet to check the latest news on Nigeriaworld.com or Nigerian online newspapers that one would not see all sorts of headlines of bribery and corruption involving men and women holding public offices. The scandals for bribe, tax evasion, embezzlement, looting and money laundering by the very people entrusted with public service and treasury are just alarming. Whether we are talking of the Siemens and Wilbros bribery scandals for contracts, Halliburton, Chevron, Texaco, Royal Dutch and Bake Hughes bribe for tax evasion, or looting and money laundering by former governors; not to mention the billions of Naira spent by INEC chairman that regaled PDP, the most fraudulent election in the history of Nigeria, the National Identity card project fraud, the N300 billion for road construction without any good road to show for it,

PTDF looting, privatization of Federal Establishments to friends and families, trillions of waste in the energy sector etc. One can revisit the last eight years and make a long list of fraudulent contracts, stealing, embezzlement, looting and all kinds of waste by our so-called leaders.

Before the 2007 presidential elections, the Economic and Financial Crimes Commission, EFCC indicted thirty-one ex-governors for abuse of public treasury, financial mishandling, money laundering and corruption. Nigerians also learned from the chairman of EFCC that the past military rulers squandered over 380 billion US dollars in the last forty years. In the same week, the World Bank and other international organizations reported that Nigeria risks collapse and disintegration if the current looting, corruption, killings and criminality do not stop. The $380 billion that our military rulers looted and embezzled in the last forty years is thirty times more than the $13 billion Marshall Plan economic aid and technical assistance that was packaged to rebuild sixteen European countries after the devastation of World War II in 1945. Today our leaders travel to those European countries for holidays and medical treatment or send their children there for studies. The public funds that Nigerian past military and politicians looted and embezzled could have been utilized to rebuild the entire African economies and create the same luxury they see today in Europe and America. Rather our rulers preferred to steal loot and launder these public funds into their private accounts in secret banks overseas where these financial resources are then loaned to residents of those countries to start businesses and carry out major infrastructural projects and human development. Today, the loots of General Abacha are not only located in secret banks in Switzerland and other foreign banks, but are being discovered hidden in juju houses in Nigeria while poverty, disease, corruption and hopelessness buffet the people. What a shame!

There is no doubt that corruption has become the major crisis in our nation. It is not only an endemic problem but a scourge in our nation. I would even argue that apart from poor leadership, bribery and corruption are the greatest challenges facing our country today. Corruption is a serious and deadly threat to Nigeria's human and infrastructural development. It is the bane of our country's development and has been the road block and hindrance for any human and meaningful infrastructural development in Nigeria for nearly half a century. Corruption is a crisis of ethical and moral values. It is a complete and total decay of societal value system. The level of corruption that exists in our nation today is not only to be blamed on a cult of personalities and visionless leaders that took over the affairs of the nation by force since forty years ago; but it is also a failure of all religious leaders who have failed to teach, rebuke and hold accountable citizens within their sphere of influence because of greed, lack of character and courage. Corruption is a deep crisis of ethical and moral values and religious leaders in the country have failed to uphold the sanctity of good and moral behaviors as a result the entire system is corrupt. No country can ascend to any meaningful human and infrastructural development with the level and cesspool of corruption that exist in our land today.

Few years ago, a reputable international organization, Transparency International (TL) rated Nigeria and placed her in the 152$^{nd}$ position as the most corrupt country in the world. By the time, President Obasanjo left office in May 2007, Nigeria scaled up to 32$^{nd}$ position, which was quite an astonishing achievement. President Obasanjo was able to fight corruption through the establishment of organizations such as ICPC and EFCC. Mallam Nuhu Ribadu, an unknown police commissioner then was elevated to head EFCC. He quickly took the bull by the horn and courageously fought against the cankerworm which has been the bane of our nation's development. Mallam Ribadu demonstrated courage, character and fearlessness. His fearless attitude and integrity quickly earned him international reputation. Even though his fight against corruption has been criticized as lopsided for his failure to investigate the ex-presidents friends and family members, yet Mallam Ribadu created such awareness that our economic systems and political leaders are frighteningly corrupt. With his fearless and courageous attitude against corruption, Nigerians began to believe that bribery and corruption in our society can be eradicated.

But since President Yar'Adua took office in May 29, 2007, it seemed as if we have stepped into the trenches again. President Yar'Adua came into the office with such high hopes that he would continue the momentum on the struggle against corruption. He is reputed as a man of character, integrity, transparency, rule of law, due process, and most especially a servant leader. He also said that he will be a listener and lead with fear of God. Seven months into his presidency, we are yet to see some of these fine virtues boldly claimed by our servant leader. What some of us have seen so far is lack of clarity and courage to keep the momentum against abuse of public treasury, money laundering and corruption in high places. During his presidential campaign tours, he promised that he will continue the policies and economic reforms of ex-president Obasanjo. He stated that he will have zero tolerance for public officials who steal and embezzle pubic funds. Yet, the reversals of policies of the last seven months and most recently the removal of Mallam Nuhu Ribadu as the chairman of the anti-corruption agency, the Economic and Financial Crimes Commission (EFCC) Mallam Nuhu Ribadu seems to confirm the much anticipated feud between AGF, EFCC Chief and IGP.

Several theories have been postulated on President Yar'Adua leadership style. It may be true that Alhaji Ya'Adua wants to distance himself from the immediate past administration and be his own man and leader. But my question is how can he achieve that when most of his cabinet is made up of tycoons from the Babangida, Abacha and Obasanjo era? How can someone who is claiming to be a servant leader surround himself with a team of people who are only promoting their selfish agenda? The president's team is a cult of confused individuals, who are fighting among themselves for their selfish interest and personal power. There is no synergy in this current cabinet at all. The impression of their actions especially the AGF, Finance minister, IGP and others demonstrate abuse of personal power and selfish interest. Former President Obasanjo brought in a few technocrats in his cabinet who really made significant impact. Today, one of the few men in that cabinet who is still standing is being eased and compelled to go to school at Kuru, Jos. What's it that Mallam Nuhu Ribadu is going to study at the Institute for Policy and Strategic Studies (NIPSS) in Kuru that he has not experienced first hand at EFCC operatives. Moreover, is the training tailored to help him do his job more efficiently and effectively? This is a man who has become a symbol of courage, character and strength in the fight against corrupt and wicked leaders of our land but now being forced out perhaps over an alleged style in which he waged war against the corrupt ex-governors, who apparently sponsored the elections of most men and women in power today.

Some have also argued that seven months is not enough time to evaluate President Yar'Adua because, since he came into power, he's been battling with legitimacy question and putting together his cabinet. I would rather argue that seven months is long overdue for our new president to clearly define his leadership strategy on how to move this monstrous nation called Nigeria forward. Rather what he has been doing is reversing old reforms, soften on scandals, petting corruption and not showing strength and courage at all. No leader can truly lead anything or anyone without courage. Courage is the essence of leadership and one of the greatest virtues of great leaders. Leadership is about making decisions. Decision making is perhaps the highest and greatest task of the leader and an effective and great leader must be willing and courageous enough to make tough, fair and wise decisions.

Throughout history, leaders who have made impact are those who have led with strength and great courage. The father of the American nation, Abraham Lincoln did not only abolish slave trade through the Emancipation Proclamation of 1863, but he was courageous enough to unite a nation and preserved the Union through a policy of reconciliation despite the apposition from his party. The British Prime Minster, Sir Winston Church and his American counterpart, Franklin Roosevelt provided courageous leadership that led to the defeat of German Adolph Hitler. Their decisive leadership helped rebuild Europe and restored the world from economic crisis and world war. Rev. Dr. Martin Luther King Jr. prophetically and courageously inspired the United States of America and the world to judge people by the content of their character and not by the color of their skin. His powerful oratory and courageous leadership freed an entire nation from hate, bigotry and self-destruction and gave millions freedom and hope around the world.

Nelson Mandela an anti-apartheid activist and international icon of freedom defeated the apartheid regime of South Africa because of his courage, strength and character. Mandela courageously stood against apartheid and won an insurmountable war against apartheid and discrimination. The late American president, Ronald Reagan challenged his Russian counterpart, Mikhail Gorbaceov to tear down the walls of Germany otherwise the two countries will meet in the woods. During Nigeria's independence struggles, our nationalist leaders were courageous enough to get rid of the British colonialists from our country, even though the damage was already done. Recently Mrs. Bhutto paid the ultimate sacrifice for her unbridled faith in the democratization of Pakistan and fight against the tyranny of Islamic fundamentalism. These leaders made significant impact and contributed immensely to world peace and prosperity because of their courageous leadership. They epitomized the true essence of leadership.

We can also learn from biblical leaders that courage, strength and character are the essential virtues of great leadership. After the death of the great Jewish leader Moses, Joshua his protégé became Israel's new leader. Despite his forty years with Moses, Joshua was overwhelmed with the enormity of the task of taking more than 3 million Israelites into the fortified cities of Canaan, a land flowing with milk and honey. God had to command Joshua to be strong and courageous because he will lead the children of Israel into the land of Canaan (Joshua 1: 6-8). No one can become a great leader without godly character and strong courage. Courage is the virtue and ability that will enable any leader to make wise decisions and take tough actions. According to Dr. Myles Munroe, an expert of leadership development, "Courage is resistance to and mastery of fear, not the absence of fear. Leaders without this virtue will fail to make fair and tough decisions." Leaders need courage to make tough and right decisions. Leadership is hard work and our country is in desperate need for leaders who have the courage to lead boldly, wisely and compassionately

Our problem today may not be necessarily struggle against racism or apartheid even though tribalism is deeply rooted in our society. It may not be tearing any walls or fighting a civil war, but we've got a vicious war to fight. It is the war against the scourges of bribery and corruption. Corruption is the greatest challenge facing Nigeria as a nation today. Corruption is endemic in the fabric of our society and without godly courage, strength and character especially from those in position of power and authority; we would not be able to enjoy the freedom and dividends of democracy. President Yar'Adua popularized himself as the servant leader that Nigeria desperately needs. A servant leader is a leader who works hard to provide for the needs of the people. Most Nigerians are not asking for luxury but basic necessities of life such as good and drivable roads, electricity, drinkable water, clinics, and hospitals and enabling environment in which they can tap into their God-given talents, skills and potential. I think that these basic things should be the top priorities of those elected in various positions of power and leadership in our country.

## IBB PRESIDENTIAL AMBITION, HIS CHARISMA, AND CULTURE OF CORRUPTION

*The presidential ambition of General Ibrahim Babangida is unwise, presumptuous, arrogant, despicable and demonic. It is only driven by greed, jealousy and retaliatory - Rev. Dr. CK Ekeke*

This past week has been a very pleasant week as well as painful one for me in particular. It was pleasant because I heard from many old friends including one of my favorite high school friends. I was glad when I talked to him this weekend and learned that he is doing very well in Nigeria, after-all a first class engineering graduate from a reputable university in Nigeria should do well. If he had studied in the United States, he would probably be a great engineer or scientist by now. I also rejoiced with him when he told me that he is married to a beautiful wife and they have four children – two boys and two girls which met and satisfied the family law decreed by IBB during his reign in 1980's. But this past week was also a painful week due to some sad news especially the passing of people who are well known to my family and me. I had to sit quietly few times this

135

week to cogitate, meditate and once again ask our creator the essence and purpose of our life here on earth.

However, the most painful news was when I read about IBB's entry into the 2007 presidential race and all his cronies who are exalting him for the top job again. Immediately I felt very sorry for the man. My sympathy for him heightened when I read where he said that he had consulted with his family, friends, and associates far and wide within and outside Nigeria before making his decision to run for the top job. I then realized that IBB is an unwise person and that his supporters and associates are deceitful and sick individuals. In the past, I heard and read what I consider to be rumors about ex-military dictator's aspiration to run for the nation's presidency in 2007. I did not feel any need to wink at such noises or ideas. But after his declaration and registration with PDP last week and reading some of the writings, comments and even events supporting and promoting him, I could not but join in the fight to stop this brutal dictator from going to live in Aso Rock again.

Initially, I shed tears for our dear nation. I cried before God of heaven, recited Islamic prayer for love and wisdom on his behalf and then poured libation to our great political ancestors who have passed on to have mercy on our people and heal our land. The heaviness in my heart because of the foolishness of his decision and the crop of Nigerians supporting him necessitated me to write this article. I just have to write so that God will purge my heart and soul and vindicate me for speaking out against this unwise and demonic decision. My purpose really is to enlighten all Nigerians of the consequences of Babangida's ambition and to warn the people supporting this evil agenda to desist from deceiving themselves and the people of Nigeria. With all due respect, let me say that the presidential ambition of

136

General Ibrahim Babangida is unwise, presumptuous, arrogant, despicable and demonic.  His ambition is only driven by greed, jealousy and retaliatory.

I know that it is un-African and disrespectful for a young person to advise and criticize older people.  As I said earlier, I am compelled to write because of the foolishness of his decision and sadly enough because of the ignorance of all those Nigerians who are supporting a brutal dictator like IBB. If I were a part of his family, friend or close associate, I would certainly muster the courage to advise him to find other areas to lend his leadership if he has acquired it now and stopped being deceived by crop of Nigerians who have a rapid love for money. The Bible is so right for saying that, "People who want to get rich fall into temptation and a trap and into many foolish and harmful desires that plunge men into ruin and destruction. For the love of money is a root of all kinds of evil. Some people, eager for money, have wandered from the faith and pierced themselves with many griefs (1 Timothy 6:9-11)." It truly makes me sick when I read or hear comments that exalt IBB or hear his supporters including those in the US and Europe inviting people to come to a forum designed to elect Babangida's the next president of Nigeria.  In fact all IBB supporters are deceitful, money mongers and insane.  They are just enemies of Nigeria and her people.

It is really disgusting and despicable to read about these Nigerians who are supporting IBB to become the next president of Nigeria.  Where do we begin to remind these visionless and myopic followers of his past treacherous, murderous and incompetent leadership?  This is a man who committed multiple murders during his brutal and rigid regime, authorized and orchestrated the killings of several of his critics and opponents including one of the brightest and promising Nigerian journalists. For instance, during his regime in the mid 1980's, the highly published economic package "Structural Adjustment Program (SAP) that was aimed to establish a realistic exchange rate for Nigeria and restructure the economy was a dismal failure. It cost millions of US dollars to implement and ended up being an economic crime strategy to enrich himself and his cronies. Billions of US dollars were borrowed from the International Monetary Fund (IMF) and World Bank, which were squandered by his beefcake business cronies. He used SAP economic package to loot the national treasury and created one of the largest and monumental foreign debt in the history of our country. He institutionalized 419, corruption at high levels and plundered the economy. Additionally, in 1993, he demonstrated such a disdain for democracy when he cancelled what has been described as the only fairest and freest election in the history of our nation, which was surprisingly won by his friend, M. K. O Abiola.

Reading and hearing comments from IBB associates and followers including those who have lived in the US and Europe for many years compels me to ask the question: where is our sense of decency and patriotism? Are these people Nigerians at all? Why are these people so blinded by money and what they can get rather than the progress of our society? IBB has not answered all the charges been leveled against him including the Okigbo panel report which accused him of mismanaging US$12.4 billion of oil windfall during the desert storm. I have just come to realize that the attitude and behaviors of followers of these leaders are the reason why our leaders have not shown any responsibility and accountability. How would anyone expect genuine leadership if the followers are mentally and financially dysfunctional? It is time we demand true and pure leadership from those who aspire to leadership positions. At the Abuja Leadership Seminar which was organized by Gathering of Champions in collaboration of Peculiar People's Ministries, USA recently in FCT, Abuja, one of my mentors, Dr. Myles Munroe talked about leadership that is driven by vision. Off-course, the Bible teaches that where there is no vision, the people perish. However, he made a very significant point when he talked about getting people who are angry and passionate for pure and genuine leadership. I think this is seriously lacking in our nation. And no wonder these leaders over the affairs of things in Nigeria are behaving anyhow they like. There are no angry followers. What we have are passive followers, people who are only after pot of porridge for their empty stomachs, which will get hungry again if they can't find a way to feed it permanently.

Before you ask me if I know that every Nigerian has the fundamental right to run for any political office in the land? I am glad that you thought about it and asked it. If your statement or question is true and practicable it means then that all the Nigerian criminals including military personnel, politicians and ordinary citizens locked up in jailhouses also do have the right to run for political office. They should be released and allowed to run for political offices. If that is not the case, then IBB has no moral authority or ethical privileges whatever to stand for any political office in the country. This year, the chairman of EFCC, Mallam Nuhu Ribadu, accused Babangida of being the patron of fraudsters in the country. In a nutshell, this is a man that should be locked in prison for his atrocities during his 8-year dictatorship and for failure to appear before Pius Okigbo panel to answer charges that are being leveled against him.

In addition to IBB candidature which I am sure would not pass the PDP Code of Conduct or even Dr. Gowon's criteria for leadership, I'll like to tackle some of the

139

babblings by his strong supporters and campaigners regarding his charisma and strong leadership character. I am compelled to talk about it because of the ignorance I sense from his supporters as well as to enlighten my audience and Nigerians who are not familiar with the word – charisma. One of my cousins used to say all the time, "it is better to shout-up your mouth than to open it and remove all doubt." I feel so for most of IBB ardent supporters including unfortunately those who reside all these years in a country like the United Sates.

There is no doubt that charisma is an essential ingredient of leadership and influence. It is a necessary quality of all great leadership. However, a call to such a level of leadership position cannot depend or be decided only on the character trait of charisma or charm. There are far more important and essential ingredients of leadership such as character, courage, wisdom, vision, core-values, integrity, honesty and strategy that must be present in a leader. In fact charisma cannot be compared or measured with the above listed leadership qualities. General Babangida may be charismatic, inspired, and passionate to desire to live in Aso Rock again but he appears to lack in abundance what I consider as the divine ingredients of pure leadership such as character, compassion, wisdom, vision, core-values, integrity, honesty and strategy.

Now, let's define charisma and analyze its relationship with leadership and try to understand how IBB acquired his charisma that is being ignorantly spoken by his supporters. What is charisma? Where is the source of charisma and how does this gift add to leadership influence? First, let me tell you what charisma is not. Charisma does not mean appearance, handsome, big, strong, intimidating person, slim, tall or beautiful.

According to Random House Dictionary, charisma is defined as the special quality that gives an individual influence, charm or inspiration over large numbers of people. A person or leader is charismatic when certain qualities such as communication skills, listening abilities and other skills are evident and abundantly superior to other people around him or her. Encyclopedia Britannica defines charisma as attribute of astonishing power and capacity ascribed to the person and personality of extraordinarily magnetic leaders. Such leaders may be political and secular as well as religious. The word charisma is derived from the Greek *charis* ("grace") and *charizesthai* ("to show favor"), connoting a talent or grace granted by God. Charisma is also often equated to charm, which is the power of pleasing or attracting, as though personality or beauty, allure, spell, enchantment, attractiveness, magic, witchery, amulet, talisman, lure, enchant, bewitch, and fascination.

From the above definitions, we can deduce that charisma can be acquired at least by three ways namely:

1. True charisma is a divine gift from God, which is an essential quality of leadership.
2. Charisma is possession of great talents like communication and listening skills.
3. Charisma can come from charm, talisman and witchcraft, which are obtained from manipulation, hypnotism and Satan.

141

Now, you compare any of the names below with Generals IBB and Abacha

**Dr. Nnamdi Azikiwe, Chief Obafemi Awolowo, Rev. Dr. Martin L. King Jr., President Nelson Mandela, Pope John Paul II, Mother Teresa, Archbishop Desmond Tutu, President Bill Clinton, Princess Diana, Ronald Reagan, Margaret Thatcher, Abacha, etc**

Obviously people flock to a leader who possesses such distinct and unique abilities. However, true and excellent leadership is not achieved by charisma alone. Great leaders must not only be charismatic but humble and compassionate. IBB has demonstrated that he is not a humble and compassionate leader looking at his past bad leadership example and even his present disdain and arrogant ambition proofs the fact. Charisma is a powerful leadership ingredient and can sometimes be used negatively. If IBB is charismatic as his supporters are saying, I do not see it from his personality. First, he is not a godly man. Second, he does not have powerful communication and listening skills. If he had charisma, it should be worldly charm which can be obtained by manipulation, tactics and talisman and that is why his is being used negatively. Charisma cannot be divorced from other leadership qualities like godly character, courage, compassion, wisdom, vision, integrity and strategy. Ibrahim Babangida lacks these qualities in abundance. How do I know? I am glad you asked. I know by this replaying his past reign and activities as Nigeria military leader in the 80's and his present decision to rule again now in 2007. It is such an unwise, envious and greedy decision. In fact his ambition to become Nigeria's president in 2007 is demonic.

Another leadership quality that is being yelled by IBB associates is his strong character. Before I talk about this essential quality of leadership, let's not confuse it with decree, intimidation, force, killings, murder etc. Character is not about outward technique to manipulate and deceive people. It is an inner quality that produces sound behavior. Character is perhaps the greatest ingredient of moral and authentic leadership because every expectation from a leader will depend on his or her character. The Bible clearly teaches us in the book of Exodus 34:6-7 and other places the qualities that make up a godly character, which is paramount for excellent leadership. Any great leader must cultivate sound character that commands respect from all, even his enemies. Any great leader must be beyond reproach. In the history of this world, we have seen only a few of such leaders. So for IBB parrots to credit him as possessing strong character makes them a laughing stock before all.

IBB supporters and followers are enemies of Nigeria and destroyers of progressive society. They are completely ignorant of the expectations of those who aspire to serve as leaders. These crops of Nigerians are superficial, cryptic, inept, unqualified, and ignorant and incompetent group of individuals, whose stock in trade is to steal, embezzle, diminish and rubbish the potential of Nigerian people and society. They are cultic followers that is crippling and denying the enormous human and natural potential of the Nigerian people. They are supporting IBB presidency for their own personal power, influence and selfish interest. They are greedy, incompetent and hungry for personal power and negative influence. They manipulate and abuse power for their personal gain and pleasure undermining the masses of the Nigerian public. They live lavished lifestyle showing their ill-gotten wealth, cheap sex and superficial charms. They lie, manipulate, compromise, harass, threaten and even kill in order to attain temporal influence and superficial power. And this is because of the political culture in our society today. It is a culture of cultic associations that has become a necessary requirement to become a leader rather character and good virtues. The political culture is full of money worshippers, egotism, greed, avarice, envy, hatred, jealousy, sin, immorality, idolatry, atrocities, ignorance, darkness and death. Political rituals, divination, astrology, sorcery, witchcraft, magic, and all manners of evil and satanic manipulation have become the order of the day in today's Nigeria political landscape. Otherwise how could anyone justify all these political motivated killings since the last 20 years? Why would anyone plan and murder his or her political opponent? Who gave them the right to take someone's life?

It is my prayer that President Obasanjo and PDP leadership follow proper guidelines in making sure that the genuine presidential flag-bearer emerges in their primary next month. They must strictly follow the party's Code of Conduct which listed the criteria for leadership which includes the following: patriotism; integrity; ethno-neutral; rule-driven; tolerance; transparency-driven; knowledge-driven; community/constituency service; and, leadership. Any one aspiring to lead millions of people in addition to all the above must be a person of great wisdom. The first

144

impression I gained from reading about IBB justification for running 2007 presidential elections under PDP showed that he lacked wisdom. He clearly lacked a very essential ingredient of great leadership. He does not exemplify a man of wisdom and discernment. Any one aspiring to lead millions of people must be a person of wisdom. The Bible clearly informs us to ask for wisdom (James 1:5). Wisdom is more precious than rubies and nothing you desire compare with her (Proverbs 8:11). How much better to get wisdom than gold, to choose understanding rather than silver! (Proverbs 16:16).

King Solomon realized the need for wisdom and anointing from God despite his charisma, heritage and material blessing, when he prayed in 1 Kings 3:7-9 for wisdom and discerning heart to govern the people of Israel. IBB lacks this quality of leadership and no one can be a leader over millions of people without divine wisdom. IBB lacks insight and foresight about things. If those he consulted were wise individuals, they would have advised him differently. His decisions to join the 2007 presidential elections showed lack of discernment, insight and careful thought. He does not seem to have any insight and foresight about leadership. He showed lack of caution in his decision.

IBB should retire to his Minna mansion, which he built with the country resources or migrate to France where his wife has the world's best boutique. Otherwise, he can search around the world and find what ex-presidents and leaders of other countries are doing after leaving office. Many of them are involved in good causes such as fighting diseases, poverty, hunger or supporting youth education and empowerment. It is rather shameful that after 8- years of brutal dictatorship, IBB wants to rule Nigeria again. If PDP allows him to win their party primaries, I am packing my bag to return home and join in this divine war. Nigeria, the giant of Africa and hope of black race will become a mockery of the entire world if IBB becomes the president of Nigeria in 2007. Nigeria has many credible leaders, people who have godly charisma, genuine character, compassion as well as vision to pacify the nation and continue president Obasanjo's and Mallam Ribadu's fight against corruption. Ebutu Ekiwe will make a better president anytime than Ibrahim Babangida. We must get angry in this country in order to stop this vicious circle of corrupt and inept leadership. Enough is enough. This nonsense must stop.

## IBB – A CHALLENGE TO YOUNG GENERATION

Since the Senate passed a Bill on March 11, 2010 barring all former military heads of state that came to power by force or through undemocratic process from benefiting in the new remuneration package for heads of state, the former military president, Ibrahim Badamosi Babangida – aka IBB has raised his ugly head again. Once again, IBB supporters - political jobbers of Nigeria want to force General Babangida to throw his weight into the 2011 presidential elections simply because of the political muddle and nightmare that the country is in at the moment.

And so, IBB, being such an unwise person despite his gray hairs, has decided to contest the presidential elections in 2011 under the PDP platform. Already, his cronies have begun to saturate the landscape with IBB photos and political slogans for 2011. At the meantime, IBB is going around giving political speeches at any opportunity he could find. Earlier in the month, the so-called Maradona of Nigerian politics, spoke at the 54th birthday of the Ogun State Governor, Otunba Gbenga Daniel, where he gave a condition for any Nigerian who wishes to contest the 2011 presidential election to see true federalism as a critical issue. Yes, most well meaning Nigerians want to see true federalism in our nation and by the way, Dim Chukwuemeka Odumegwu Ojukwu talked about it almost 50 years ago.

Also, at the 55th anniversary of Nigeria Union of Journalists (NUJ) held in Abuja last week, Mr. Babangida spoke on Nigeria's unity, arguing that the Nigerian nation had lived together for 50 years and the citizens should not look back. This is in response to bitter and hard truth that Col. Maummar Gaddafi made about Nigeria after the Jos mayhem last month.

However, the recent interview that IBB granted to the British Broadcasting Corporation (BBC) over the weekend, in which he allegedly said that there is no young people capable of leading Nigeria and so feels that even in his 70's, he still has the capacity, wisdom, and experience to lead Nigeria again was foolish and unfortunate statement.

In fact the entire interview on BBC this past weekend exposes the arrogance, ignorance and the greedy attitude of Ibrahim Badamosi Babangida. IBB is unwise, presumptuous, and a jealous human being. I believe that his ambition and quest to govern Nigeria again are driven by a jealous, retaliatory, and demonic spirit. This is a man who recently lost his wife of 38 years to cancer and should be mourning for her demise rather than aspiring to rule Nigeria again after his despicable and bastardization of Nigeria political entity and social systems during his 8-year dictatorship.

Where will I begin to analyze his BBC interview? First of all, despite his acclaimed charisma and political wisdom, IBB does not know that Barack Obama before been elected the 44th president and first black president of the United States of America on November 4, 2008, served as Illinois State Senate from 1997-2004; and then served as Democratic Senator from January 3, 2005, to November 16, 2008.

How does he aspire to lead Nigeria in the 21st century when he does not have the correct facts on the most important political event of our recent time? His idiotic statements and unwise decision compel me to ask this question – what must have been in his head when he took over the affairs of Nigeria in 1985 by force as a relatively young military man - still then in his early 40's. No wonder, the man caused such havoc and wrecked the Nigerian economy with his Structural Adjustment Program known as SAP. In the 1987, IBB introduced a highly publicized economic package "Structural Adjustment Programmed" that was aimed to establish a realistic exchange rate for Nigeria and restructure the economy, which was a dismal failure. It cost hundreds of millions Naira to implement and ended up being an economic strategy to enrich himself and his few friends. Millions of U.S. dollars borrowed from the International Monetary Fund (IMF) and World Bank to implement the program were squandered. He used SAP economic package to loot the national treasury and plundered the nation's foreign reserves.

SAP, which was later known as "Suffer and Perish" had such devastating effects on the economy and severe consequences on thousands of Nigerian students abroad. According to Babangida's economic team and their Western friends then at World Bank and IMF - the writers of the economic package argued that SAP would restructure the economy and achieve a realistic exchange rate for Naira. Rather than achieve the economic benefits promised by General Babangida and his protégées, SAP created a comatose economy with wrenching problems - severe inflation, massive unemployment, declining foreign reserves, huge balance of payments and a valueless Naira, which we still have today.

He institutionalized 419, corruption at high levels and plundered the economy. His brutal and rigid regime authorized and orchestrated the killings of several of his critics and opponents including one of Nigeria's brilliant journalists-Dele Giwa. Until today, IBB and his crony friends have not answered the charges leveled against them including the Pius Okigbo panel report which accused IBB of mismanaging US$12.4 billion oil windfall during the desert storm. In 2003, the chairman of EFCC, Mallam Nuhu Ribadu, pointedly accused Babangida of being the patron of fraudsters in the country. In short, IBB should be locked in prison for life for his atrocities during his 8-year dictatorship and for failure to appear before Pius Okigbo panel to answer charges that were leveled against him, yet he is going around giving talks and insulting the young people he vandalized and destroyed their lives. It is only in Nigeria that this sort of nonsense will happen. If I were president of Nigeria, he will be the first person I will arrest and lockup in prison for life.

General Babangida celebrated corruption and made illiterate people such as Orji kalu, the Ubas, and others instant millionaires. He enthroned the new super rich while millions of Nigerians suffered. In fact, the era of IBB led to the beginning of the moral decadence and purposeless society that we have today. He introduced the political culture where  money is worshipped, egotism, greed, avarice, envy, hatred, jealousy, immorality, idolatry, atrocities, ignorance, darkness, political rituals, divination, astrology, sorcery, witchcraft, magic, and all manners of evil and satanic manipulation became the order of the day during his reign. The depth of corruption and social degradation led to moral decline, ethical and spiritual decadence at all levels in our society.  His economic agenda destroyed the Naira and basically rubbished the Nigerian economy, which actually elevated greed, bribery, and corruption we see today. Naira was devalued and a dollar could buy 100 Naira at that time.

The quest for dollar and foreign currency motivated many young Nigerian girls into lucrative prostitution overseas, mostly in Italy, Holland, France, and Switzerland where most of them were infected with HIV. The rampancy of AIDS cases in Nigeria today is as a result of an uncontrollable ring of organized prostitution of young Nigerian girls that were taken to overseas for such old fashion trade in the early 1980's and forced into organized prostitution due to economic and financial hardship at home. His administration did absolutely nothing to stop such organized crime against the reproductive resources of our country. And then these young girls infect their boy friends and their Nigerian husbands in a country where basic necessities of life lack in abundance not to mention of sound medical treatment. This unbridled greed and sexual pervasion led to social and moral decadence we see in Nigeria today. IBB economic and other public policies destroyed the potential, creativity and God given skills and talents that lie within the Nigerian people.

IBB and those clamoring for his return should be ready for the young generation, which he has publicly and internationally insulted. He and Nigeria will never have peace if he maneuvers to become Nigeria's president in 2011. We will disrupt with our pen, civil disobedience and blood. Enough is enough. It is a shame that the Northerners cannot find and present capable people to run for higher offices in the land except to recycle these vicious and half educated people. This is what we have had in the last 40 years.

IBB insulted the young people of Nigeria that his administration failed to educate. During his 8-year reign, university education was bastardized and many young people and professors fled the country in search of better education and teaching environments elsewhere. IBB talks about unity, yet he was responsible for the political disunity in our nation today with his senseless states creation.

151

During his 8-year reign, IBB spent $38 billion to build a new capital – Abuja. Abuja was a vast area of land without any single structure but forest. Today, it is the pride of Nigeria. Even though, I still consider it a good federal investment – moving the capital from the congested city of Lagos to a structured, organized and centric city, yet it was a huge capital investment. My question then is, why the federal Government unable to undertake such development and infrastructural development in other regions of the country. What about Niger Delta region that has become an eye sore and un-livable today? Why is this injustice and wickedness in allocation of federal capital projects, federal appointments, revenue allocation, etc even though the oil resources from South-South and Southeast account for more than 80% of the revenue income of the nation. Why does our federal government continue to hold the power in the center rather than allow the states and local government to be more autonomous? And by the way, when will the true federalism become a reality in Nigeria?

In conclusion, if General Babangida aspires to contest the 2011 presidential elections, which the constitution allows him to, he must be ready to answer the following questions:

1. Who killed Dele Giwa, Mamman Vatsa, M. K. O. Abiola and others?
2. What did he do with $12.4 billion oil windfall?
3. Why did he cancel the 1992 presidential election - fairest and freest election in which his friend Moshood Abiola clearly won?
4. Why did he institutionalize corruption and created the illiterate millionaires in likes of Orji Kalu, the Ubas that we have today in our land?

5. Why did he cause such enmity between the people of south-south and southeast?
6. Why does he have such a disdain for Nigeria and the Nigerian people?
7. Why is he insulting the young people of Nigeria?
8. When will he stand and answer in the courts the Pius Okigbo panel report?
9. Will IBB pass the PDP Code of Conduct or Dr. Gowon's criteria for leadership?
10. What is his true identity? Is IBB a true Nigerian?

Finally, has IBB and his cronies considered these young and intellectual Nigerian leaders of international repute – Mrs. (Dr). Ngozi-Okonjo Iweala, Mrs. Oby Ezekwesili, Prof. Dora Akunyuli, former Senate President Ken Nnamani, Prof. Charles Soludo, Mallam Nuhu Ribadu, Prof. Pat Utomi, Governors Donald Duke, Otunba Gbenga Daniel, Babatunde Fashola, and many others who are 1000 times more qualified than IBB to lead Nigeria in this highly technological and information age.

## INCOMPETENT GOVERNMENT, VISIONLESS POLITICIANS AND GREEDY BANK CEO'S – NIGERIA IN A STATE OF EMERGENCY

*I still believe prophetically that the sovereign state of Nigeria came into existence for the emancipation of the Black Race; if this generation of Nigerians fail in this divine purpose, we will stand before our creator one day to give account – Dr. C. K. Ekeke*

I want to thank all of you who called or sent email to ask of me during my absence from contributing to this forum on issues of national interest. There comes a time in life's journey when one must take time off to reflect on life's purpose, aspirations, interests, successes, as well as mistakes in life. The last two years for me have been a time of reflection and learning experience for which I am truly grateful.

In the last two years as I reflected much about life and the backwardness of people of color especially in the continent of Africa, I feel strongly the call to dedicate my energy to be an advocate of moral, ethical, compassionate, courageous and wise leadership – excellence in leadership, governance and public policy, because I believe firmly that the number one reason under-development, poverty, violence, diseases, and evil abound in society such as ours is due to lack of skilful, courageous, compassionate, wise and visionary leadership. Research studies have shown and support that fact.

Having said that, I want to call on all true and lovers of Nigeria to shade ethnic, tribal, religious, political, social, cultural and economic background aside and join together in the fight to reclaim the soul of Nigeria. The Nigerian state is in a state of emergency. There is crisis in the home, crisis in the church, crisis of conscience, crisis in the government, and crisis even in the business sector. We must work together to fight the enemies of human progress, flush out incompetence, inefficiency and combat violence, disease, evil and wickedness in our society. This is not unrealistic call like Boko Haram to eradicate Western education and values in Nigerian society but a call to save the soul of Nigeria. A year from now, Nigeria will celebrate her 50$^{th}$ year of independence. There is a growing tension and energizing movement to destabilize the Nigerian state. The threat of Niger Delta militants has been quenched temporarily when this government negotiated with the militant leaders by bribing them to lay their weapons, which is not the best way to solve the yearnings of people and their grievances against social and economic injustice being meted against the people and region of a lucrative oil-producing area.

Since Umaru Yar'Adua was elected president of the most populous black nation in the world two years ago, he has not demonstrated the servant leadership, which he clearly and boldly advocated for. He has not shown any bold and courageous leadership. He has kept mum over matters of national discourse and interest. All he has done is to northernize the government again, by reshuffling the federal and political appointments, reversing some of the major laws of President Obasanjo, his mentor and political godfather. He has traveled several times to Germany and Saudi Arabia for medical treatment. At one time, he was out from the public scene for weeks that caused the rumor whether he was still alive or not. Even the vice president did not know his where about. What a government?

Recently I watched a documentary about animal kingdom. The documentary showed the levels of leadership in the animal kingdom. To my amazement, an elderly lioness lost her position of leadership among this particular group of lions when she sustained injury on the left eye during a fight with the cobra. Because of that handicap, the group of lions made decision for her to relinquish her leadership role and it was given to another lioness. It was astonishing to me. Here are animals that do not have soul as spiritual scientists have argued, and yet they have the emotional intelligence to govern themselves. We human beings sometimes need to learn from these animals, which we butcher and eat.

Comparing President Yar'Adua with President Obama will be like comparing apple and orange. President Obama was just elected a year ago as the first black president of the United States of America. He is the son of a Kenyan, child of Africa and inherently has African blood in him. Despite all odds against him, he won the democratic nomination and went on last November to win the presidency of the United States of America. Obama made history. I have often said that his book, "The Audacity of Hope" should been entitled "The Audacity of Courage." From community service job in the down-trodden Chicago downtown, he ran and became an Illinois state senator, then elected national senator and ultimately went on to become the first president of the free world. The love affair between an immigrant student from Kenya at the University of Hawaii and Kansas white female student at the same university produced one of the most brilliant political figures of our time. The election of Barack Hussein Obama to the Oval office is without doubt America's defining moment in history.

Since taking oath of office in January this year, President Obama has achieved what most political leaders may not achieve in their lifetime. He is turning around an economic depression, which he inherited from the failures of the past governments. He is pouring cash capital into the banking and financial sector to slow down unemployment and home foreclosures. He is still waging two wars – Iraq and Afghanistan, which he also inherited. He has assembled the best minds for dialogue on every major issue he promised during his campaign; to exchange ideas and strategies on how to re-brand America and make her the leader of the free world again. President Obama has put together a team of the best and brightest to handle issues such as the Economy, Defense, Foreign Policy, War in Iraq & Afghanistan, Nuclear & Terrorist Attack, Education& Poverty, Healthcare, Energy Environment, Homeland Security & Immigration, Seniors & Social Security, Ethics, Faith, Family, Civil Rights and Technology.

Early this year, the Chief Executive Officers of major Telecommunication/IT companies in America were invited to Washington DC to meet with President Obama to talk about how to use Information Technology and social networking media to drive transparency, engage citizens, improve government performance and lower the cost of government operations. He has called on the ingenuity and spirit of American innovation to use the power of technology to create jobs by exploring untapped areas such as Healthcare IT, Green IT, Solar Energy, Global Warming and Environment. President Obama has visited many countries since he took office energizing the peoples of Europe, Middle East, Asia, Africa and world leaders on

157

America's leadership role and how to work together to achieve global peace and prosperity. He is rebranding America in the international scene which his predecessor, President George W. Bush damaged while in office. Just one year in the Oval office, President Obama has received a Noble Peace Prize for his extraordinary efforts to strengthen international diplomacy and cooperation between peoples and his vision of and work for a world without nuclear weapons. President Obama's name in just one year is now rated among national and international icons like President Nelson Mandela, Rev. Dr. Martin King Jr., Mother Teresa, Bishop Desmond Tutu, and others who received Noble Peace Prize for life long work against social injustice, civil right, and apartheid and world hunger.

Without doubt, President Obama is a charismatic leader. He is a keen intellect, with deep listening and communicating abilities. President Obama can speak on any national issues – from the state of economy to healthcare, climate change, and environment, and foreign policy, social and ethical issues for hours with facts and figures. His speeches are insightful, inspiring, encouraging, challenging and even prophetic. His speeches have been compared to that of President John Kennedy and Dr. Martin Luther King Jr. As I write this article, President Obama and Nancy Pelosi, speaker of the House have scored another major political point. Early this morning, the Lower House voted to pass the Healthcare Reform Bill, which President Clinton and his wife tried unsuccessfully. All this President Obama accomplished within one year in office.

I said all this about President Obama just for those who are floating this dangerous idea on the Internet that Nigeria needs time to develop. They are defending and condoning incompetence, mediocrity, visionless and cultic leaders that have hijacked the affairs of our beloved nation for the last 50 years. They cite from biased history books to justify the length of years it took some of the Western nations to be where they are today. These writers blame the Nigerian masses for poor governance, pandemic corruption and backwardness in our country today. They clearly blame innocent Nigerians as the reason why the government has not made much progress. This is wrong, unwise and faulty thinking in this day and age in which we live where ideas, strategies and power of technology are driving innovation, development, progress and prosperity.

What has President Yar'Adua accomplished since two years he was elected in office? We have heard bogus slogans such as servant leadership, seven point agenda, rule of law, and re-branding of Nigeria without any substance to it. Again President Obama's rebranding of America's image as the world leader is not the kind of rebranding we hear and read about Nigeria where millions are spent without results. President Obama is changing America's image through powerful and energizing speeches, vision, and ideas that are appealing to other world leaders.

What has President Umaru Yar'Adua done even within the context of Africa? How many speeches has he given? One of the primary responsibilities of a leader is decision making, but also a leader must talk and communicate vision to the people. A leader is someone who ignites and inspires

159

the best in people. Good leaders are great visionaries who inspire people with powerful ideas and work with their teams to create strategies for the masses to achieve shared vision. President Yar'Adua has skipped visits to United Nations for two years in a row now. The UN is a world stage where presidents of nations, head of states and leaders of thought come to dialogue and exchange ideas and strategies on how to confront and combat challenges of government, poverty, and seek ways to foster global peace, progress and prosperity. Nigeria's president has refused to show up despite the fact that in this last occasion he was selected as one of the speakers to address the UN body. While the Libyan, Iranian and Venezuela presidents took the center stage to dialogue on the matters of international politics and air their grievances against the United States, our president went to Saudi Arabia for an opening ceremony of a private university. The chancellor of the university received him, while diplomats and leaders of thought; business and government leaders converged at UN headquarters in New York. What a missed opportunity for Yar'Adua to defend the challenges President Obama leveled against poor governance in Africa and the recent charges of Mrs. Hilary Clinton on government corruption in Nigeria.

Today in Nigeria – the so-called giant and heart of Africa is a dungeon with poor infrastructures that hinders genuine business. Leaders at all level of our society have failed the people. Most of them are inefficient; incompetent, corrupt, have no vision, no ideas at all, not to talk of strategies to get anything accomplished. Millions of Nigerians are wallowing in abject poverty, corruption is endemic, no clean and equipped health or medical facilities, education is at zero levels, tribalism, religious idolatry and ignorance loom all over our society, witchcraft, voodoo, violence, crime, diseases while Nigeria's workforce remains one of worst educated in Africa with no performance management and efficiency at all.

For those who are now writing to defend this kind of incompetence and mediocrity in governance should also defend our business leaders and blame innocent Nigerians for their cronyism and beefcake businesses. The recent rot in the banking and financial sector calls for a state of emergency as well. The appointment of Mallam Sansui to sanitize the banking sector is a welcome idea. I was suspicious of Prof. Soludo when he called President Obasanjo the Moses of our time. I knew even as a scholar himself, he has bought into the cultic leadership of the federal government. Today, we can see his incompetence at the Apex bank, despite the awards he received from all corners of the globe. Even his recent involvement in the political saga of Anambra state exposes his character and public leadership. It is rather unfortunate that Anambra, a state that has produced the best Nigerian minds and leaders of our time has now become a paradise of political nonentities and hooligans. I think that these CEOs who were involved in these scandalous and un-collateral loans that were given to themselves by using fictitious names and non-existent companies should be locked-up for life. Mrs. Cecilia Ibru, one of the admirable Bank CEO's, who received worldwide recognition, is now Nigeria's nightmare and a disgrace. The primary task of our banking sector is to encourage companies to compete, invest, and hire a strong and well-educated workforce. The banks today should have a vision to use information technology to benefit consumers and stimulate investment, innovation, and create jobs. Rather, these greedy CEO's were issuing un-collateral loans – savings from poor Nigerians to themselves by using fictitious names and sometimes non-existent companies abroad to steal and stash billions of Naira on the detriment of the poor Nigerian masses. I support any action to lock these Bank CEO's in prison for the rest of their lives. What a greedy group of selfish individuals.

I think that those who are now suggesting that we need to give Nigeria time, or blame innocent Nigerians for Nigeria's backwardness are unrealistic in their assessment and unwise in their thinking. There is a deep leadership crisis in Nigeria. The country is fractured and frazzled from bad governance and poor leadership. Nigerians have always been resourceful and resilient people. I believe that Nigeria is blessed with natural resources, human potential, artificial intelligence, ideas and strategies to take our country from despondency to where it supposed to be among the comity of nations. Our problem is poor leadership, endemic government corruption, and colonial mentality, ethnic, religious and tribal factors. These are some factors that have truly hindered and continue to hinder the nation's progress, prosperity and peaceful society. The reality of a great and prosperous Nigeria can only come true from courageous and energetic visionary leadership.

## RELIGIOUS INTOLERANCE, MILITANCY AND TERROR

### MALLAM MUTALLAB FOILED TERRORIST ATTACK ON U.S FLIGHT 253 - A NATIONAL TRAGEDY AND GLOBAL IGNOMINY

Paul Marshall, a victim of his own rage once wrote this, "We live in a world of cynicism, cruelty and corruption." Paul Marshall was right then and even now. Most of you if not all will agree that what we are seeing on the television, hearing on the radio and reading on the media, Internet and worldwide web on this solemn holiday season is not fun thing to talk or even write about. It is sad, sordid and shameful news altogether for a nation that has been struggling with tarnished and battered image. The fact that Nigerians are now being labeled "TERRORISTS" thanks to the young Mutallab and perhaps other Islamic extremists and fanatics in the making is not only a national tragedy but also a global dishonor.

The global community woke up on December 25th, 2009 to read the sordid news about a terrorist attack on US Northwest Flight 253 from Amsterdam-Schipol airport heading to Detroit, Michigan by a relatively young Nigerian man, Umar Farouk AbdulMutallab, 23 years of age on a Christmas Day. AbulMutallab's evil attempt to detonate some explosive powder substance strapped to his underwear with a syringe filled with chemical solution foiled due to his amateur at the game and certainly the bravery of Jaspar Schugringa and some passengers on board who jumped on him to stop the dastardly explosion.

Umar Farouk Abdul Mutallab, we learn is a 23-year-old Nigerian man, and to the surprise of many, were educated in Mechanical Engineering at a prestigious University College, London. He is the 16th and youngest son of a wealthy Nigerian in the name of Alhaji (Dr.) Umaru Mutallab, a staunch member of the Northern Oligarch and one of the huge beneficiaries of Nigeria's oil wealth. The young Mutallab had been previously educated at British School of Lome, Togo, a school established by the British colonial masters to train the sons and daughters of their protégées who'll continue to rule over their commonwealth nations. When the young Mutallab finished high school there, he showed some signs of religious fanaticism. But his British mentors and teachers decided to send him over to UK to attend the prestigious London University, where he studied Mechanical Engineering from 2005-2008. One of his classmates quipped, that the young Mutallab barely did his part of the group study, but rather prayed all the time, had no social life and lived in a posh central London apartment home with prize tag about $10m, from where he walked about ten minutes to school for lectures. He managed to finish his program receiving a diploma in Mechanical Engineering in 2008.

The young Mutallab, a beneficiary of stolen wealth, unlike millions of Nigerian within his age brackets have resorted to 419 fraud, prostitution, political thuggery, kidnapping and violence or doing any menial jobs just to survive. The young Mutallab, who is silver spooned instead of pursuing his graduate program in UK or even transferring to an American university, where he would be easily accepted, decided to pursue further studies in Arabic and Islamic studies in Egypt and Yemen, where he was instead brainwashed by Al Qaeda to kill Americans, Jews, Christians, non Moslems or so-called infidels. The ranting of his religious beliefs, radicalism and extremism led to a fall-out with his father. He disobeyed and disowned his wealthy father and chose to flirt with the irrational Jihad terrorists.

His father, Alhaji (Dr.) Umaru Mutallab, is a billionaire, who own real estate around the world. Yet no one is asking how a one time minister and retired First bank chairman amassed the millions of dollars to own houses in katsina, Abuja, Lagos, Yemen, UK, USA and other nations around the world. People are talking about his courage and bravery for reporting his rebel and prodigal son to the CIA at the US Embassy in Abuja for his religious fanaticism and extremist terrorist tendencies. Why wouldn't he report his irrational, irresponsible and potential terrorist son, who denounced his family and threatened to kill Americans, Jews and Christians with a shout, "ALLAH IS GREAT? Why would a father who frequents the United States every year for medical treatment and owns multi-million dollar property in the US risk his own life for a derailed son, who after all, is not the firstborn, perhaps the son of one of his concubines from Yemen? Moreover, he has read how Ambassador Adeniran was rejected by the United States government as Nigerian ambassador to the United States because his 23 years old son involvement in a group gang rape of young white and black American girls. He knew

165

that his own case would be much graver and in fact put Nigeria in serious trouble if he had not reported his rebel and fanatic son before he attempted this horrendous and evil attack on the NWA flight.

I think that Alhaji Umaru Mutallab courageous action will exonerate Nigeria from global condemnation and any possible U.S. attack. He reported his son's extremism connection with Al Qaeda to the CIA at Abuja. The US intelligence failed to disseminate that critical information to other security agencies. I believe the United States department made a huge mistake not to take the report on the young Mutallab seriously. When a desperate father reports his child to the CIA authorities, that should have been be a vital piece of information to disseminate to various agencies especially when this young and depressed Mutallab leaves in a terrorist nation such as Yemen and has connection with Al Qaeda. Additionally, I do not understand why US security agents should maintain all these different lists on suspected or potential terrorists. The list for suspected terrorists should be on one huge database – the Terror Watch, Selectee and No-Fly lists are just bunch of beaurocratic nonsense.

The TIDE, which is smart and intelligent database software should return within seconds any database query according to last name and country no matter how many millions of rows of data on the database object. With more intelligent filtering, such dataset should return just in matter of seconds, which then could be transmitted within minutes through many available sophisticated technologies to the electronic databank, which would have triggered more scrutiny at the Amsterdam-Schipol airport. The United States security agencies should be blamed for not piecing and filtering the information that was given by Alhaji (Dr.) Umaru Mutallab on the young Mutallab to various security agencies. I think the American people are already having hot discussion and debate on that. I believe President Obama will be on top of this matter to break the wall of bureaucracy and any act of incompetence in the various security agencies such as the CIA, FBI, DIA and Homeland Security. Also the U.S. should be asking their British ally, why they didn't inform the US embassy in UK about Umar Farouk AbdulMutallab religious extremism. They refused him visa to continue his studies in UK and yet, the young Mutallab went to US embassy in London and secured a multiple visa entry to the U.S.

The United States is at war against Al-Qaeda, Taliban and Islamic religious extremists. It is a war of religious, political and even economic ideology and I have no doubt that the US securities agencies, CIA and FBI will do whatever it takes to fully investigate this horrendous attempted attack. So far, most of the details we are reading are coming from what Americans are telling us. I learnt that the US security agents have flooded the northern states of Kano, Maiduguri, Sokoto, Bauchi, Abuja and other Northern cities where Boko Harams sect are currently operating to take out Al-Qaeda operatives, even undermining the Nigerian SSS, Police and the army. That's what you get in a country where leadership has failed at all levels. This is just a national tragedy and global disgrace.

I don't want this piece to focus just on the Mutallabs, their privileged lifestyle in Nigeria, and the failure of international intelligence collaboration on terrorism. Rather, I like to focus on the national opprobrium that the young Mutallab and others like him have brought on every single Nigerian citizen, the root cause of religious extremism, and the failure of Nigerian leaders to deal with religious extremism in Nigeria and what this terrorist attempt on US flight 253 portends for Nigeria as nation and Nigerians especially those who reside abroad.

There is no doubt that the horrendous attempt by Umar Farouk Abdul Mutallab to detonate some explosives strapped to his underwear with a syringe filled with chemical solution on NWA U.S Flight 253 from Amsterdam-Schipol airport heading to Detroit, Michigan is a national tragedy and global embarrassment for all Nigerians. The Nigerian name is gravely dishonored by this wicked evil act and will take more than the ranting of Prof. Dora Akunyili, minister of Information and Communications to remedy. This is the time for strong leadership and wise diplomacy to restore the tarnished and battered image of Nigeria.

Nigeria is now labeled a "TERRORIST NATION" by the US state department. For some years now, as a nation we were dealing with the battered image due to drug peddling, prostitution of young girls, 419, credit card forgery, human body parts trafficking and all sort of illegal and illicit ways of survival thanks to Ibrahim Babangida – aka IBB. During his 8 years rule 1985 – 1992, corruption rose to all time high and his governors and senior government officials looted the national treasury. His SAP agenda, which was later known as "Suffer and Perish" had such devastating effects on the economy and severe consequences on millions of Nigerians. IBB institutionalized 419, corruption at high levels and plundered the economy. In fact the era of IBB led to the beginning of the moral decadence and purposeless society that we have today. The depth of corruption and social degradation led to moral decline, ethical and spiritual decadence at all levels in our society. His economic agenda destroyed the Naira and basically rubbished the Nigerian economy, which actually elevated greed, bribery, and corruption. Naira was devalued and a dollar could buy 100 Naira at that time. The quest for dollar and foreign currency motivated many young Nigerian girls into lucrative prostitution overseas mostly in Italy,

Holland, France, and Switzerland through an uncontrollable ring of organized prostitution of young Nigerian girls that were taken to overseas for such old fashion trade in the early 1980's. His administration did absolutely nothing to stop such organized crime against the reproductive resources of our country. That era of unbridled greed and sexual pervasion led to social and moral decadence we see in our country today.

President Obasanjo first introduced the ranting to restore the battered image of Nigeria overseas thanks to the advice of leaders at the World Bank and IMF. Mr. Frank Nwaeke Jr. was appointed the information and communication minister and he became the beneficiary of such huge project to reclaim our lost glory and reposition Nigeria to be the "Heart" rather than the "Giant" of Africa. Billions of Naira was spent to clean Nigeria's image abroad while religious extremisms were breeding at home. Then came Prof. Dora Akunyili, the current minister of information and communications with her ranting and passion about rebranding Nigerian yet she does not know that Nigeria, especially that the Northern states are a breeding ground for religious extremism and Jihad when she made this senseless statement recently, "Federal Government of Nigeria received with dismay the news of an attempted terrorist attack on a US airline. We state very clearly that as a nation, we abhor all forms of terrorism."

This is a shameful, despicable and outrageous statement. Does our information and communication minister not know that Nigeria especially the Northern states are breeding ground for Jihad, religious extremism and international terrorism? The men and women in various position of leadership in Nigeria are just sissy, cowards and ignorant. Does Prof. Dora Akunyili not know the history of the religious extremism that has been terrorizing Nigeria for the last forty years. First of all, is the minister of information and communication the right person who should be speaking on behalf of the nation during this time of national disagree and global shame? Where is the Vice President of Nigeria, since the President is currently bedridden in Saudi Arabian hospital? Where are the leaders of national security agencies? Where is the minister of Aviation, an industry that is comatose thanks to the pandemic corruption at the highest levels that put Nigerian Airways out of business? What steps are being taken to fully investigate the Mutallabs and actually figure out if these are truly Nigerian people or not? This country does not have leadership at all. What we have are ignorant, inept and bunch of cowards as leaders.

Prof. Dora Akunyili should know that religious ignorance, intolerance and violence have been one of the banes of our nation's development. Religious conflict and violence have been a big problem in Nigeria and a major threat to the security, unity and national progress of Nigeria. Religious ignorance and intolerance breed violence. Religious violence has decimated more lives in Nigeria in the last 40 years than hunger, disease, and accidents combined together. Nigeria has been a battleground between Islam, Christianity and traditional religions. Since 1960, Nigeria has had some many incidents of religious extremism and Islamic fundamentalism in their attempt to Islamize the nation. We have had religious riots in Jos, Kano, Maiduguri, Kaduna, Sokoto, Bauchi and other major Northern regions in which thousands of Christians were killed, their businesses looted and their property worth billions of Naira destroyed. Many of us still have vivid memories of the dastardly and despicable rash of rampage and violence in the major cities of the Northern Nigeria being carried out by Islamic fanatics and fundamentalists.

In 2003 when Nigeria had a rare opportunity to host the Miss World contest, a young and talented journalist wrote an article jokingly saying that if Prophet Muhammad had been alive, he would have chosen one of the beauty queens as wife. The Moslem fanatics took that as an excuse to carry out their carnage on Christians in the Northern states especially of Igbo descent looting their business and

171

destroying their properties. That ignorant and irrational rampage led to the loss of over a thousand precious lives and Nigeria missed the unique opportunity to showcase her to the world. The Miss World contest was moved to London, England, and Nigeria was denied the economic and business opportunity to attract foreign investors. Off-course the perpetrators of the heinous violence went scot-free.

In 2004, not even a year later the Islamic religious extremists again went on another rampage in Jos and Kano over a controversial cartoon which was drawn by a Danish cartoonist and published in Denmark and other European countries that sparked peaceful protests in Iran, Turkey and other major Arabic countries. The cartoon in question was not drawn by a Nigerian or published in any Nigerian newspaper or magazine, yet the Nigerian Islamic adherents and fanatics jumped on that occasion to kill their Christian brothers and sisters in Nigeria. Even the worst violent protests in the major Arabic nations did not claim but a few lives and injuries but in Nigeria hundreds of Christians were massacred; businesses and churches were burnt to ashes. Also this time, the perpetrators got away with it and justice was not meted.

Even until today, we continue to read and witness these acts of rampage and atrocious extremism including the ongoing religious riots, vandalism and killings in Bauchi state between the Maitatsine, Boko-Haram and Kala-kato sects. These acts of vandalism, violence, and killings of fellow human beings compel one to question the teachings of Islamic faith and its adherents. Why such acts of violence in the name of Allah? The radical Islamic fundamentalists can go to any extreme to defend their questionable religious sect and beliefs. These acts do not portray the attitude and behavior of people who follow a true prophet and genuine religious leaders.

What is the root cause of all this. There is a historical and biblical reason for this craziness and both are intertwined.

**First the historical**: Dr. Anis A. Shorrosh, a Palestine Arab Christian, an expert of Islamic and Christian theology, in his book: ISLAM REVEALED brilliantly explained the driving force behind the fanatical sects of Islam. He argued that one cannot understand the tensions, attacks, and violence and continuing explosion of Islamic fundamentalist until one understands the contradictions and intricacies that form the basis for Muslims' beliefs. The book was a product of series of debates he had in 1980's with Ahmed Deedat, considered the foremost Islamic scholar and great orator. These debates took place mostly in the prestigious Royal Albert hall in England and thousand of Muslims and Christians flocked to attend these debates. In that book, Dr. Shorrosh brilliantly compared the God of Heaven and Allah, Christianity with Islam, The Holy Bible with Koran (Quran), the fundamental teachings of Christianity and Islam and most importantly the turbulent life of Islam's sixth-century prophet Muhammad with the holy, virtuous life of the first century Jewish Messiah - Jesus Christ. In a nutshell, he traced the root cause of this despicable, irrational and senseless violence to religious hypocrisy, intolerance, ignorance and bigotry.

Make no mistake about it; Christianity and Islam do have

major fundamental differences and tenet of beliefs. The Muslim concept of sin and salvation is radically different from that of the New Testament Bible. These two biggest faiths in the world cannot be both right. It is either one is right or the other is wrong. Both cannot be right at the same time. Muslims want to make Islam a worldwide religion. Muslims want Africa beginning with Nigeria to be the indigenous home of Islam. Saudi Arabia is already pumping millions of dollars to promote Islam in many countries around the world. Today, Islam has spread to more than 60 countries with over one billion adherents. They assert that Christianity is white man's religion and claim that Islam is the true religion and the only religion with a message of peace and preserver of human civilization. They feel that Christians have been deceived and that Moslems have an obligation to lead them into the truth of Islam. Most importantly Moslems claim that Allah is the only one true God. And they believe the best way to achieve their Allah given mandate is through violence, terrorism, and jihad.

**Second the biblical:** The major root cause of Islamic fundamentalism is not found in their claims but in the pages of Holy Scriptures. In Genesis 16:11, 12; "The angel of the LORD also said to her: "You are now with child and you will have a son. You shall name him Ishmael, for the LORD has heard of your misery. He will be a wild donkey of a man; his hand will be against everyone and everyone's hand against him, and he will live in hostility toward all his brothers."

The biblical account of Genesis 16 - 21 details the

impatience of Abraham and Sarah and the sad mistake they made which explains the reason why we have such a religious paradox and conflict today between two brothers - Christianity and Islam. If you recall, in Genesis 12:1-3, The LORD called Abraham to leave his pagan country, his people and his household to go to an un-known land - a land flowing with milk and honey. God promised to give him and his descendants the land of Canaan. He promised to bless him and make him into a great nation and through his descendants all the nations of the earth would be blessed. At that time, Abraham was 75 years and his wife Sarah was 64. In Genesis 15, God makes a covenant with Abraham and reconfirms His promises to him. At that time, Abraham believed and God credited it t him as righteousness (Gen. 15:6).

In Genesis 16, Sarah became very impatient; she gave her Egyptian maidservant Hagar to Abraham. Abraham went into her and she became pregnant and bore Abraham a son and they named him Ishmael which means God hears. However, Ishmael was not the child that God had promised Abraham. Abraham was 86 years at this time. And so Sarah began to despise Hagar her Egyptian maidservant because she has bore Abraham, her husband a son. Eventually, Abraham listened to his wife Sarah and sent Hager away. The Angel of the LORD appeared to Hagar at a well near Kadesh and Bered and then spoke these words to her in Genesis 16:11, 12.

In Genesis 17, God makes another covenant of circumcision with Abraham and this time reminds him that He will make him the father of many nations. At this time

Abraham was 99 years old and Sara was 90. In Genesis 18, Sarah laughed at the discussion between Abraham and three visitors who came to visit Abraham to give the news of the birth of his son. To make this story short, In Genesis 21, Sarah became pregnant and bore Abraham a son and they named him Isaac. Abraham was 100 years old and Sarah his wife 90 years. Isaac was the son of the promise. Through Isaac, God would continue His covenant promises to Abraham. Isaac became the father of Jacob who becomes the father of the twelve tribes of Israel and great grandfather of Jesus, the founder of Christianity. God knew what was best for the Egyptian maidservant Hagar and her son Ishmael. God did not forsake them but rather He blessed them. Ishmael and his children became the originator of Islam faith. As you can see, Christianity and Islam are brothers and came from one great grand father - Abraham even though their mothers are different. However, God's covenant promises and purposes were with Abraham through Isaac his son and not Ishmael.

This is without doubt the root cause of religious extremism, fanaticism and conflict that we see today between the adherents of Islam and Christianity. The religious riots, violence, vandalism, extremism and killings in the name of Allah will not abate until the true God fixes the problem through the return of His Son, Jesus Christ who is the prince of peace?

Thank God Almighty that the derailed Mutallab did not succeed in his wicked act and ignominious plot to blow-up the US flight 253. Otherwise, those of us who still carry the green passport or go by our Nigerian name and still carry the thick accent would have life terribly miserable in the US. There is no doubt that even with the failure of this evil plot, Nigerians are going to be subjected to sever scrutiny in every area of their life here in America and elsewhere in the West. Few years ago, I learn that banks and financial institutions stopped hiring Nigerians in that sector because of 419 and credit card fraudulent activities. Qualified Nigerians were looked with scorn and with four eyes in everything they do here in the States. With the recent re-branding of Nigeria as a "Terrorist Nation", we are doomed. I think it is time for the variant groups that make up Nigeria to sincerely look each other in the eye and decide what kind of country we want. Christianity and Islam cannot cohabit without acceptance and tolerance of each other.

Our generation is doomed if courageous men and women would not stand up against the evil of nation building. Even though Umar Farouk AbdulMutallab's attempted terrorist attack on U.S Flight 253 failed and foiled up, yet his terrorist attempt is a national tragedy and global disgrace for all Nigerians. Young Mutallab terrorist attempt is reminiscent of Richard Reid, who tried to destroy a trans-Atlantic flight in 2001 with explosives hidden in his shoes, but was subdued by other passengers. The Richard Reid, a British got a life sentence. I'm sorry for young Umar Farouk Abdul Mutallab, a Nigerian.

## JOS MASSACRE – TERROR, JIHAD, AND THE CHALLENGE OF LEADERSHIP

*"The LORD saw how great man's wickedness on the earth had become, and that every inclination of the thoughts of his heart was only evil all the time. The LORD was grieved that he had made man on the earth, and his heart was filled with pain"* (Genesis 6: 5-6).

*"The angel of the LORD also said to her: "You are now with child and you will have a son. You shall name him Ishmael, for the LORD has heard of your misery. He will be a wild donkey of a man; his hand will be against everyone and everyone's hand against him, and he will live in hostility toward all his brothers." (Genesis 16:11, 12).*

*"Now I say to you that you are Peter, and upon this rock I will build my church, and all the powers of hell will not conquer it"* (Matthew 16:18).

*"Jesus turned and said to them, "Daughters of Jerusalem, do not weep for me; weep for yourselves and for your children…..Jesus said, "Father, forgive them, for they do not know what they are doing" (Luke 23:28, 34).*

*Furthermore, since they did not think it worthwhile to retain the knowledge of God, he gave them over to a depraved mind; to do what ought not to be done. They have become filled with every kind of wickedness, evil, greed and depravity. They are full of envy, murder, strife, deceit and malice. They are gossips, slanderers, God-haters, insolent, arrogant and boastful; they invent ways of doing evil; they disobey their parents' (Romans 1:28-30).*

When the U.S. intelligence came out with the report a few years ago that Nigeria risks disintegration by the year 2015 if she does not deal with government corruption, Niger Delta militancy, security issues, electoral reform and infrastructure problems, many especially within the PDP party rebuffed the report, arguing that the nation is strong, prospering, and united. These assertions were made despite the seemingly myriad and very serious problems confronting the nation.

On December 25, 2009, Nigerians were shocked to read that one of her citizens, a relatively young, rich and educated kid, Umar Farouk Abdul Mutallab carried a terrorist attack on US Northwest Flight 253 from Amsterdam-Schipol airport heading to Detroit, Michigan. As a result of that attempted terrorist act and other U.S intelligence sources, Nigeria was listed as a terrorist country and today many of her citizens are subjugated to all kinds of shameful treatment at the airports – local and international.

At the same time, Nigeria's ailing President Musa Yar'Adua is not where to be seen while his wife and his kitchen cabinet lied to Nigerians about his health. In addition, the religious extremism, violence and killings of Christians continued in the North, coupled with political thuggery and assassinations in Southwest, the scourge of armed robbery and kidnappings in Southeast, and off-course the Niger Delta militancy in South-south.

While the gory pictures of crushed skulls and brains of passengers crushed alive with a lorry truck on Lagos – Benin during a broad day light armed-robbery was published over the Internet, the Hausa/Fulani Muslim herdsmen went on killing rampage at Dogo Nahawa, Zot and Ratsat Christian villages in the remote area of Jos, Plateau State.

The horrifying pictures of children, women and young people massacred with machetes, guns or burned alive, a dastardly and satanic act carried out by the Hausa/Fulani Muslim herdsmen on the Berom Christians of Jos are direct result of years of ethnic hatred, religious intolerance, tribal politics, cowardly leadership, visionless politicians, and conspiratorial government.

This is simply jihad. It's so sad that we don't want to call it what it is. Our leaders and media people are simply cowards. What are they afraid of? What are they living for when the precious lives of children and women are being extinguished and snuffed out in such a savage and barbaric manner? Nigerian politicians, the army, police and journalists have mortgaged their soul for a pot of porridge and thereby compromised the dignity of their profession. The souls and blood of the innocent children and women are crying out. I'm sorry for Nigeria. I weep for her.

Oh yes, the true God of the universe will forgive you Hausa/Fulani Muslim herdsmen but He will not forget your satanic atrocities. He will avenge even to the 4$^{th}$ generation of your family line. You have brought a curse upon your land, Oh Hausa/Fulani herdsmen and upon those who paid you to commit these acts of evil, and wickedness upon innocent children and women.

Our God will also dry the tears of those who have lost everything. For Priscilla Sunday, who lost her seven children to this dastardly devilish act and many other women, God will avenge for you. The God of Abraham, Isaac and Jacob will dry your tears and give you the fortitude and strength to bear this incalculable loss. Know that your beloved children, even though their lives have been snuffed out of them in such a brutally manner by these agents of Satan, know that your little precious ones are resting in peace in heaven.

Nigerians should brace up for the resurgence of Islamic fundamentalism and Jihad, unless well meaning Nigerians and leaders rise up to the occasion because our corrupt and visionless politicians will not. This is the political and religious reality of the day. It is not the time to hide under the pretense of prayer asking God to answer by fire and sword of the Holy Spirit and He will. But it is also a time for self-defense and protection. It is a time for wise thinking and courageous action because your cowardly government and leaders – including unfortunately the federal biased army and police will not defend you.

What is taking place in Nigeria is not new, however, I could not believe that in the 21$^{st}$ century, when people and nations are making progress, Nigeria and most Nigerians are still stuck in crude thinking, savage lifestyle, and uncivilized behavior. These are horrifying and dark time in Nigeria. Will she survive as a nation? Fifty years after independence, Nigeria sits on the brink of collapse and disintegration. Nigeria is no longer a crawling nation, but now a dysfunctional nation, with an unfortunate people.

Are these ominous signs of an end of Nigeria as one nation? Why is Nigeria burning and risks disintegration? Why is the so-called giant, heart, and jewel of Africa on the brink of collapse? Why is evil, wickedness, violence, killings in the name of Allah, power, and oil so rampant in a country so blessed with abundant natural and human resources? Why are Muslims and Christians killing each other in Northern Nigeria? Can Nigeria survive as a nation? Is our country cursed because of oil and religion?

In the past, I had written papers and articles to explain the biblical root cause of this hostility between Christianity and Islam. This is not a political issue or ethnic hatred alone. This is purely religious. Before, Mohammad died in 632; he managed to unify Islam and the Arab empire into a powerful religious and political force. So for Muslims, there is no separation between religion and politics. One cannot function without the other. The introduction of Sharia in the North is a powerful and perfect example. Sadly enough, it is Christians that continue to separate religion from politics. Woe to you for your biblical and theological ignorance.

The irrational killings of Christians in Northern Nigeria is filled with deep-seated animosity and hatred because of the fundamental and distinctive religious, doctrinal and theological beliefs that separate the two biggest world faiths. For the purpose of this article/paper, I will deal with the resurgence of Islamic fundamentalism, which calls for the sixth pillar of Islam faith – Jihad.

Please, let's understand that no world religions today – Animism, Buddhism, Confucianism, Hinduism, Marxism, New Age Movement, Secularism, Shinto, and Taoism, etc are in such horrifying conflict except unfortunately Islam, Judaism and Christianity. Christianity is an offshoot of Judaism just like Islam is. In fact Christianity and Islam are brothers. Christians claimed to have descended from

Abraham through the line of Isaac, Jacob, and Jesus. Muslims, in fact, its founder Mohammad claimed his descendant from Abraham through Ishmael. Isaac and Ishmael were two sons of Abraham, Isaac being the son of promise and Ishmael, the son of Haggai, the Egyptian slave who served in the household of Abraham, Sarah's maiden. Realistically, Judaism, Christianity, and Islam are family members. Christianity is the spiritual son of Abraham, Isaac and Jacob. Muslims are also the spiritual sons of Abraham and Ishmael.

But the question is why they are in such hostility today. Why are there deep-seated rivalries, animosity and hatred between Muslims and Christians? There are biblical, historical, theological and religious reasons for this hostility. But for the purpose of this article, Let us review the sixth pillar of Islam faith to find out the reason for this ferocious orgy to kill Christians.

In Islam faith, there are 6 pillars of namely:

1. Shahadah – the creed of witness

2. Salat – the creed of rigid and ritual prayer life

3. Zakat –the creed of almsgiving

4. Saum – the creed of fasting

5. Hajj – pilgrimage to Mecca, and

6. Jihad – Holy War to kill infidels

Jihad or Holy War is the sixth and most important religious duty for any serious Muslim. The Kharjites, a powerful sect of Islam raised Jihad to a sixth pillar of Islam in the early days of Islam. Muhammad himself declared it is the duty of every Muslim to subjugate the whole world to Allah, if need be by holy war. When the situation warrants, men are required to go to war in order to spread Islam or defend it against infidels. One who dies in a Jihad is guaranteed eternal life in Paradise. All male, free and adult Muslims must become involved in Jihad if they want to go to heaven. Jihad is a holy war against those who are non-Muslims, those who do not believe that Allah is the only God and who do not believe that Mohammad is a true prophet of God. Jihad is regarded as a divine institution, and it is used to advance Islam and repel evil from Muslims. Muslims who die fighting in a holy war are assured of a place in paradise and special privileges there.

The Islamic faith is deeply rooted in violence and Jihad in the name of Allah. The call for Jihad has always been used to conquer people, land, territories and nations. The radical Muslims who perpetrate terror, behead, kill, participate in suicide bombing, or kidnappings etc always justify their actions from Koran, the holy book of Islam. Mohammad, the founder of Islam claimed he received "revelation" from Angel Gabriel, while meditating in a cave in Medina. Many Islamic and Arabic Christian scholars question the validity of his revelations and off-course his writings. There seems to be many fables and borrowings from biblical texts of Jewish and Christian faiths.

Let me stay on the Jihad because how Islam began, its founder, its spread and conquest by sword, conquest of Africa, its doctrines, beliefs and its holy book, Koran are not the purpose of this piece.

Why do Muslims hate and kill their Christian brothers?
Why do they also kill their own Muslims brothers when
they renounce Islam?

The answers to these questions are found in the pages of
Koran. Dr. Anis A. Shorrosh, a Palestine Arab Christian
scholar and eminent professor Emeritus of world religions
at my alma mater, in his masterpiece book, "Islam
Revealed" brilliantly and eloquently explained the driving
force behind the root causes of Islamic fundamentalism and
fanaticism. He argued that one couldn't understand the
tensions, attacks, and violence and continuing explosion of
Islamic fundamentalism until one understands the
contradictions and intricacies that form the basis for
Muslims' beliefs. In fact the Koran itself gives many
passages that advocate, promote and justify violence and
killing of infidels – anyone who is non-Muslim, who does
not believe that Allah is one true god and who does not
recognize Mohammad as prophet. Examples of such are
found all over Koran. In Koran, 9:5 teaches, "Kill those
who join other gods with Allah wherever you shall find
them; seize them, besiege them, and lay wait for them with
every kind of ambush: but if they shall convert, and
observe prayer, and pay the obligatory alms, then let them
go their way." Other passages that call for killing infidels
are: 2:92; 2:245; 2:276; 3:27; 4:102; 4:143; 5:56; 8:40;
9:29; 9:74; 9:111; 9:123; 22:39.

The Koran also teaches, "And if you shall be slain or die on
the path of Allah, then pardon from Allah and mercy is
better than all your amassing; for if you die or be slain,
verily unto Allah shall you be gathered. "And they also

185

who have fled their country and quitted their homes and suffered in my cause, and have fought and fallen, I will blot out their sins from them, and I will bring them into garden beneath which the streams do flow ((3:151-52; 3:194). Koran further states, "Fight the infidel and you will go to heaven. Turn way, and you will go to hell. In all of Islamic theology, this is the only way a person can know for sure that heaven is his destiny: wage a holy war and give up your own life."(8:12-18)

I have read and heard some modern, moderate and conservative Muslims teach that Islam is a peaceful religion and that Koran is opposed to violence. I know there are many sects much like Christianity, but Christians are not going around, at least not today killing other people who disagree with them. It is true that students of history especially biblical historians cannot forget the Crusades – Roman Catholicism bloody warfare against Islam or Islam against Hinduism, the Catholics against Protestant, Lutherans, the Irish Catholics, or even the Holocaust, etc, which were all religious and political motivated warfare. The truth of the matter is that human history has been dominated with wars - religious, political, economic, social, ideology, race, classicism, sexism, etc. All kinds of warfare have been waged throughout human history. But none of these had been divisive and destructive than religious wars. Fortunately, today, humanity has made progress and such wars have been minimized and replaced with tolerance, freedom, peace, progress, scientific and technological advancement, etc except only Islam that continues to wage blatant warfare against Christianity.

Today, Islam is the main persecutor of Christians all over the world. Thousand of Christians are dying under Islamic persecution, especially in the Middle East, Africa and Asia. In the continent of Africa, religious violence and ethnic cleansing are enormous. Africa and Middle East have been called a "Bloody Continent." Africa is a battleground between Islam, Christianity and traditional religions. Muslims and Christians kill each other in Nigeria, Sudan, Somalia, Rwanda and Burundi. Religious and ethnic killings have decimated nations like Senegal, Sierra Leone, Sudan, Somali, Ethiopia, Rwanda, Liberia, etc. Muslims with the help of repressive government have decimated their Christian population in Senegal, Rwanda, Sudan and Algeria in order to make their nation a 100% Islamic state. Islamic fundamentalists kill and execute hundreds of women every year for unveiling their face or any sensitive body publicly. Women who commit adultery are stoned to death while Muslim men marry as many wives as they want or can afford. This is purely insanity.

In a CNN interview, after 911 terrorist attacks, Osama bin Laden, the new leader of Islamic fundamentalism said, "We declare jihad against the US government, because the US government is unjust, criminal and tyrannical. It has committed acts that are extremely unjust, hideous and criminal whether directly or through its support of the Israeli occupation. For this and other acts of aggression and injustice, we have declared jihad against the U.S., because in our religion it is our duty to make jihad so that god's word is the one exalted so the heights and so that we drive the American away from all Muslims countries." Since then, he had made several tapes and given several speeches calling young and able Muslims worldwide to rise up against Israel, America and Christians.

On February 22, 1998, bin Laden issued an edict calling for death to America, including civilians. At that time, he announced the creation of the 'International Islamic Front for jihad Against the Jews and Crusades." In a subsequent interview with Time magazine, bin Laden said, "Thousands of millions of Muslims are angry...hostility toward America is a religious duty, and we hope to be rewarded for it by God. "I am confident that Muslims will be able to end the legend of the so-called superpower that is America" - Time, December 23, 1998.

For fanatical Muslims, it is pure joy to kill and be killed for Allah. Radical Muslims believe that they have a mandate from Allah to wage jihad against Israel, America and anyone who oppose Muslims. They believe what they are doing is for a righteous cause. Moreover, if they believe that by doing this evil they are serving Allah, nothing will dissuade them from doing it.

Today, Muslim fanatical sects are recruiting and training young people in Africa, including camps in Nigeria to carry out Jihad on the West. Currently, there are Muslim sects like Maitatsine, Boko-Haram, Kala-Kato sects, and now Hausa/Fulani herdsmen located in Jos, Kano, Maiduguri, Kaduna, Sokoto, Bauchi and other major Northern regions training and educating the young people to hate America, Israel and kill anyone who is non-Muslim, who oppose Islam, Muhammad and Allah. Last Christmas, Nigerians were shocked to read that one of her citizens, Umar Farouk Abdul Mutallab attempted to detonate some explosive powder in a way of terrorist attacks on US Northwest Flight 253 from Amsterdam-Schipol airport heading to Detroit, Michigan.

Religious conflict is a huge leadership challenge and a major threat to the security, unity and national progress of Nigeria. Religious ignorance and intolerance breed violence. Religious violence and war have decimated more lives in Nigeria in the last 40 years than hunger, disease, and accidents combined together. Northern Nigeria especially has been a battleground between Islam and Christianity. Since 1960, Nigeria has had some many incidents of religious extremism and Islamic fundamentalism in its attempt to Islamize the nation.

Islamic fundamentalism, fanaticism, terrorism and jihads are a big threat and enormous challenge for our nations' leaders. I call upon Nigerian government, political leaders, religious and civil leaders, Imams, clerics, Islamic scholars, moderate, modern and conservatives Muslims and business leaders, to work together in resolving the imminent threat to Nigeria's unity. Nigerian religious leaders must work together to ensure that Christians, Moslems and paganisms become partners in this 21$^{st}$ century rather than enemies in solving the social, economic and political obstacles facing our nation. They must work together to hold our politicians and government leaders accountable to the promises and principles of fairness, justice and equity.

They must be involved in shaping public policies, laws and decisions that hinder Nigerian people from fulfilling their God-given purposes on planet earth. Our religious leaders must work together to educate their followers about

189

tolerance and peaceful cohabitation? As human beings we cannot accomplish much in isolation rather we develop, mature as people and achieve greatness in the context of love, relationship and fellowship. And until we learn the cardinal principle of Islam and Christianity, which is forgivingness and reconciliation, we will never live in peace. Without genuine forgiveness and reconciliation, there cannot be unity and peace. Without love, another cardinal truth of Christianity and Islam, we cannot have genuine relationship. Relationship is the most vital aspect of life. Genuine relationship and love are the greatest human assets and the essence of every major faith in the world. Christians and Muslims must understand that they are brothers from the same great grand father – Abraham. Let's surrender to the true heir and heritage of Abraham.

## THE URGENCY FOR NATIONAL CORE-VALUE LEADERSHIP

## NIGERIA STILL CRAWLING AT 45 - THE URGENCY FOR NATIONAL CORE VALUES

---

Every October 1st, since 1960, Nigerians everywhere celebrate the Independence Day anniversary. So in just a few days, Nigeria will celebrate the 45th anniversary of her independence from Britain. Big celebrations, large parties and great speeches will be the hallmark of October 1, 2005. School children will match in clean uniforms; songs and bands will be played to entertain the Nigerian masses in various cities and states. The Nigerian foreign missions will also throw huge parties to showcase Nigeria's false image as a rich country. Other nation's ambassadors, diplomats and host country government officials will be invited to party with the Nigerian people. Assorted Nigerian as well as foreign dishes will be provided. Whiskeys and expensive wine will also be in abundance. Local embassy staff will also have the opportunity of the year to enjoy the country's lavishness. Nigerians in Diaspora will also celebrate in big ways. There will be basically an exhibition of custom designed cultural outfits and various costumes being worn. Luxurious cars like Hummers, Mercedes, Lexus, and Jaguars will roll in the parking lots like a fashion parade night in Paris, New York or London. I remember one

191

particular Independence Day celebration in Dallas, a white American couple who lived not too far from the conference hall where the independence party was organized, asked me and my company if we were having a fashion parade. In a nutshell millions of dollars are always spent to celebrate the first of October in Nigeria and abroad.

There will be many people giving speeches. However, the keynote speaker everybody will be watching to hear what he says will be the president of the federal republic of Nigeria. Millions of Nigerians will watch President Obasanjo on the national television as he speaks to the entire country where we are as an independent nation. He will extol eminent leaders like late Dr. Nnamdi Azikiwe, Chief Obafemi Awolowo, Alhaji Abubakar Tafawa Balewa, Alhaji Ahmadu Bello, Ernest Ikoli, H. O. Davis, Chief S. L. Akintola, Dr. M. I. Okpara, Solanke and Eyo Ita among many other nationalists who fought for Nigeria's independence. The president will also give an inspirational speech on the achievement and accomplishment of his government while encouraging Nigerians to be patient in-order to reap the so-called "dividends of democracy". He will also list his plans and strategies for the future.

Nigeria's independence was granted due to the activities of people like Dr. Nnamdi Azikiwe, Chief Obafemi Awolowo and Ahmadu Bello, who were the pioneers of the nationalist grievances against the British system of indirect rule. The British imposed a system of administration in which the local affairs were largely left in the hands of African traditional rulers: the Emir, Oba, and Eze, while the national affairs were completely controlled by the British officials. These nationalists aspired to share in the national government, which was the exclusive preserve of the British. Those elected to the congress were all British officials and the nationalists thought that the national administration did not represent the Nigerian masses and therefore they protested against the British government to revise the 1922 constitution to include Nigerians in the Legislative Council. The history of Nigeria's independence was largely due to the history of the struggle by these men who fortunately gained their education through British established missionary schools in Nigeria. Few of them like Dr. Nnamdi Azikiwe had a rare of opportunity to travel abroad where he gained quality education that enabled him to wisely challenge British style of government which was established for the people of Nigeria and most of Africa then. As a result of such pressure through wise and careful reasoning, Nigeria was granted independence in October 1, 1960 without blood shed.

The struggle of these nationalists even became more necessary because of the variant groups and kingdoms that the British lumped together in 1900 to create a nation we know today as Nigeria. It was the wife of Lord Lugard Nigeria's second governor general who named us Nigeria. In 1900 before we were lumped together, we were great empires and nations for instance, the kingdoms of Oyo, Bornu, Hausa, Benin, Bonny, Jukun, Idah, Aro, and Igboland. The peoples of these kingdoms and empires had deep political, social, religious, tribal and linguistic differences. Nevertheless, there were enormous business and trade among them. When the British invaded and conquered these kingdoms, these variant groups of people with profound linguistic, social and cultural differences were forced to live together for benefit of the colonial masters and struggle of power between them and the French people. The British created this monstrous nation for their political and economic interest. The peoples of Hausa, Kanuri, Igbo, Yoruba, Kalabari and many other various groups were forced to live together. It is like asking various animal species like the camels, cows, tigers, lions, goats, sheep, dogs and chickens to live together. You guessed right what would happen! And this was done without a well-defined set of core values that addressed national unity, patriotism and parameters to discourage social, cultural, religious and linguistic differences between the peoples of this new nation.

The amalgamation of these variant groups has been very problematic and difficult. At forty-five years, Nigeria has not yet grown-up. At a perfect middle age, she is still immature and crawling with her belly. The tendencies and acts of childishness are still evident. Since she was granted independence for self-government, she has had only turbulent times of political crisis, tribal and religious violence that led to unforgettable genocidal civil war of 1967-70 that decimated more than three million lives and left her with so much bitterness, anger and hatred toward one another. I think it is time for Nigeria to genuinely forgive one another before God or Allah or Supreme Being whichever one you prefer and bury its tumultuous and fractured history in-order to live together and peacefully again. Without genuine forgiveness and reconciliation, there cannot be unity and peace. The declaration for the end of the war slogan: "No Victor No Vanquished" should be revisited and properly implemented, otherwise Nigeria will fight again and this time, I have a perfect end of war slogan: "To Your Tents O All Tribes."

A lot has been said and written about the amalgamation of Nigeria as a nation. The late visionary leader, Chief Obafemi Awolowo once observed that Nigeria is not a nation, but merely a geographical expression. Many notable visionaries and leaders of thought have also referred the Nigerian nation as merely a political expression for the economic and political interest of the colonial masters. Today, we are also witnesses of the renewed fight, revival and formation of new militant groups calling for peaceful separation. This similar call, demand and secessionist movement made by former Major General Emeka Odumegwu Ojukwu in 1969 by is even louder today. Chief Ralph Uwazuruike, the leader of the revived movement for the actualization of the Sovereign State of Biafra (MASSOB) is strong, courageous and passionate about the movement he leads despite threats, imprisonment and killings of his followers by the federal government. Recently we read that the Biafra currency, which was used during the civil war era, has resurfaced and is being accepted as a legal tender in many African countries.

As I write this article, the Nigeria headline headlines are abundantly full of the story of the arraignment and arrest of Alhaji Mujaheeden Dokubo Asari, the fearless and outspoken leader of the militant Ijaw youth. He has threatened to blow up the Idama Flow stations being controlled by the Chevron Nigeria Limited. He has

195

persistently and passionately called for an independent state of Ijaw people and a peaceful separation of Ijaw people from Nigeria. The military dictator Abacha was able to silence the people of Ogoni after the brutal killing of Saro Wiwa, a man of high intellectual ability. The Ogoni's were persecuted which led to the United States and Canadian government to grant them political asylum and refugee status into their countries. Today, Mr. Ledum Mitee is the leader of the Movement for the Survival of Ogoni people and he is very active and fighting hard for his people. President Obasanjo and his government will have to be very careful in dealing with leaders of these kinds of civil rights activists and freedom fighters like Alhaji Dokubo, Chief Uwazuruike, and Mr. Ledum Mitee. This is a democratic government and the world is watching how this government handles such sensitive issues.

The reason for all the anger, frustrations and fighting is not just because of the economic and political denial but lack of coherent national core value system that gives sense of patriotism and empowers the peoples of Nigeria to believe in themselves and their national leadership. Since Nigeria gained independence, she has had many kinds of government – Unitary, Parliamentary, Military and now Democratic Presidential system. Despite Nigeria's enormous human potential and abundant natural resources, the promise of these various governments has been a dismal failure. They have not kept their promises but floundered and left the Nigerian masses worse than when they were slaves under the British.

For instance, during President Babangida's government in 1980's, the highly publicized economic package "Structural Adjustment Programmed (SAP) that was aimed to establish a realistic exchange rate for Nigeria and restructure the economy was a dismal failure. It cost hundreds of millions Naira to implement and ended up being an economic strategy to enrich himself and his few friends. Billions of dollars were borrowed from the International Monetary Fund (IMF) and World Bank and squandered. He used SAP economic package to loot the national treasury and plundered Nigeria into a serious national debt. I am sometimes disgusted when I read that some Nigerians still call on Ibrahim Babangida to run for presidential elections again. Where do we start to remind these visionless and myopic followers of Babangida of his treacherous and incompetent leadership? This is a man who murdered one of the brightest Nigerian journalists and cancelled perhaps the only genuinely democratic elections in the history of Nigeria? No wonder these leaders are not accountable because the led are very dysfunctional and perhaps mentally and financially challenged. Their stock in trade is to steal, steal and steal from the national treasury.

The government of Abacha was practically visionless and did not have any economic plan but political agenda in-order to entrench himself as a life president. He looted the national treasury and left Nigerian economy in such a horrendous national debt that we have today. Up till today, the present government is negotiating the billions that he stashed away in Swiss banks. The act of God removed him from this planet before he could destroy more lives through poverty, hunger and authorized killings and murder.

197

Even this present government has not lived up to its promises. After nearly six years of democracy, people are yet to see the so-called "Dividends of Democracy". Nigerians are yet to see the benefits of NEEEDS and SEEDS, another government economic propaganda. As a former World Bank executive, I believe that Nigeria's finance minister, Mrs. (Dr.) Ngozi Okonjo-Iweala is capable of a workable economic plan to improve the economy and help poor Nigerian masses, but it will not be easy for her. She has to deal with the corrupt systems of the Nigerian government as well as the un-cultured populace. Nigerians are good at sabotaging any economic plan that will affect their illegal way of doing business and livelihood. I also believe that these economic acronyms are vicious strategies to deceive Nigerians and loot the national treasury while the Nigerian people are being impoverished and thousands of lives wasted each and every year.

I have often heard about this government boast about how it gave Nigerian people wireless phones. The wide circulation of cell phones in Nigeria today is not an achievement rather it is big business for the foreign wireless companies who have found opportunity for lucrative business in Nigeria. If the past Nigerian governments had successfully implemented line telephones in 60's, the use of cell phones today would have been very minimal. However, with the rapid technological advancement and the easy implementation of wireless technology makes it easier for these companies to invest in poor countries. Nigeria with a population of nearly one hundred thirty million is a huge consumer market for wireless communication companies. Before the arrival of cell phone, we can count the number of people who had line phones in their homes. The technology and infrastructure were not there to dig up wire lines and plant telephone poles. Wireless technology that Nigeria enjoys today is not an achievement that any government should not boast about. If these sophisticated cell phones and the chips were made in Nigeria and then Nigerian companies are the providers, then I can really praise this government for its visionary accomplishment. But for now, it is just the 21$^{st}$ century phenomenon. Even cell phones are commonly used in Bangladesh and many other poor nations that are rated with Nigeria.

Lack of genuine leadership has been blamed for poverty and the travails of the Nigerian society. There is no doubt that Nigeria's or even Africa's problem is due to of lack of leadership. There are at-least three mains areas of leadership failure:

1. Lack bold and courageous leadership
2. Lack of moral ingredients of leadership and
3. Premature exposure to leadership


However there cannot be moral and courageous leadership without a well-defined set of core values that will shape the lives and especially those who are called to lead. Core values are constant and passionate beliefs that drive people lives, business decisions or nation's priorities. Core values determine and shape daily actions of people, business or government leaders. They are hidden motivations that dictate every decision and determine life's priorities. Vision, passion and purpose are driven by core values. Without core values or code of conduct, people, families, businesses or even nations will have a broken focus? Dr. Mike Murdock, one of the greatest wisdom teachers of our contemporary time said, "The passion of our daily routine is the hidden secret for our success, people fail because of broken focus." Daily routines are core values or value systems that drive and determine life's success. Daily routines determine and shape our daily actions.

The same is true of a nation. Core values ask the question, why do I do what I do? Developing national core values and the passion for why we as a nation do what we do will be the secret to our nations success. Well-defined strong national core values will not only contribute to our nation's success but also will also inspire people to reach their fullest potential, embrace good change, communicate what is important and enhance credible leadership. Core values are not only applicable to individuals or business organizations, families or churches, but also to nations, states and cities. Without a strong national value system no individual, family, church ministry, business enterprise or even a nation can be very successful.

There has to be patriotic decisions and passionate actions that determine and drive our nation's priorities. This has nothing to do with the constitution. By the way, Nigeria's first constitution was written-up for us by the British people in 1922. These are people who do not understand our culture or social systems. Since then, our constitution has been revised many times without our constitutional experts radically revamping the constitution to accommodate the social, cultural, religious and tribal norms of all the variant groups that make up Nigeria. The fundamental rights as defined in our constitution today are not the same as a well defined set of core values such as character, honesty, genuine integrity, discipline, character, trust, truth, commitment, dedication, patriotism just to mention a few that that will enhance credible leadership, spur nation's building, promote good business culture and inspire people to embrace good change in-order to reach their potential. I was disappointed that the recent concluded CONFAB conference was setup to determine how to divide, distribute and allocate oil revenue rather than how to establish core values to unite the nation. I am convinced that in order to build a respectable and prosperous Nigerian nation that we aspire and dream to have, there must be first of all a set of well-defined core values or code of conduct that will help to create an environment in which government, businesses, investment and people can thrive and prosper.

In a nutshell, we have to figure out the moral ingredients that make citizens of the civilized Western nations like the USA, Britain, France, Germany, Japan and many others very patriotic and self serving. It would be a taboo to hear that an American governor or senator was arrested in Africa for money laundering. It would very uncivilized that an American or European government official will steal money and took it to Africa or bought a million dollar mansion some where in the African continent. I remember vividly how former and late Italian prime Minister – Bettino Craxi was chastised when Italians found out that he owned a vacation home in Tunisia. He was chastised and forced to resign as prime Minister. Within few years, He died in his fifties, a very sad and sudden premature death.

Nigerian politicians do the incredible without any chastisement from the people. Last Thursday, September 15, the governor of Bayelsa State Chief D.S.P Alamieyeseigha was arrested at the Heathrow airport for money laundering. Two weeks earlier, the London Metropolitan Police had arrested Governor Joshua Dariye of Plateau State over alleged money laundering. A month ago, FBI accosted Mrs. Jennifer Atiku, the black American wife of the Vice president for possessions of large sums of money and lavish shopping spree in the DC and Baltimore. At her "white house" mansion in Potomac, Maryland, tons of business documents were uncovered of Vice Presidents illegal business in the USA. This is the same man who is aspiring to take over from the incumbent president. Most of the senators and governors have been involved in some form of bribery, corruption or money laundering while the vast majority of people that they are supposedly leading and provide livelihood for are dying of hunger, poverty and disease.

It is unthinkable and unimaginable how these governors, senators and many of these Nigerian government officials own these millions of dollar homes in United States and Europe. Sometimes, these homes are locked up without any one living in them. These million dollar homes have high property taxes and exorbitant bills. Only God know how these Naira paid government officials are maintaining these million dollar properties in USA and Europe. It is only in Nigeria that people enter into politics in-order to make money.  In the West, most of the politicians are very rich and wealthy before running for political office.  Basically they want some power, authority and influence.  What a shame that the reverse is the case in Nigeria.

Nigeria and Nigerians can hold to fine points of tradition and cultural values but if not translated into core values that are embraced by all, we will never prosper economically, socially, politically, religiously and otherwise.  Nigeria is in dire need to construct right standards that are embraced by all.  She must translate those standards into core values that will guide personal conduct and relationship with each other.  This is what is desperately needed in Nigeria in-order for us to grow-up, start walking and forge ahead as a nation not revenue allocation.  Otherwise anything else will be uncivilized, crude, and primitive and we will continue to crawl even at 100 years.

Congratulations on your 45$^{th}$ Birthday.

## 47 YEARS AFTER – SYMPTOMS OF MIDDLE AGE CRISIS – PART I

On October 1$^{st}$, 2007, Nigeria will clock forty-seven years old. Already plans are underway even though in a modest and low profile manner to celebrate Nigeria's 47$^{th}$ independence anniversary.  For Yar'Adua, this will be his first independence celebration as president.  I understand he is quietly planning a modest celebration unlike his predecessors who spent hundreds of millions of Naira to celebrate an independence anniversary of a nation that continues to fracture into different parts. It was Dr. Joseph Nanyen Garba, the erudite scholar and Nigeria's former permanent representative to UN, who said it well when he wrote in the foreword of his book – Fractured History

*"In our thirty-four years of nationhood, we have made an unprecedented turnaround; going from a nation of hope, strength, abundance, economic prosperity and high aspirations to a nation which has become the embodiment of a degenerate society."*

I concur with Dr. Garba. The Nigerian state is surely chronically ill, ethically and morally decadent and frankly suffering from a serious and severe middle age crisis. Since Nigeria gained independence, she has had various systems of government – Unitary, Parliamentary, Military and now Democratic Presidential system. Despite Nigeria's enormous human potential and abundant natural resources, the promise of these various governments has been a dismal failure. They have not kept their promises but floundered and left the Nigerian masses worse than when they were as slaves under the British kingdom.

Few days ago when I coined the title of this article, I did not hesitate to place a call to an expert, a friend who was trained in Psychology and Psychiatry as well as a Mental Health Counselor. He approved the title and confidently convinced me that nations like human beings do suffer "Middle Age Crisis." Frankly speaking, I became more aware of this "Middle Age Sickness" few years ago when some people I know who are in their 30's, 40's and 50's all

204

of a sudden began to behave irrationally and senselessly. Most of us who came from Africa where witchcraft is unfortunately still rampant and commonly practiced would attribute voodoo as the cause of such irrational behavior. But since middle age crisis attack people from other societies, attributing it to voodoo would be a wrong analysis. However, after forty minutes into the discussion, I came to the realization that middle age crisis is a present reality that affects both men and women. It usually begins somewhere around age 35 and sometimes last until lifetime. It occurs to both male and female but probably affects men more than women. Middle age crisis does not discriminate. It attacks both poor and rich respectively. He cited many famous names in this country who are suffering from middle age crisis.

However, I was profoundly amazed when he cited examples of nations and countries that have suffered or currently suffering some sort of middle age crisis. Unfortunately, my country – Nigeria was quick to be named in that list. In this article, unlike my previous ones, I do not intend to rehearse history or extol our eminent nationalists leaders who fought for Nigeria's freedom and independence against the British Empire and bequeathed us a nation endowed with abundant natural resources and many talented human beings. Rather, I would discuss briefly some of the areas I believe are serious crisis issues facing our nation since she gained independence from Britain. Today, some of those visionary leaders like Dr. Nnamdi Azikiwe, Chief Obafemi Awolowo, Alhaji Abubakar Tafawa Belewa, Alhaji Ahmadu Bello, Ernest Ikoli, H. O. Davis, Chief S. L. Akintola, Dr. M. I. Okpara,

Solanke, Eyo Ita among many others would sometimes look out from their heavenly abode with despair at a nation that is now fragmented and a people without much hope and future. With the embrace of a new colonial master – the Chinese, the future of Nigeria looks windswept than ever.

**Bad Leaders**

The first middle age crisis facing our nation perhaps more than anything else is that of bad leadership. Governance in Nigeria for the last forty years or so was hijacked by a group of selfish, greedy, egoistic, visionless malicious, mischievous and treacherous rulers. Since she gained independence in October 1$^{st}$, 1960, she has not had good leaders to pilot the affairs of the country. Nigeria as a nation has not really enjoyed any genuine political peace and national prosperity despite enormous blessings that God endowed on her. Instead, the country has been ruled and governed by military and political dictators that denied the people of Nigeria security, order, peace and basic needs of livelihood. For forty seven years, what we've had is a military dictatorship, political hypocrisy, idolatrous religious system, and extravagantly indulgent corrupt judicial system that oppressed the poor, children and minority members of the family. In a nutshell, Nigeria's rulers have failed to fulfill their obligation to the nation and its people.

The eminent scholar and International poet, Prof. Chinua Achebe in his famous book entitled: The Trouble with Nigeria, writes,

*"The trouble with Nigeria is simply and squarely a failure of leadership."*

Many concerned Nigerians as well as foreigners have also attributed the pandemic poverty, diseases, corruption, violence, ethical and moral decadence in our society due to lack of leadership.

Dr. Joseph Nanven Garba in his treatise of governance in Nigeria said this:

*"Nigeria, to my mind, does not lack real men and women. The ingredients for creating a formidable nation exist. What is lacking is leadership with the political will and the selfless dedication to galvanize the entire nation."*(Fractured History - Elite Shifts and Policy Changes in Nigeria)

Fortunately Nigeria does not lack competent people who can lead. Rather what we lack are visionary and courageous leaders that are transparent in their discharge of domestic, public and foreign responsibilities. Nigeria can brag of men and women with reputable education and impressive resume for leadership positions but most of them lack the ethical and moral qualities of leadership. Nigeria does not lack human resources but she abundantly lacks courageous leaders who are sincere, genuine and truly understand the divine tasks, obligations and purposes of leadership. Therefore the truly missing ingredient is failure to understand the divine dimensions of leadership. Nigeria's biggest problem in this age and time is not just economic, social, religious or political but lack of God fearing leaders. It's a leadership crisis.

I have often said that leadership is not a career or a profession but a service, a sacred duty, an enormous sacrifice and service to humanity. It is a divine duty that was designed by our creator to govern his creation and harness the resources found therein justly, fairly and equitably. Leadership was designed to provide order, security and to enthrone peace, justice and righteousness on planet earth. Therefore those aspiring to lead must not only have basic education but sound moral and ethical development as well. Today, many people who in charge over the affairs of our country lack the moral and ethical qualification and as a result the Nigerian society is ravaged with many problems.

As I read and witness the crop of corrupt leaders currently running the affairs of our nation, I am afraid to say that Nigeria and Nigerians alike are suffering from the so-called middle age crisis. Despite the enormous progress being made by many countries to correct the anomalies in governance and establish sound democratic systems and transparent leadership, Nigeria's current leaders continue to ignore the opportunities within their disposal to truly transform our beloved nation. Instead, our leaders continue to mismanage the enormous human potential and abundant natural resources within their disposal because of greed, personal power, profit and pleasure. Even more disheartening and disappointing a times is the activities of followers, who are also completely ignorant of the expectations of their leaders. Therefore what we have today in our country is a superficial, cryptic, unqualified and incompetent group of leaders; a leadership cult that is crippling and wasting enormous human potentials. What we have today in our society is a group of leaders that is only after their own personal profit, power and influence. They are greedy, incompetent and hungry wolves who abuse power for their personal gain and pleasure. They enjoy lavished lifestyles, showing of their ill-gotten wealth, enjoying cheap sex while millions go hungry. Sadly enough, what we have in Nigeria today as leaders are people driven by greed, corruption, jealousy and hatred of the Nigerian people. They extort, levy heavy taxes on poor citizens, take bribery and loot the state treasury. They lie, compromise, harass, threaten and even resort to murder in order to attain and solidify their temporal influence, superficial charm and evil power.

## Ethnicity, Tribalism and Injustice

Lack of genuine and courageous leadership led to the second crisis - ethnic hatred, tribalism and injustice that exist in our nation today. It is a well known fact that before the white men came as missionary workers with pretense to colonize the territory known today as Nigeria; the various inhabitants of that vast area lived in peace and traded with each other. To subjugate and dominate this vast area for their economic and political purposes, these variant groups of people with profound linguistic, cultural, religious and even political differences were coerced to amalgamate into one country. A name was chosen for the people without due consultations. Since then this marriage of inconvenience has been very problematic and difficult to manage especially after they were granted freedom and independence to live together and govern themselves. The marriage became more turbulent following the 1960's political crisis, tribal and religious killings that led to unforgettable genocidal civil war of 1967-70 in which more than more than three million lives were massacred. That bitter civil war left an unforgettable anger, bitterness and hatred among the peoples of Nigeria. Even the end of war slogan "No Victor No Vanquished" could not bury the tumultuous and fractured history of a people that had been traumatized and to live peacefully and to trust each other became a very challenging problem to fix.

Many in the past had written on the economic and political amalgamation of Nigeria. The late visionary leader, Chief Obafemi Awolowo once observed that Nigeria is not a nation, but merely a geographical expression. Other notable visionaries and leaders of thought have also referred the Nigerian nation as merely a political expression for the economic and political interest of the colonial master - Britain. The amalgamation of Nigeria as a nation is an issue that must be addressed if we really desire to live in peace and fulfill the assignment that God, Allah or the Divine Creator has put us together to accomplish for mankind and especially for the oppressed black race of this planet. I believe that without genuine forgiveness and reconciliation, there cannot be order, unity and peace in our country. We cannot move forward as a nation and fulfill our common purpose and destiny if ethnicity, tribalism and injustice are not addressed in our country. We truly need a national identity that harbors ethnicity and discourages tribal identity.

Speaking of injustice, the Holy Scriptures clearly teaches that righteousness and justice exalt a nation. Righteousness and justice are the foundation of any nation. No nation can flourish; have order, peace, security and prosperity without righteousness and justice. Justice is ought to be a prominent concern of any credible leader who loves and cares for the citizens. But that has not been the case in Nigeria as far as I can remember. Ours has been a society barricaded by injustice, an openly conspicuous in the manner in which the nation's revenue are shared, award of business contracts, infrastructural development and obviously distribution of political positions. Instead of our leaders to administer justice, they mete injustice on the poor, children, elderly, widows and minorities. No nation can truly flourish if she treats her people that way. Injustice is sin before Almighty God and He hates it with a passion. One fine day, God will severely punish those or nations that promote and practice injustice (Note: This is not my opinion – read the Minor Prophets: Amos, Hosea and Micah).

The injustices in our nation led some courageous men to form peaceful groups and unfortunately some militant groups as well to battle against the biased, discriminatory and satanic system that they live in. Today, we have Chief Ralph Uwazuruike, who heads the revived movement for the actualization of the Sovereign State of Biafra (MASSOB). He is peacefully protesting against the injustices in our system. I also believe that his continued detention in maximum security prison especially after leaders of other similar groups have regained their freedom is an obvious example of injustice in our system. And I humbly and politely call on the President Yar'Adua to do the right thing to free Chief Ralph Uwazuruike on this Independence Day. He has been in detention for over two years while other similar leaders, even more militant than him, have been released. The injustices in our system must be eradicated otherwise; we cannot truly flourish as a nation. The negative effects of injustice will always hunt and prevent us from reaching our potential as a nation. It must be eradicated.

## 47 YEARS AFTER – SYMPTOMS OF MIDDLE AGE CRISIS – PART II

Part one of this article generated quite a few comments including insults and attacks. First of all, let me say that my comments on Chief Ralph Uwazuruike do not mean that I support his revived movement for the actualization of the Sovereign State of Biafra (MASSOB). The truth is that his continued detention in prison when other similar leaders, even more militant than him are freed is an example of injustice in our system. I do believe in the unity and continued existence of Nigeria as a nation. I do believe that there is a sovereign and divine assignment for Nigeria as a unified nation. The colonial master may have amalgamated the variant groups of people that make up Nigeria for their economic and political gains but in actuality God allowed it, so that Nigeria can fulfill her divine mandate – and that is the redemption of black race on planet earth.

As far as bad mouthing our country is concerned, especially my capacity as a reverend does not mean that I have to keep quiet where corruption, unrighteousness and injustice reign high. All my education till date and especially my Theological training did not only prepare me to be an ambassador of God on earth, but it prepared me to be a scholar, a social and moral activist who speaks to public issues that confront and challenge humanity. My training empowers and encourages me to be passionate for justice, ethics, and cultural diversity. Also, let me make this humble assertion that I'm called to be a prophetic voice to our nation. So there is nothing you can do to me. I am not bothered at your insults, attacks, innuendos and threats. I must obey God rather than men in carrying out the task that God has assigned me to do. Our country must rise above ethnicity, tribalism and injustice.

## Bribery and Corruption

The third major crisis facing our nation is bribery and corruption. Bribery and corruption is an endemic practice in Nigerian society. The political culture is very corrupt and our people love and worship money more than God. Our leaders and followers alike are money worshippers, egotistic, jealous and envious haters who are willing to commit all kinds of atrocities to satisfy their sinful lifestyle. It was during the era of General Babangida that corruption was staunchly enthroned and celebrated. He destroyed the Nigerian economy and basically rubbished our societal values by elevating greed, bribery, and corruption and enthroning most of the crooks, cronies and pathetic individuals we have as leaders in our nation today. Ours is a culture of corruption filled with greed, debauchery, chaos and confusion. Political rituals, divination, astrology, sorcery, witchcraft, magic, and all manners of evil and satanic manipulation are rampant and sadly have become the order of the day in today's political environment.

In the last forty years or so, especially during the reign of IBB, Abacha and President Obasanjo, the country witnessed monumental corruption, looting of state and national treasury, ethnic and religious violence and off-course political motivated killings. On September 15, 2006, the trans-gender ex-governor of Bayelsa State Chief D.S.P Alamieyeseigha was arrested at the Heathrow airport for money laundering while more than two thousand teachers in his state had not received any wages for six month. Two weeks earlier, the London Metropolitan Police had arrested Joshua Dariye, ex-governor of Plateau State over alleged money laundering in UK. Up till today, the British government is still recovering their loot and stolen assets and returning some of them to our country. It is so sad that Nigerian leaders loot their country and invest their stolen riches and wealth into the economy of Western rich nations while their own countries and people wallow in pandemic poverty, chronic diseases, misery and death. It is a curse indeed. May God deliver us from this slave mentality?

Prior to last year's primary elections, the Chairman of Economic Financial Crime Commission (EFFC), Alhaji Ribadu, charged 31 out of 36 governors with financial mishandling, money laundering and corruption. The crime commission czar also indicated that the past military rulers had squandered over 380 billion US dollars in the last 40 years. The World Bank and other international organizations also reported that Nigeria risks collapse and disintegration if the current looting, corruption, killings and criminality do not stop. In addition to all that, we witnessed the finger pointing between President Obasanjo and his vice, Atiku over the scandalous PTDF looting, the impeachment saga of four governors and state of emergency declared in three states. Not to mention the scandalous looting and money embezzlement of the former IG, Chief Balogun, who looted hundreds of millions and acquired house practically in every major State of Nigeria including a few overseas. He depleted the police department budget, paid the police personnel meager salaries that forced most of them to openly ask for N20 bribe at checkpoints. Yet the new police boss in this new government has not done anything to stop the shameful act. In fact most of the shooting at checkpoints and armed robbery have been attributed to our police officers. The police force is suppose to protect the citizens and provide order and security but rather they openly and shamelessly ask for bribes at checkpoints and if people refuse to give, they risk being killed on the spot with impudence. What a shame to our police leadership and a disgrace to a nation that supposed to uphold law and order.

Even the new government of Yar'Adua has not taken any significant leadership action to abate corruption and looting of state and national treasury rather his Attorney General and Minister of Justice, Chief Michael Aondoakaa is in a power tussle with Mr. Ribadu, a courageous man who has

215

given some relief and measure of hope to Nigerians worldwide. As I write, a monumental scandal of N628 million to renovate the official residences of the Nigeria's first female speaker and her deputy is tearing apart the Nigeria $2^{nd}$ big house. The salon beautician and the first Madam speaker of Nigeria lower House is battling to save her position and shame after a contract award of N628 million naira to renovate her official residence and that of her deputy without due process. This is happening under a president who proudly tells Nigerian that he is a stickler of due process and rule of law and in a country where millions earn less than one $1 a day.

First of all, it is a disgrace that a hair beautician without any credible academic qualification and legislative expertise is leading the largest House of Representative in Africa. To add salt to injury, this is a woman who came from a humble background and should understand the plight of millions of Nigerians who don't have food to eat not to talk of a roof over their head. Even more disturbing and annoying is the fact that this is happening under a president who parades himself as a servant leader, a stickler to due process and rule of law. Yet the House leadership is still debating and playing politics over such a selfish and debased act by a woman whom millions of women have come to look up to help promote and enact laws that would alleviate their problems and save their children from shackles of injustice, hopelessness, joblessness and economic slavery. There is no doubt that what we have in our nation today is a reckless abuse of power, a desecration of the position leadership and a lack of quality stewardship and transparent leadership. In a nutshell, Nigerian leaders

216

are driven by greed, envy, jealousy, corruption, use of threat and innuendos to achieve political power, superficial authority, bad influence and temporal material gain.

## Religious Ignorance, Intolerance and Militancy

Religious conflict is another big threat to the security, unity and prosperity of our country. Religious ignorance and intolerance breed violence. Religious ignorance, intolerance and violence are also a big problem in Africa. In the continent of Africa, religious violence and ethnic cleansing are enormous. Religious violence has decimated more lives in Africa in the last 50 years than hunger, disease, accidents and even wars combined together. Africa and Middle East have been properly called a "Bloody Continent." They are a battleground between Islam, Christianity and traditional religions. Muslims and Christians kill each other in Nigeria, Sudan, Somalia, Senegal, Rwanda, Burundi and other places in Africa and the world.

In addition to the bloody violence and conflict between these widely known religions, we have the pagans and African traditional religions with thousands of fetish shrines such as the Okija shrine all around the country. Their Fetish priests use hypnotism and witchcraft to deceive ignorant, debased and hopeless people looking for quick and magical ways to achieve success or solve their problems. Some of these fetish priests kill and slaughter new born babies for rituals.

Then we have the adulterous religious systems and satanic religious leaders who parade themselves as the moral authorities in our society and yet the land suffers from all kinds of violence. Our religious leaders have woefully failed in their divine duties to rebuke sin and wickedness in high places. They have compromised and contaminated themselves with the Devil and corrupt practices of these shrines and their pagan priests. And it is so evident and reflective in our culture by peoples' mannerisms and ways of life are pompous of voodoo, juju, witchcraft, sorcery, spirits, mediums and all manners of demonic powers.

And then there are those who profess to be truly followers of Christ and tongue speaking Holy Spirit filled believers who claim to be miracle workers. Despite the visible presence of many magnificent houses of worship and religious centers around the country, all kinds of social, moral and unethical behavior exist abundantly in our land. They promise people healing, prosperity and God's favor when their lives and hearts are completely in disobedience to the Word and Commandments of God. Therefore what we have is spiritual ignorance and bankruptcy due to desperate economic conditions. How many times have we read stories and seen cases of wickedness, violence, prostitution, rape and rituals in our Churches? Bribery and corruption are accepted behavior and rampant. There is a persistent idolatry and wickedness all over our land, oppression of the poor and the needy and crush of the weak. Biblical ignorance is also a big disease in our churches today. I am amazed that about 65% of Nigerian population claim to be Christians attend Church every Sunday and sit under so-called pastors and teacher of Scriptures and Holy Law and yet rituals, divination, astrology, sorcery, witchcraft, magic, and all manners of evil and satanic worship remain rampant in our society.

Greed, hatred, corruption, idolatry, jealousy and envy continue to flourish among the people. The Word of God is His presence and where there is presence of God, evil, unrighteousness and ungodliness cannot be in abundance as it is in our society today. What we are seeing today is moral bankruptcy, biblical ignorance and spiritual capitalism.

May I appeal to Nigerian religious leaders to work together to ensure that Christians, Moslems and paganisms become partners in this 21$^{st}$ century rather than enemies in solving the social, economic and political obstacles facing our nation? They must work together to hold our government leaders accountable to the promises and principles of fairness, justice and equity. They must be involved in shaping public policies, laws and decisions that will help the Nigerian people to fulfill their God-given purposes on planet earth. Our religious leaders must work together to educate their followers about tolerance and peaceful cohabitation? As human beings we do not grow in isolation rather we grow, develop and mature as people in the context of love, relationship and fellowship. And until we learn the cardinal principle of Islam and Christianity, which is forgivingness and reconciliation, we will never live in peace. Without genuine forgiveness and reconciliation, there cannot be unity and peace. Another cardinal truth of Christianity and Islam is love and without love, we cannot have genuine relationship. Relationship is the most vital aspect of life. Relationship is in fact the greatest human asset. Character, courage, love and relationship are the greatest assets of every major faith in the world.

**Moral and Social decadence**

Another major crisis facing our country Nigeria is moral confusion and social degradation. Despite the wealth and opulence of the Western world, their cultures and societies are declining rapidly. There is a huge social apathy, moral degradation and spiritual capitalism. In the Western nations, the anti-family activities, radical feminists group and the liberal agenda are working tirelessly to destroy the family, which is the foundation and bedrock of any civil society. The homosexuals, lesbians and radical feminist movement want to redefine the institution of marriage and family by advocating sex-same marriages. In United States, Canada and many European countries, anti-family agenda is strong, active and fighting hard to destroy the most important institution that exist in the entire universe. The recent scandal of legalized prostitution and cheap sex in Germany during the last 2006 world cup is also an indication of how the family is being hit negatively by anti-family agenda.

This liberal agenda is also spreading furiously in the Third World countries. Few years ago, we were all astonished when the Changing Attitude Nigeria (CAN), which is unfortunately, an Anglican gay movement, protested and were seeking for freedom to express openly. They were also asking for sex marriage recognition like their counterparts here in the West. And this is exactly what our young people are borrowing from America, Britain and other Western nations today. They emulate their lifestyle, mannerism, etc and as a result, sexually diseases are transmitted unhindered. Despite that President Obasanjo opposed such a shameful and abominable request, yet I was astonished to read a report recently indicating that Nigeria is in 3<sup>rd</sup> position after South Africa and India as the most infected HIV and AIDS carriers in the world. This is a serious indictment and severe consequence to a nation that has refused to take care of her citizens through sound laws, fairness, justice and righteousness. Our country is already ravaged with many problems and to add deadly diseases show how morally and socially decadent we are rapidly becoming. Managing the consequences of indecent, illegal and illicit sexual pervasion would lead to a major and monumental crisis in health sector that is non-existent.

It was during the era of General Babangida that the depth of corruption led to the social degradation, moral chaos, ethical and spiritual decadence at all levels in our society. His economic agenda destroyed the Naira and basically rubbished the Nigerian economy, which actually elevated greed, bribery, and corruption. Naira was devalued and a dollar could buy 100 Naira at that time. The quest for dollar and foreign currency forced our young girls into lucrative prostitution overseas mostly in Italy, Holland, France, and Switzerland where most of them were infected with sexually transmitted diseases. The rampancy of HIV cases in Nigeria today is as a result of an uncontrollable ring of organized prostitution of young Nigerian girls that were taken to overseas for such old fashion trade in the early 1980's. The heads of state then, General Babangida and others absolutely did not do anything to stop such organized crime against the reproductive resources of our country. And then these young girls infect their boy friends and their Nigerian husbands in a country where basic necessities of life lack in abundance not to mention of sound medical treatment. Medical and sex education are practically zero. This unbridled greed and sexual invasion has led to social and moral decadence in our country. And today, the country is reaping the severe consequences of such a sinful, unholy and greedy lifestyle.

Our society is doomed if courageous men and women would not stand up against this inhumanity and deliberate agenda to destroy the innocent and peace loving people of Nigeria. The World Health Organization (WHO) reported recently that more than 30 million children and 20 million women are infected with HIV and AIDS in Africa. About 13,000 children die daily in Africa. Treatable diseases such as meningitis, malaria, polio, tuberculosis are on the rise due to lack of clean water and public health care facilities. Rather than building hospitals and clinics in their country, Nigerian rulers and wealthy people travel to America and Europe for medical treatment while millions of poor Nigerians die from common treatable diseases. This is a gross injustice against humanity and God will not spare us for it.

**Conclusion**

There is no doubt that lack of genuine leadership can be blamed for poverty and the travails of the Nigerian society. Even the pandemic poverty, diseases, violence, religious and ethnic war ravaging the continent is due to blind leadership. And that leads me to the cure of these problems. According to my Psychiatrist friend, even in treating patients, the first step toward cure, healing and restoration is to admit that you have the problem and then find ways to solve, stop and eradicate the problem. The same truth holds for any country or nation that sincerely admits that the problem does exist. Today, in our society, we read and hear from people who do not believe that we have any problem. They see greatness. And it is okay to be optimistic and hopeful. However, let us not have a blind optimism and empty hope. Even God Himself did not ask us to have blind faith in Him. He demonstrated through many sources and creation that He does exist. Nigerian rulers, leaders and stakeholders must demonstrate that optimism and hope by putting something on the ground for people to see.

They must begin by showing good example, leading with character and integrity. They must lead with vision that is embraced by all Nigerians and a mission that will provide a sense of momentum and rekindle the passion and patriotism of every Nigerian. They must be willing to inspire and motivate all Nigerians to make impossibilities possible again. They must be willing to establish a plain level environment for all Nigerians to succeed. They must be willing to give every boy, every girl, every old and young person the privilege and opportunity to succeed in Nigeria. They must work hard and together to establish a value system irrespective of religious beliefs that will shape our daily routines, drive our lives, dictate every decision and determine our life's priorities. In so doing, the Nigerian people will not only contribute to the nation building but will create peaceful environment for good change with great opportunities for all Nigerians to live peacefully and responsibly in order to fulfill our God given potential.

Our leaders must accept responsibility and show good stewardship and transparency in their leadership duties.

They must be compassionate and servant leaders who truly and genuinely understand the yearnings of every human being, which is the inalienable right to life, justice and pursuit of happiness. Our leaders must show vision, courage, insight, wisdom and discernment in handling the feelings of those under their leadership. Our leaders must help their citizens to participate and share actively in the limitless opportunities of global economy and prosperity. Our leaders must understand that leadership is not just an honor but a sacred duty that entails hard work and sacrifice. The Nigeria people need leaders who can guarantee their God given and basic necessities of life such as housing, clean water, electricity, medical care and access to quality education. Please let us accept that we have problems, so that we can work together to fix them in order to salvage our nation and eradicate the enormous waste of human resources. Otherwise anything else is evil, satanic and blind leadership. Remember this Nigerian proverbial saying, that one fine day, "all we do on earth, we will account for kneeling in heaven."

God bless Nigeria and happy 47th

## SERVANT LEADERSHIP – A FOUNDATIONAL
## LEVEL OF LEADERSHIP

### HAND OVER TO RESPONSIBLE LEADERS NOT DIGITAL LEADERS

---

President Obasanjo's public utterances have been a major concern for many Nigerians including the Upper House of the legislator that cautioned him recently. Last year the president scolded at Ekiti leaders to shut-up because their intelligence is useless and has yielded nothing to the state. In January this year, he publicly announced that Governor Yar'Adua is medically fit to be president despite credible rumors that he is a sick man. The president even contradicted himself for saying that he has been diabetic for over twenty years and yet has been able to lead the country during all these years. The president has been making other disturbing and dangerous comments such as: "April election is do or die for me; I am fighting Atiku to stop corruption; I will not hand over to crooks and criminals; not to mention the feud between him and his vice, the PTDF allegations and the name calling of those who have fallen out favor with him. This presidential attitude especially at the end of his 8-year term and national election time clearly reveal signs of uncertainty, anxiety and desperation on the part of the presidency as well for the Nigerian people. His last days should be the best and the most glorious days of his leadership but I am afraid that he is blowing it. There is no doubt that his presidency looks as bad as that of General

Babangida and Abacha. I am sure that no matter who writes his biography, Nigerians will be watching to read fair and balanced report about his leadership especially in this democratic dispensation.

However, the statement that necessitated my writing this article was the president's comment through his special adviser on political affairs that he'll hand over to digital leaders. Dr. Bolade Osinowo, the special adviser on political affairs speaking on behalf of the president during a campaign meeting said, "The president would ensure that digital leaders take over the reins of government after he leaves on May 29. What Nigerians require after Obasanjo's exit, according to Dr. Osinowo, is "great discipline of craftsmanship and that is why the next generation of leaders must be digital." (Nigerian Tribune of Wednesday, February 21, 2007).

When I read that statement, I counted it as one of those presidential phrases, which sometimes sound funny and humorous. I did not give any serious thought to it. But at my routine dental appointment last Tuesday, I had arrived at the dentist office about forty-five early for two reasons: first to browse through the pile of magazines for latest news on dental hygiene and second to try my luck at getting treatment before my scheduled time so that I can catch up with other activities that day. As soon as I signed in, the attendant ushered me in to see a hygienist who finished another customer a little earlier. As I walked into the treatment room, I noticed a flat panel computer monitor and a keyboard beside it. I have seen other systems and equipment in this dental treatment room but not flat panel computer monitor. The young and beautiful hygienist simply typed my name on one of the fields on the dashboard of the computer screen and within seconds, all my dental records displayed. She immediately told me that I am also due for an x-ray as well. While I hesitated she muttered sir, it won't take but two minutes because everything is digital now. I looked at my wristwatch and also took note of the time on the wall clock in front of me as she pulled the x-ray equipment around that is connected to the computer. Within three minutes, she took four x-rays on both sides of my both sides of my teeth – lower and upper jaws. As she took them, the results showed on the dashboard, while she gave compliments of my good strong set of teeth.

Then, she took another couple of minutes to review my dental treatment history. Before, she could get busy with the cleaning because I know, I may not be able to chat with her while she poked in my mouth, I asked who developed the software that they are using? It is an out-of box application called eagle, she said which makes the job of dentists and dental hygienist much easier. Then she added, since everything is going digital nowadays, the job that we do as dentist and dental hygienist has gone digital as well. While the young lady worked on my teeth, I began to analyze and process the word digital especially as it relates to the statement made by Dr. Bolade Osinowo on behalf of the president.

The dental hygienist was right. Everything nowadays is going digital including Nigerian leaders. For me the above statement sounded very artistic as well as high tech. As a corporate consultant working primarily in the area of technology leadership, the word digital was very familiar. You cannot work in the computer and technology field without knowing the word digital. Even without working in technology field, the 21$^{st}$ century has been rightly designated as a digital century where everything is going digital. Almost all consumer electronic gadgets are digitalized these days such as digital phones, digital cameras, digital televisions, digital channels, digital cables, digital radios, digital cars, digital computers, digital systems, digital application, digital software etc. Sometimes when I visit patients at the hospitals, I am amazed at the number of computers, medical technology system and equipment in the hospitals and patients' rooms that doctors, physicians, nurses and various medical practitioners have to work with. To put it into prospective, we live in digital age and we are going digital. In fact it is very difficult to get a decent job especially in the U.S without some knowledge of computers and information technology.

There is no doubt that technology has radically changed the way we live in the society today compared to 25 or 50 years ago. And today's leaders are tapping into the limitless opportunities of technology. Here in the U.S, business and government leaders no doubt have gone high tech in their approach to business, campaign and raising money. Today, many of them are using the Internet to communicate their vision, agenda and strategies to the public. Most of them are also raising millions with catchy campaign programs and promises through their websites. About four years ago, Dr. Howard Dean, raised millions of dollars through his sleek e-business website. Even though he lost the democratic nomination to Senator John Kerry, his fund raising skills are today sought after by many corporate business and non-profit organizations. Senators Barack Obama and Mrs. Hilary Clinton are using the same tactics to raise millions today. They have IPTV websites where they deliver ten minutes video clips as well as share their vision and agenda for 2008 presidential elections. Some of the other leaders are also getting their campaign programs out through emails, Internet pop ups, cell phones, and other electronic media gadgets. In a nutshell these leaders are tapping into the limitless opportunities of technology and Internet to reach their followers and general public.

But in Nigeria, this is not the case. Despite the boom of wireless communication, email, Internet and other electronic gadgets in our society today, Nigeria is still rated among the least in terms of number of consumers who have access to wireless devices and Internet. In fact the wireless technology boom is favoring the third world countries more because it is much easier and probably more affordable than old technology. And so if our leaders go high tech, it means that they can reach only about 18% of the population. However, what we need today is not digital leaders or even high tech leaders but responsible leaders. We need leaders who are compassionate and who truly understand the yearnings of the people. We need leadership that understands that the Nigerian people have inalienable right to life, justice and pursuit of happiness. We need leaders who are visionaries, courageous, insightful, wise and discerning. We need leadership that

229

understands globalization and the digital age in which we live. We need leaders who can be trusted to assist its citizens to participate and share actively in the limitless opportunities of global prosperity. We need leaders who are responsible, wise, and who truly understand that leadership is a duty, an honor that entails hard work and sacrifice. What Nigerians are in dire need of today is leadership that can guarantee them their God given right to basic necessities of life such as housing, clean water, electricity, medical care and access to quality education.

But the word craftsmanship gave me hard time to correlate with leadership. Since I am not an artist, I quickly consulted the Merriam Webster Collegiate dictionary. Dr. Webster defines craftsmanship as the noun form of craftsman, which means a worker who practices a trade or handicraft. Another meaning is one who creates or performs with skill or dexterity especially in the manual arts. When I put craftsmanship and digital together, I found it very difficult to connect with leaders. First of all, leadership is not an art according to some proponents of that theory but a service. Leadership is not a profession or a career but a calling. Leadership is duty. Even the essential skills of leadership such as character, courage, vision, compassion, integrity, and charisma are not art but inherent gifts or virtues that can be learned.

The sobering question therefore is what does the president and his special adviser mean by digital leaders. Who are these digital leaders in Nigeria that our president is talking about? This is the first time I am learning about digital leaders. And our president may be right. Since the beginning of this year, he has repeatedly said that he will not hand over to liars, crooks, and criminals and corrupt politicians referring off-course to candidates from other political parties and off-course those who have rebelled against him. The president has employed all manners of political antics to bring them down. The unfortunate thing about the whole affair is that some of these enemies were former PDP stalwarts. The great PDP family appears to be in some crisis because all their illegal businesses and illicit affairs are now public knowledge. Those who are sick of the double standard are flirting around and joining with other political parties. What a society of dysfunctional and political prostitutes!

The digital leaders that the presidency talked about may be referring to Governors Umar Musa Yar' Adua and Goodluck Jonathan, who have been selected and anointed by the president himself to move into ASO Rock after May 29th. Even though some of the other contestants were not happy about the selection because they thought that the two are weak links and could cause PDP to loose the national election. However, the two earned the president's blessing primarily because of their humility and loyalty to the president. Secondly both men were quite educated. But wait a minute what about Governors Odili, Duke, Attah, Egwu and other contestants who were highly educated as well. The reality is that the president needed stooges who could still listen and take orders from him while at Otta farms. Someone has written that this is the first time in the history of Nigeria, that university graduates will occupy the exalted office if they win. Personally, I am removing the tiny word "if" because it portrays uncertainty. For me, it is a done deal for both men. Even though their selection seemed coerced and imposed against the choices and wishes of most PDP members. I think that most Nigerians will be proud anyway for the first time to have two highly educated men occupy ASO Rock unlike in the past when we had elementary school teachers and uneducated military men govern us.

Alhaji Umar Musa Yar' Adua and Dr. Goodluck Jonathan are therefore the digital leaders that the president is talking about. The president must understand that Nigeria is not in shortage of university graduates, highly educated men and women and professionals who have excelled in their various careers, qualified and competent people who can lead. Our society can boast of men and women who are educated, qualified with impressive resumes and who are capable of genuine and sincere leadership. Some of these Nigerians are very cautious to join the political terrain because the political philosophy is still dictatorial and the political playground very risky and murderous. The beauty of democratic governance is the freedom to debate, dialogue and disagree without resorting to violence and vendetta. But in our situation, when we disagree, we kill our opponents. What a society and a people with very poor and low level thinking. Once again, Nigeria's problem is not lack of human potential or natural resources but lack of competent and courageous leaders who truly understand the divine purposes and obligations of leadership. What we lack in Nigeria is not educated men and women, but wise and responsible leaders who truly understand what leadership are all about. Nigerian politicians have weird understanding of leadership.

The leadership landscape in our nation does not show that our politicians know what they are doing. Eight years of democratic government has yielded no results at all except looting of public treasury, money laundering, violence and killings. For instance, the recent exclusive interview of the so-called strong man of Ibadan and the king maker of Oyo politics demonstrates my point. It also revealed the depth of trouble that we are in Nigeria as far as governance is concerned. This is an interview, which was conducted in the comfort of his London residence. There was no distraction and yet Chief Adebibu could not articulate well and wisely. In fact this interview speaks volumes not only about Oyo politics but also about the Nigerian political quagmire. This interview clearly reveals the trouble with Nigeria and the problem with Nigerian leaders. Here is a 76 years old man who has been in politics since 1951 and yet the kinds of words coming out of his mouth do not show any wisdom at all. To make the matter worse, he is the kingmaker of a state that has produced the likes of Chief Obafemi Awolowo, Chief Bola Ige and so on. It is the same that is happening everywhere in the country and particularly in Anambra State, where an uneducated Chris Uba is in control of a state that has produced the best minds and politicians in Nigeria. It is a shame that Nigeria has deteriorated and degenerated to such a low level at an age when societies are getting smarter, doing things wisely and going digital.

The Nigeria people are wary of good leaders. We want to enjoy the dividends of democracy. This year will be twenty years since Nigeria became part of the global effort to reform the economy and entrench democracy. General

Babangida introduced the first major national economic reform in the 1980's. IMF gave hundreds of millions of dollars for successful implementation of the so-called SAP program. IBB and his cronies looted the whole thing and made a mess of SAP program. This second major economic reform NEEDS again from world bank, thanks to Mrs. (Dr.) Ngozi Okonjo-Iweala could yield some results 10-15 years from now but again the cronies in PDP have frustrated the finance czar to resign in order to loot the excess oil windfall and pocket the foreign debt interest accruals. Countries like South Korea, Taiwan, and Brazil just to mention a few that became part of the globalization effort almost the same time with Nigeria are already reaping the benefits of stable government and dividends of democracy. Why is Nigeria's situation different?

I want to challenge as well as encourage whoever ascends to Aso Rock to lead with character, integrity, courage, and compassion and with vision that is embraced by all Nigerians. The next president must focus on an agenda that will provide a sense of momentum and hope for all Nigerians. The next president must rekindle the passion and patriotism that will inspire and motivate all Nigerians to have a sense of belonging. The next president must establish the structure and strategies that will shape the nations future and provide the environment for Nigerians to make impossibilities possible again. The next president must establish core vales and value system irrespective of religious beliefs that will shape our daily routines, drive our lives, dictate every decision and determine our life's priorities. In so doing, every Nigerian will not only contribute to the nation building but will create peaceful environment for good change with great opportunities for all Nigerians to live peacefully and responsibly in order to fulfill the potential that God has deposited inside each and every one of us. We must rise up to our nation building otherwise history will judge all of us as selfish, ignorant, haters and cowards. Let us rise up and reclaim our nation from corrupt and incompetent leaders.

In conclusion, I will like to humbly and politely advise the president to choose his public statements wisely. I have had the privilege of meeting the President a couple of times especially during his visits to the United States. For one thing he looks like a strong man physically. He is also likeable and very humorous. However, his demeanor does not portray presidential at all. He is not charismatic and does not speak eloquently. He also speaks arrogantly and unintelligently sometimes. In a nutshell, he lacks presidential courtesies and etiquettes. Hoverer, despite all his shortcomings, God chose him to be the leader of the most populous and richest country in Africa. It is his destiny and God's divine timing for Nigerian nation. He has accomplished his mission if nothing the well-known fact but hidden truth (REVELATION) that Nigerian leaders and politicians are extremely corrupt, incompetent and visionless. However, as you vacate office in a few months guard your comments and examine them very carefully before delivering to the public. You should also let your advisers know that they cannot go to the public places and make ignorant and senseless statements. As the father figure of our country your words must come with some degree of wisdom, hope and strength to the people. I am sure by the time the president bags his PHD in Theology, he will tell all the pastors, bishops and spiritual leaders in the country to shut up and listen to him.

May God give our leaders wisdom for leadership – Amen!

## BEYOND SERVANT LEADERSHIP

*"But be sure to fear the LORD and serve him faithfully with all your heart; consider what great things he has done for you" (1 Samuel 12:24)*

*Servant leadership is a foundational and basic model of leadership. The ultimate design is supernatural leadership – God empowered leaders; for no one has truly led unless followers are turned into leaders and until their talents, skills, abilities and potentials are unlocked and activated – C. K. Ekeke, Ph.D.*

President Yar'Adua's inaugural speech on May 29th, 2007 was without doubt a great speech. It was written similar to "Sermon on the Mount" and delivered like Christ Himself. Since he was dragged into contesting the last presidential election, Alhaji Yar'Adua has consistently spoken like the Messiah. Some of his messianic statements are as follows: I will serve with the fear of God; I will serve with humility; and recently I will be a servant leader. No wonder some of his loyalists have already dubbed him Nigeria's Messiah. Yar'Adua's loyalists remind me of Chief Olusegun Obasanjo's men whom also referred him as the "Moses of our time" and the "Father of modern Nigeria."

The concept of servant leadership is not new. However, I must commend the president elect for popularizing the concept in Nigeria recently. For the first time in the history of Nigeria as far as I can remember the number one citizen is talking about serving the people rather being served. His servant leader speech has suddenly awakened the consciousness of many Nigerians - young and old. In fact many have written to welcome the concept as well as look at the practicability of the concept in present day Nigeria where our leaders do not serve but want to be served and lord over the rest of us. Time will tell if President Yar'Adua will be an exception and become a servant leader, which is by the way a foundational and basic form of leadership.

As I said earlier, servant leadership model is not new. In the later part of 20th century, an AT&T executive, a deeply religious man by the name Dr. Robert K. Greenleaf popularized the concept of servant leadership in the business world. His book - Servant Leadership: A Journey into the Nature of Legitimate Power and Greatness was a masterpiece on the theory and practice of business organizations and management worldwide. Dr. Greenleaf established a Center for Servant Leadership where he developed servant leadership theories that brought a new paradigm shift to the concept of management and business organizations. Since then hundreds of books have been written on the subject of servant leadership.

Servant leadership concept and practice however date back to the time of great Jewish leaders such as Moses, Joshua, Gideon, Esther, Deborah, Nehemiah and others who served the Israelites according to God's instruction and directives. They were men and women who sacrificed and risked everything – their life, family, comfort, wealth, recognition etc in order to serve. However, it was Jesus Christ who coined the concept, taught it to his disciples and modeled it before the world. He constantly told his disciples and followers the cost and sacrifice of being a leader (Matthew 8:18; 10:39).

His life and ministry was characterized in the service for mankind. Six hundred and fifty years before his divine birth, Prophet Isaiah announced that Jesus would be a suffering servant (Isaiah 53). While the Jews looked for a King and a Messiah who will deliver them from their Roman bandage, Christ came like a humble and suffering servant for the purpose of emancipating mankind from the shackles of injustice and bondage of sin. His mission and leadership was to suffer and die in order to redeem mankind from the bondage of sin, which he clearly communicated when he said, "For even the Son of Man did not come to be served, but to serve, and to give his life as a ransom for many" (Mark 10:45).

One of the dramatic demonstration of servant leadership occurred the night prior to Christ crucifixion (John 13:1-17). While they were in a room just before the Jewish Passover Feast, Jesus began to wash the disciples' feet. When he had finished, he said to them,

*"I have set you an example that you should do as I have done for you. I tell you the truth, no servant is greater than his master, nor is a messenger greater than the one who sent him. Now, that*

*you know these things, you will be blessed if you do them" (John*
*13:15-17).*

In this passage Jesus did not ask the disciples to become feet washers. He symbolically taught his followers that to lead is to serve. Genuine leaders serve the people. They do not wait to be served. The object lesson here was about service. My heart aches when I read about Pastors and religious leaders who practice such symbolical rituals including washing feet in their churches. There are many things they can do to serve their church members not foot washing.

The crucifixion of Jesus was perhaps the most dramatic demonstration of his servant leadership. The Apostle Paul wrote to the Saints in Philippi saying,

*"Your attitude should be the same as that of Christ Jesus: who, being in very nature of God, did not consider equality with God something to be grasped, that made himself nothing, taking the very nature of a servant, being made in human likeness"*
*(Philippians 2:5-7).*

Jesus lived his life as a humble servant and showed the entire world that humility and service are the secret and pathway to greatness (Matthew 20:28). No wonder the Apostle Paul identified Jesus as the ultimate example of servant leadership and attests that God has highly exalted him to the highest place and given him a name that is above every name" (Philippians 2:9). The Apostle John also bears witness that Christ is the Lord of Lords and King of Kings (Revelation 17:14).

Jesus also challenged and changed the mindset of his disciples on leadership. On more than one occasion, Jesus' disciples argued among them as to which of them was considered to be the greatest" (Luke 22:24). As they debated among them who will be the leader of the group, Jesus said to them,

*"The Kings of the Gentiles lord it over them; and those who exercises authority over them call themselves Benefactors. But you are not to be like that. Instead, the greatest among you should be like the youngest, and the one who rules like the one who serves" (Luke 22:25-26).*

Jesus wisely taught them that, "if anyone wants to be first, he must be the very last and the servant of all" (Mark 9:35). Again, Jesus continued to emphasize that those chosen to lead must serve; they must become the servant of all. He encouraged them to emulate his life and leadership style.

After Christ resurrected from the dead, he commiserated with the Apostles who seemed to have forgotten the leadership lessons and powerful demonstrations he taught them. Some of the disciples quickly went back to their fishing profession. Jesus had empathy for them. Suddenly Jesus realized that his disciples needed something more than servant spirit, they needed supernatural empowerment in order to serve effectively. He promised to send them the Holy Spirit. He said to them,

*"And I will ask the Father, and he will give you another Counselor to be with you forever - the Spirit of truth. The world cannot accept him, because it neither sees him nor knows him. But you know him, for he lives with you and will be in you" (John 14:16-17).*

The night before his ascension, Jesus said to his disciples,

*"It is not for you to know the times or dates the Father has set by his own authority. But you will receive power when the Holy Spirit comes on you; and you will be my witnesses in Jerusalem, and in all Judea and Samaria, and to the ends of the earth. After he said this, he was taken up before their very eyes, and a cloud hid him from their sight" (Acts 1:7-9).*

Here Jesus promised a supernatural helper, who would empower them for service. He is like another Christ, invisible, the world would not see or recognize him. He is the Holy Spirit – the spirit of truth, wisdom, understanding, counsel, teacher and empowerment. He is the one who will empower them to become selfless and supernatural leaders.

*"When the day of Pentecost came, they were assembled in the Upper Room; suddenly a sound like the blowing of a violent wind came from heaven and filled the whole house where they were sitting. They saw what seemed to be tongues of fire that separated and came to rest on each of them. All of them were filled with the Holy Spirit and began to speak in other tongues as the Spirit enabled them" (Acts 2:1-4).*

At this supernatural event, the disciples received power for leadership. Their life, ministry and leadership were never the same again. The disciples trusted the Spirit of God to teach, guide and lead them in everything they did. With such supernatural empowerment, they turned the Roman world upside down and achieved supernatural success. The Apostles Peter, James and other disciples such as Mark, Luke and Barnabas led supernaturally. Barnabas especially became one of the great leaders of the church. Barnabas believed that his existence was for the cause of Christ and service to humanity. He mentored Paul, who became the greatest Church leader of all time. At the later end of his life, the Apostle Paul echoes one of his mentors, Barnabas saying, "However, I consider my life worth nothing to me, if only I may finish the race and complete the task the Lord Jesus has given me - the task of testifying to the gospel of God's grace" (Acts 20:24). These men ruled supernaturally. Supernatural leadership became the model of leadership that guided the Apostles and early church fathers.

Some of you had asked me in the past based on my previous writings on this subject, what and who exactly is a supernatural leader (ship). My shortest answer has always been, "God empowered leader." We must understand that God is the one who designed and ordained government in order that his people may have peace and order (Romans 13). God also chooses leaders to preside over his government. When he chooses, he empowers that leader in order to accomplish his purpose because God's vision is always too big for a natural man to accomplish. Today people seek to lead without being called, commissioned and empowered. Seeking to be a leader is an honorable ambition and a noble task (1 Timothy 3:1), however to lead another fellow human being requires godly wisdom and supernatural ability. King Solomon realized the need for godly ability to lead the children of Israelites despite his courage, charisma and wealthy heritage, when he asked for godly wisdom and discerning heart to lead the people (1 Kings 3:7-9).

A supernatural leader therefore is someone who is called by God to possess virtuous character and who effectively motivates, mobilizes resources and directs people toward the fulfillment of a joint embraced vision from God. Supernatural leadership is a spirit-empowered, courageous, compassionate and visionary leadership. It is leadership that involves divine initiation and less of human intervention. It is God's inspired and empowered leadership. Supernatural leadership is the ability to set goals in accordance with God's purpose and to communicate those goals to others in such a way that they work together to accomplish those goals for the glory of God. Therefore Spirit-empowered leadership is the ability to create a peaceful, orderly, stable and enviable environment in which people can be mobilized, motivated and inspired to achieve their God given potential. To lead is hard work and a great service to humanity. Leadership is also a sacred task and a divine duty that requires God's guidance and mentorship. In fact you cannot truly and genuinely lead if God is not leading you.

According to Prophet Isaiah in the book of Isaiah 11.2, a supernatural leader must:

1. Have the Spirit of the Lord rest upon him or her
2. Have the Spirit of Wisdom and of Understanding
3. Have the Spirit of Counsel and of Power
4. Have the Spirit of Knowledge and of the Fear of the Lord, and
5. Delight in the Fear of the Lord.

I have always maintained that the plethora of problems facing our dear nation and the world at large cannot be solved by the kind of leadership we have today. I believe that lack of God empowered leaders is probably the root cause of most societal problems. Lack of ethical, moral, authentic, courageous and compassionate leaders is the primary cause for poverty and the travails of our society. As I have said before, the Nigerian nation does not lack leaders, what we lack are leaders who truly understand the divine dimension of leadership. The Nigerian people do not lack men and women who are fascinated with power, authority and influence. What we fail to cultivate are the ingredients that lead to true power and influence. Outside the shore of the continent, Nigerians as well as many Africans are achieving great success and making supernatural accomplishments. But back home, we are stuck with inept and superficial leaders. We truly need supernatural leaders, God empowered leaders who are divinely gifted to deal with the social, economic, moral and political problems facing our nation today. The societal ills that confront our nation and its people cannot be completely solved through service-oriented leadership but by supernatural leading.

Is supernatural leadership obtainable, practicable or even possible in our world today? I believe it is possible. In the early 1900's, the leaders of the world thought the same about servant leadership. Servant leadership was written off as unattainable and impracticable but today, not only that the leaders of many nations have embraced servant leadership model but the egoistic corporate community has embraced it in their management and leadership training programs. Most of the major business schools in the North America, Europe and Asia teach the theories and principles of servant leadership model. However, we need to move beyond servant leadership to supernatural leadership – God empowered and Spirit led leadership. What we need today are men and women who understand that leadership is a godly call and a divine duty.

We need men and women who demonstrate godly character, courage and compassion. We need men and women who are visionaries, wise, discerning and can be trusted with human lives and destinies. We need men and women who are God fearing and willing to be led by God as they lead their fellow human beings. So, I believe supernatural leadership is possible today. I believe that supernatural leadership is the way of the future. It is the key solution to most of societal problems. Nigerians can set that example by becoming supernatural leaders - God led and Spirit empowered leadership.

I believe the leaders in our country can do better by being God fearing and allowing trusted religious and spiritual leaders to advise them. We are known to be very wise, courageous and compassionate people. We are also very interesting and intriguing people. Nigerians are known for great and unexplainable achievement. Recently, the entire world stood in amazement as Rotimi Adebari, a Nigerian who arrived in Ireland seven years ago as an asylum-seeker, was elected Mayor of Portlaoise, a bustling commuter town west of Dublin. It is unexplainable but that's how most Nigerians are known outside world. Here in the USA, many Nigerians as well as Africans head major business undertakings, civic and religious organizations. They are company presidents and directors, college deans and president of many colleges, medical directors, physician consultants, doctors, engineers, nurse managers, and writers winning global prizes, sports achievers, working in NASA and among the best immigrant college student's achievers. Just name it; they are always among the top in the North America.

President Yar'Adua may be the servant leader that Nigeria needs today. Most of the time an effective and true servant leader understand the struggles and sufferings of those under his leadership. Recently President Yar'Adua admitted that Nigerians are going through hell and promised to create 40 million jobs within 10 years. He wants to boast economic growth and empower all Nigerians to become small business owners rather than meddling into politics of greed, violence and corruption. However, he's yet to demonstrate that he is tribal blind, a good listener and who genuinely cares for all Nigerians irrespective of their tribal, religious, cultural and linguistics differences. Because a servant leader loves all people, has genuine concern for them and cares for them. A servant leader is also a problem solver, who demonstrates empathy for the people he serves, who's concerned about people's welfare, works with people of all background, does not discriminate or judge people based on their social, cultural, linguistic or religious affiliation. A servant leader also teaches his subordinates and serves God as he serves the people. Time will tell if President Yar'Adua may be the servant and savior of millions of the suffering Nigerian people.

In conclusion, we need to move beyond servant to supernatural leadership because it will take supernatural leaders to salvage our nation and eradicate the enormous waste of human resources. We are in desperate need of men and women who truly understand the divine obligations of leadership. We need men and women who have the calling, anointing, preparation and the commission to lead. What we need in Nigeria today is not superficial, inept and visionless leaders but wise, courageous and supernatural leaders who truly understand why they are placed in their position of power, authority and influence. We need leaders who have vision that is embraced by all, leaders who are committed to serving the people, and leaders who are patriotic, passionate and compassionate toward those they are leading. More than anything we need leaders who have the godly capacity to transform our country into a society of freedom, prosperity, righteousness, peace, joy and happiness. We need supernatural leaders who have the ability to harness the enormous human resources present in and out of the continent into a continent of light, enlightenment and productivity. This is my life's call and cry for many years now. I have such an eternal hope that the leaders of tomorrow, the 21$^{st}$ century leaders will heed this divine call.

## LATE PRESIDENT YAR'ADUA – AN APOSTLE OF SERVANT LEADERSHIP

I like to express my deepest sympathy to First Lady Turai Yar'Adua, her daughters and members of Yar'Adua's family over the passing into glory of President Umaru

Musa Yar'Adua, who died on Wednesday May 5, 2010 after a protracted illness of acute pericaditis - Churg Strauss Syndrome at the age of 58. During this time of mourning, may Almighty God fill your heart with love, compassion, and with hope knowing that your husband, Umaru Musa Yar'Adua has departed this wicked world to a place where sickness, pain, suffering and especially misguided friends do not exist? May God give you and other members of your family the fortitude and strength to bear this huge loss!

Having expressed my condolences, I wish to state that Nigeria has lost an apostle of servant leadership. The late President Yar'Adua popularized the concept of servant leadership in Nigeria. I truly believe that the late President had wanted to genuinely serve the Nigerian people but his illness and bad advisers – most of whom were his friends, family members, and those political godfathers misguided his good intentions. And then, his wife and close aides exploited his illness for their personal ego and selfish interests.

For instance, during his inaugural speech on May 29th, 2007, President Yar'Adua's delivered a great speech filled with inspiration and hope. His inaugural speech was written similar to Sermon on the Mount and was powerfully delivered just like Christ Himself. Someone of the messianic statements that stood out in that speech were as follows: "I will serve with the fear of God", "I will serve with humility", and "I will be a servant leader." The late Yar'Adua popularized the concept of servant leadership and even became a believer of servant leadership model.

The late President Yar'Adua in his quest to serve recognized that millions of Nigerians are struggling and suffering. He understood that after eight years of democracy that Nigerians had not seen the dividends of democracy promised by Chief Olusegun Obasanjo. The late President Yar'Adua admitted that Nigerians are going through hell and promised to create forty million jobs within ten years. He promised that he would spur economic growth and empower willing Nigerians to become small business owners rather than meddling into politics of greed, violence and corruption. The late President promised to declare war on the energy sector. His seven-point agenda was lucid and translucent that many felt that the messiah had truly arrived. During that period many of his loyalists named him, "Nigeria's Messiah" in the same manner Chief Obasanjo's loyalist referred OBJ as the "Moses of our time" and the "Father of modern Nigeria."

However, for President Yar'Adua to actualize those explicit and loft goals, it would require for credible, capable and visionary Nigerians from all walks of life irrespective of tribal, linguistic or religious differences. The late Yar'Adua refused to be tribal blind. He refused to be a good listener, who genuinely listens and cares for all Nigerians no matter their social status, tribal affiliation, cultural and linguistics differences. Rather, he surrounded himself with unwise and greedy political figures.

249

As a servant leader, President Yar'Adua should have expressed love for all Nigerians, show genuine love for all Nigerians without discrimination or bias, because no one can truly lead without first loving the people. As a proponent of servant leader model, he should have been a problem solver, who demonstrates empathy for the people he was called to serve. As a servant leader apostle, Yar'Adua should have listened to the people of Nigeria rather than the cronies that hovered around him. As a servant leader, he should have served the people first rather than his friends and tribal folks. Those were the missing ingredients in Yar'Adua's government and in fact the missing ingredients of true, pure and genuine leadership in Nigeria and in all over Africa.

There is no doubt that the late President Yar'Adua had a passion for honor and integrity. Despite his passion for service and the awesome privilege he had to lead Nigeria, he neglected to abide by the golden and guiding principles of servant leadership concept but rather surrounded himself with jobless political enemies of true democracy, progress and unity of Nigeria. Those folks eventually ruined his presidency and rubbished his presidential legacy.

Some of us had written in the past portioning blame on the former President Obasanjo for the sad political events of the last three years. It is a known leadership principle that one of the key legacies of great leadership is the joyful transfer of power and authority to a healthy, courageous, compassionate, trustworthy, and honest individual. Former President Obasanjo did not do that and has never done that in all his opportunities to serve our great nation. He knew about Yar'Adua ill health.  He knew that when Yar'Adua was governor of Katsina State, yet Obasanjo imposed him as president on a great and complex nation like ours.  Today, I hope that those greedy for political power can see that tyranny and mediocrity cannot be imposed on the people.  Either by social disobedience or act of God, the people will overcome evil.

Also, I must point out that the attitude of First Lady Turia Yar'Adua and the so-called kitchen aides of the late president were a public disgrace and dismal failure.  Mrs. Turai Yar'Adua did not act wise – either as a wife, mother or even as the First Lady of Nigeria.  She lusted for power and her attitude in this whole thing was despicable.  Nonetheless, I blame those who listened and carried out her orders.  All of them have failed in their understanding of democratic principles, constitution of Nigeria and dereliction of duty.

For instance, the last saga in which Moslem clerics were invited to visit the late president at Aso Rock was a noble act but with wrong purpose.  What First Lady Turai Yar'Adua did by inviting the Islamic clerics was religiously right no matter how long it took her to fulfill that requirement.  However, the Christian clerics were angered and questioned why only the Moslem Clerics were invited to see the ailing president then.  The agitation prompted Mrs. Yar'Adua to arrange for the Christian clerics to visit ailing president as well.

There are several biblical accounts in which Men of God were invited to intercede on behalf of Kings and the nation.  When Lazarus was sick, Mary and Martha invited Jesus to come and pray for him (John 11:1-44). Jesus did not go immediately but waited for four days. When Jesus finally arrived to Mary and Martha's home, Lazarus was already dead and buried; Jesus being anointed still offered prayer of faith that raised Lazarus from the dead. Such anointing to heal the sick, cast out demons and raise people from the dead is still available to those who believe.

Throughout the history of humanity, prophets of Most High God and religious leaders have been involved in the affairs of the nation. True prophets of the land are always consulted in matters of serious national discourse such as wars, crisis, uncertainties, etc. True prophets also promote justice and righteousness by calling the nation's leaders to order and rebuking when they mislead the people. Even the United States which we modeled our presidential system of Government, has always consulted national pastors and religious leaders for advice, counseling, divine wisdom and prayers. In this critical time of financial devastation and economic crisis due to unbridled greed at Wall Street and the resulting consequences on the lives and unity of the nation, the White House has called on religious leaders asking for their prayers, wise counsel, and moral support.

God will not do anything without first revealing it to His true servants and prophets (Amos 3:7). God is interested in all nations, "for the kingdom is the Lord's and He is governor among the nations (Psalm 22:28). God is interested in the political, economic, and social and leadership challenges of every nation, tribe, tongue, kindred and people. Moses was not only a priest and prophet of

252

God but a great politician and spiritual leader who brought the law, which formed the foundation of civil and criminal law in many countries today. He was used by God to bring the children of Israel out of bondage, slavery captivity in Egypt. David was a king and a moral leader. Daniel was the adviser to the powerful king of Babylon. Joseph became the prime minister of Egypt because of his divine wisdom and prophetic insights into future of Egypt.

It is only in Nigeria that I hear and read from writers – mostly from the South who argues Nigeria is a secular state. What an arrogant and senseless statement. The Northerners will never make that statement because for them – as Moslems, there is no separation between politics and religion. Today, all the 19 states in North have introduced Sharia law, which is an Islamic religious law in a country that presumably practicing democrat presidential system of Government. Yet these ignorant writers from the South continue to talk and write that Nigeria is a secular state. Even the United States is not a secular state despite what the liberal politicians are doing to eliminate religious values and practices. The world will see hell and suffer the wrath of God if the United States of America is secularized. There is no nation on the face of this earth that is secular. Every nation is deeply rooted in its religious beliefs and those beliefs impact how the government, business, economy and even education are designed to function.

The problem is that there is an abundance of biblical and theological ignorance among the Nigerian clerics and followers. In Nigeria today, most pastors and religious leaders emulate the American churches and pastors in preaching the gospel of prosperity without understanding that there are laws and capitalistic systems that make prosperity preaching thrive in the United States. Today, our land is filled with teachings of pragmatic and psychological philosophies to attaining success or solving spiritual problems rather than a sound exposition of the Word of God.

What we see and hear today are false prophets, fake churches, and spiritual capitalism. But the frightening thing is that some of our esteemed pastors and church leaders have failed to read their Bible and understand that we are called differently – some pastors, teachers, prophets, evangelist, and apostles. We are all called differently with clear and precise assignments. Abraham, Moses, David, Deborah, Ruth, Esther, Nehemiah, Joshua, Solomon, Daniel, Joseph, Isaiah, Jeremiah, Ezekiel, Amos, Peter, Paul, just to mention a few received God's call but very different and radical assignments.

Some of the questions that we must answer one day as Nigerians are as follows: what kind of democracy and presidential system of government does Nigeria want to practice? Is it practicable to operate two laws – Constitutional Civil law and Islamic Sharia law in a presidential system of government? Can Nigeria continue to be one united country?

The more I reflect on the political permutations and wrangling due to the passing of President Yar'Adua and the elevation of Goodluck Jonathan as president of Nigeria to finish the 2007-2011 democratic dispensation; I could not but pray that we get it right in 2011. As Nigerians, we must understand these simple but powerful truths: first, that life is transient. Second, that genuine power is given, and third, that true leadership is service.

As Goodluck Jonathan takes over the helm of governance as executive president, I hope that he will be a servant leader just like his late boss aspired to be. Even though servant leadership is a foundational and basic model of leadership because the ultimate design and call for leadership is supernatural leadership – God empowered leaders; for no one has truly led unless followers are turned into leaders and until their talents, skills, abilities and potentials are unlocked and activated.

Personally, I applaud President Jonathan's loyalty, humility and coolness during the whole ordeal of Yar'Adua's illness and ultimately death. He managed and handled the political events of the last one year very politely, diplomatically and naturedly especially during the illness of late President Yar'Adua. When he became acting president, he took some bold steps to reshuffle the federal cabinet – he has fired the former Attorney General of the Federation and Minister of Justice, Mr. Michael Aondoakaa. UK, EU, and recently the US have courted him. He has met with President Obama during the nuclear arm talks last month in Washington DC, even though I was not particularly impressed with his interviews and speeches.

Power has been rightly and by divine providence of God given to you, Dr. Goodluck Jonathan. You must not be a weak and uninspiring president. You must lead courageously with the understanding that you have just but one year to make a difference. You must begin right away to deal with the serious issues facing our dear country such as her unity and national reconciliation, constitutional amendment, electoral reform, religious extremism, violence and killings of Christians in the North, political thuggery and assassinations in Southwest, the scourge of armed robbery and kidnappings in Southeast, and off-course the Niger Delta militancy in South-south, unemployment and jobs, epileptic energy supply, poverty, diseases, lack of drinkable water, lack of good roads, bribery and corruption, injustice, lawlessness, ethnic and tribal hatred, crime, security of life, health care crisis, moral and social decadence, environment among other domestic and international issues.

It is my hope that President Goodluck Jonathan will improve on his presidential courtesies and etiquettes and most importantly surround him with wise, genuine, and trusted people.

Truly, Nigeria is in dire need of courageous leaders not cowards. Unfortunately what we have had in the last 50 years are simply administrators but not leaders. What we have as leaders today are people driven by greed and corruption – very ungodly and rapacious individuals.

Leadership is a divine duty and a great sacrifice and service to humanity. The young generation of Nigerians must rise up to enthrone people who have the wisdom, courage and vision to truly transform our nation to be among the very best in the world. I pray and hope that the passing of President Musa Yar'Adua will shut the door of bad, poor and mediocre political leadership of the last 50 years and open up a new era of brand leadership - wise, courageous, visionary, innovative, change leaders to reclaim Nigeria's lost glory as the most precious jewel of Africa.

May God give us the fortitude and strength to bear the passing of President Yar'Adua and to forge ahead with hope and anticipation for great leadership for the future? May President Umaru Musa Yar'Adua's soul rest in peace!

God bless Nigeria and Nigerians!

## SUPERNATURAL LEADERSHIP – VITAL INGREDIENTS FOR SPIRIT-EMPOWERED LEADERSHIP

Since the beginning of this century, natural disasters, ethnic strife, religious wars and violence have been more frequent than ever. There has been an unprecedented catastrophic event of unimaginable proportions. Many of us have vivid memories of the unprecedented disasters and rash of tragedies that have occurred since 2001. In September 11, 2001, there was a dastardly terrorist attacks in New York that brought down the two tallest buildings in New York killing more than three thousand people and destroyed hundreds of businesses leaving thousands jobless and devastated; the ethnic, religious, economic and political wars that decimated most of the population in Senegal, Afghanistan, Iraq and others creating the worst global refugee camps in our modern time; natural disasters such as hurricanes Ivan that destroyed the coastlines of Florida; the tsunami that devastated more than six countries in the continent of Asia and Africa and drowned thousands; the massive earthquakes that killed hundreds in Japan; plane crashes in Nigeria that in one instance killed all the three children of one parent and the unforgettable and catastrophic hurricane Katrina that ravaged the U.S. Gulf Coast killing and displacing thousands in Alabama, Louisiana, and Mississippi and leaving nearly half a million fleeing to other part of the States for shelter, food, sanitation and medical needs.

We have also seen social apathy and moral degradation especially in the West. The anti-family movement are advocating for same-sex marriages while feminist movement is fighting to redefine the institution of marriage and family. We have also vivid memories of the worst sex scandal involving catholic Bishops against children – the very ones that they ought to be protecting. The Anglican priest – Gene Robinson who was elevated to position of bishop despite his marriage to a man    In a nutshell the planet earth – God's kingdom is ravaged by terrorism, natural disasters, social and moral insanity, poverty, corruption, injustice, political instability, religious and ethnic wars, lawlessness, crime and violence, health epidemics, pandemic diseases and now bird flu. Insecurity and uncertainty is the order of the day. Individual freedom and security of life - the essential elements and basic rights of human beings are now privilege of a powerful few. Today, the common masses are being abused and assaulted for sake of security and young lives perish each day without fulfilling their purpose on planet earth. Yet those at the echelon of leadership positions remain unconcerned and unmoved. The church of Jesus Christ has also remained powerless while Christians suffer abuses, torture and persecution in many countries of the world. In a nutshell, God's greatest assets are powerless and unproductive thereby stifling God's vision and mission for planet earth.

As I ponder over the horrendous times in which we live, the Spirit of God revealed to me that lack of God empowered leadership is the root cause of all societal problems. Lack of authentic, effective, moral and courageous leadership is the primary cause for poverty and the travails of our society. Our planet does not lack those with the skills to lead; what we do lack are the divine ingredients for courageous and compassionate leadership. In a nutshell, supernatural or Spirit-Empowered leadership is lacking. First of all, let me define supernatural leadership. Many leadership authors and writers have defined leadership in many ways. From a biblical perspective, a leader is someone who is called by God to possess virtuous character and who effectively motivates, mobilizes resources and directs people toward the fulfillment of a joint embraced vision from God. Supernatural leadership is a spirit-empowered, courageous, visionary leadership. It is leadership that involves divine initiation and less of human intervention. It is leadership inspired and empowered by God. Supernatural leadership is the ability to set goals in accordance with God's purpose and to communicate those goals to others in such a way that they work together to accomplish those goals for the glory of God. Therefore Spirit-Empowered leadership is the ability to create an enviable environment in which people can thrive, prosper and reach their fullest potential. Supernatural leadership is hard work. It is about being an excellent steward of God's human and natural resources. If you are called to lead, God wants you to possess divine power and authority by instilling in you what I called the 7 divine ingredients of leadership. These ingredients if carefully cultivated and developed will turn you into a supernatural leader.

**A Call and a Commission**

The first ingredient of supernatural leadership is a call followed by commissioning. Courageous and effective leadership requires a person to be called and commissioned first by God, second by people and third by circumstances. A true leader must be called and prepared by God. This is often a painful process and involves a lot of sacrifice. Supernatural leadership is the perfect combination of calling, commissioning and competence. In Numbers 27:18-23; the LORD told Moses to commission Joshua, a man in whom is the spirit. Then Moses laid his hands on him before all the assembly of Israel and before the high priest Eleazer and commissioned Joshua as the LORD instructed. And in Deuteronomy 31:14 and 34:9, Joshua was filled with the spirit of wisdom as Moses laid hands on him. Joshua was then presented as the successor of Moses at the Tent of Meeting before all the children of Israel and they listened to him. There cannot be effective leadership without a call, commission and competence. Today a lot of people want to become leaders through the back door without any calling, commissioning and preparation. Without a call, commission and adequate preparation – training and mentorship, a person cannot be a leader that God uses. A call to leadership must be answered with humility because the leader that God uses must be a person of character, faith and obedience e.g. Abraham, Moses, Joshua, Jesus, Paul.

## Character

The second essential element of supernatural leadership is character. Character is an indispensable ingredient of supernatural leadership. A person may have impressive skills and talents, and personality but without character. Character transformation is required for supernatural leadership. The spiritual and character transformation takes place from the inside out, not from the outside in. A supernatural leader must cultivate godly character. Developing spiritual qualities of character takes time and requires a teachable mindset. It involves the acquisition of divine wisdom. As a supernatural leader, your character weaknesses, poor behavior traits and negative attitude must be pruned and conquered in-order to mature into an ultimate leader or Christ-likeness. You cannot become a supernatural leader without controlling your behavior and character weaknesses through dependence upon the Holy Spirit. The attributes of faith, goodness, knowledge, self-control, perseverance, godliness, brotherly kindness and love must be abundant in the life of a supernatural leader. A supernatural leader must have a genuine character, a consistent credibility and godly integrity in the eyes of his or her followers. Without consistent and positive character traits, followers will have a hard time believing in you. The strength of your character and convictions is a source of inspiration and encouragement to many who will follow you. A supernatural leader must strive each day to be Christ like. Without quality of character and positive integrity, you cannot be an effective leader.

Dr. Myles Munroe, the guru of leadership potential development writes in his book 'Insights for the Frontline Leader', "True leadership cannot be divorced from the basic qualities that produce good sound character. The character of a leader should be one that commands respect

261

from all, even his enemies. Leadership is born out of character and determination." Character is perhaps the greatest ingredient of pure leadership. Character is not about outward technique but of inner reality. Character and hard work are essential for anyone who wants to lead supernaturally. When God looks at leaders, He doesn't look for the tallest, biggest, and best looking or most articulate, God looks for those who will obey Him to carry the divine duties and tasks of leadership. He looks for those who are willing to exchange any sinful lust and love for power, authority, sex and money for the true and spiritual riches of divine leadership. Whether you are a husband, wife, student leader, corporate executive, a senator or a nation's president, you must display quality and consistent godly character in-order to lead effectively. A supernatural leader must display this virtue more than all his or her peers. You must lead beyond reproach.

**Courage**

The third key ingredient of spirit-empowered leadership is courage. A supernatural leader must be a person of great courage and convictions. He or she must display courage and strength like Joshua who led the Israelites into the Promised Land. The biblical account of Israel's leader Joshua and how he faced a daunting task of taking his nomadic troops of Israelites into battle against the fortified cities of Canaan after the death of their great leader Moses was an epitome of courageous leadership. God commanded him in the book of Joshua 1:6-9 to be strong and courageous. He, God promised to give the Israelites victory despite the overwhelming odds against them. Joshua courageously led the Israelites into the Promised Land. A supernatural leader must show such courage in the face of great danger and opposition. He or she must demonstrate a genuine concern for the welfare of the people, a concern that must be obvious even to your adversaries and enemies. A supernatural must be willing to die for what is right, fair and equitable. Despite oppositions, challenges and conflicts, a supernatural leader must identify with all and never waver in his or her commitment as a leader. According to Dr. Mylcs Munroe, "Courage is resistance to and mastery of fear, not the absence of fear." Leaders without this virtue will fail to make fair and right decisions. Without right and godly decisions, people will suffer and perish.

**Commitment**

The fourth ingredient of supernatural leadership is commitment. Commitment is the love of leader to his or her followers. A supernatural leader must first commit to God. Commitment to God involves personal cost, self-denial, hard work and personal sacrifice. Sometimes, it involves paying the ultimate price, which is death (Martin Luther King Jr., Jesus). Jesus Christ said; if you want to follow me, you must be willing to carry the cross. A committed leader does not compromise or sacrifice truth because of peer or political pressure like Pontius Pilate during the trial of Jesus by the Romans. A leader is called to be a person of courageous commitment, first to God and then to followers. Effective leadership flows from such commitment. As a supernatural leader, the single most important commitment is first to God. Any true and successful leader will flow from that commitment.

In Romans 12:1-2, the Apostle Paul urges us to devote ourselves to God. He encourages us to allow God's mercy to accomplish the work He has placed in us. In Eph 2:8-10, the Apostle writes that, "For we are God's workmanship, created in Christ Jesus to do good works, which God

263

prepared in advance for us to do. We must let God drive us to total and absolute commitment. A supernatural leader must be motivated by God's mercy to devote himself or herself to God. When a leader takes this step, you are acknowledging Christ's leadership in your life. You sacrifice your selfish desires and misguided ambitions as you strive to align yourself with God's Will. Once this act of commitment occurs, your talents and dreams will be surrendered to His purpose. And the more you give yourself to Him, the more He will bless and use you as a leader.

In Matthew 16:24-26, Jesus spoke another kind of commitment. He told His disciples and made it clear that He wants total commitment. Jesus said, unless one commits everything, one loses everything. He urged His followers, take up your cross and follow me. He knew better than anyone else how elusive the great prize is. But he also knew that anything less than total commitment to achieving the prize would not suffice. In leader's organizational life, total commitment to the vision facilitates success. Og Mandingo, one of the world's greatest inspirational and motivational speakers said, "The major cause of failure in life is "quitting too soon" otherwise weak and short-term commitment. God expects us to have a strong and long-term commitment to each other. Commitment will lead to trust because without trust a leader cannot get extraordinary things done. Commitment is not compromise but leads to trust and credibility.

**Change**

Change is another essential ingredient of effective leadership. Every effective leader must be an innovator – a change maker. Change and innovation are integral components of both spiritual and supernatural leadership. Without change, growth is impossible e.g. Abraham, Paul, Peter etc. Change will always lead to challenges, conflict and opposition. Challenges and conflict are unavoidable. Every leader will face challenges, opposition and conflict during the course of his or her leadership. As a leader you will be criticized, opposed and refused as you lead major changes in your home, church, organization or nation. As a supernatural leader, you must be willing to listen, learn and confront challenges. You must be an expert of conflict management and problem solving. However a supernatural leader is not called to compromise in managing conflicts but to confront it. You must not run from it but must confront conflict with courage and compassion.

**Compassion**

Enduring leadership, the kind that makes a positive, long-range difference, is always characterized by compassion. A compassionate leader cares about people. A compassionate leader seeks the greatest good for all people. As Jesus we must show compassion even when confronted with suffering. Showing compassion sometimes requires breaking the rules, often in ways that people don't understand. In Mark 1:41-42, "filled with compassion, Jesus reached out His hand and touched the leper. In Jesus' time, touching a man with leprosy violated Mosaic Law; according to the law, Jesus would be rendered ceremonially unclean, thus unable to pray at the temple. Jesus' desire to help a poor leper outweighed His obligation to the Law. As a supernatural leader; you must take care of those who come to you for help. You can only be effective when the needs of others are met. If you want to be effective, you must be become a servant leader. You must humble yourself and serve with humility, compassion and love.

Jesus said, "If we command wisely, you will be obeyed cheerfully ((Luke 22:26). If you want to be successful as a leader, you must put other people first including their families.

In the book of Exodus 33:18-19, when Moses asked God to reveal His glory to him, the LORD said, "I will cause my goodness to pass in front of you, and I will proclaim my name, the LORD in your presence". God has to shield Moses from the fullness of His glory by covering him in the cleft of a rock, and as He passed in front of Moses, God accompanied His awesome display of proclaiming perfection of His character. Here in this passage, God revealed Himself as the compassionate and gracious God who is slow to anger, who abounds in love and faithfulness, who maintains love to thousands and who forgives wickedness, rebellion and sin. Many people will admire a leader who demonstrates these qualities – love, grace, faithfulness, and forbearance. Ghandi, Martin Luther King Jr., Mother Teresa and Princess Lady Diana exhibited this great virtue that made them exemplary human beings. Compassion is perhaps one the greatest ingredients of supernatural leadership. A leader who exhibits this quality will be loved and admired by millions around the world.

**Charisma**

The last but not the least divine ingredient for effective leadership is charisma. The call of God to a position of leadership does not depend upon appearances but upon obedience. Charisma does not mean good looks, big, tall, strong or intimidating personality. According to the Random House Dictionary, charisma is defined as the special quality that gives an individual influence, charm or inspiration over large numbers of people. A person or leader is charismatic when certain abilities such as communication and oratory skills, listening abilities, wisdom and other skills are evident and abundantly superior to other people around him or her. Obviously people flock to a person who possesses such distinct and unique abilities. This is a very powerful leadership ingredient and can sometimes be used very negatively for example Adolph Hitler. In fact Dr. John Maxwell, the American icon of leadership theory and principles surmised in his book, Becoming a Person of Influence, "Leadership is influence." Charisma is influence and true leadership is achieved when those under your influence and authority become leaders by maximizing and reaching their fullest potential. To be an effective leader, a person must seek to be charismatic as well as humble and compassionate.

**Conclusion**

Seeking to be a leader is an honorable ambition and a noble task. In First Timothy 3:1, the Apostle Paul writes to his prodigy Timothy, "If any sets his heart on being an overseer, he desires a noble task." Ambition is not sin or wrong, but it must be guided with humility, wisdom, discernment, character, integrity, and vision otherwise it becomes egoistic. King Solomon realized the need for wisdom and anointing from God despite his charisma, heritage and material blessing, when he prayed in 1 Kings 3:7-9 for wisdom and discerning heart to govern the people of Israel. It also requires prayer, perseverance, passion, shared vision and strategy.

Prayer is perhaps the key ingredient that holds everything else together. Without persistent and passionate prayer life, you cannot be an effective and supernatural leader. Jesus the ultimate leader prayed before every major event major event during His earthly leadership. Time alone and team prayer is necessary for successful leadership. Certainly, prayer is important as you look toward the inevitable difficulties you will face as a leader. The times of personal and team prayer will strengthen and sustain your leadership.

As a supernatural leader, you must make prayer the first act and true mark of your leadership. Prayer is the key to dynamic faith, strength, power, success and victory. It is a noble act and a divine habit that must cultivate in your live as a leader. Fervent prayer of godly leaders will accomplish the will of God on earth. The late William R. bright, founder of Campus Crusade for Christ said this on winning the Nobel Prize for Religion, "I believe that biblical prayer is the most enriching and energizing of all the Christian disciplines and can accomplish more for the Glory of God and ensure His blessing upon the people of the earth more than anything else we can do."

According to Prophet Isaiah in the book of Isaiah 11.2, a supernatural leader must:

1. Have the Spirit of the Lord will rest upon him or her
2. Have the Spirit of Wisdom and of Understanding
3. Have the Spirit of Counsel and of Power
4. Have the Spirit of Knowledge and of the Fear of the Lord, and
5. Delight in the Fear of the Lord.

This is supernatural or spirit-empowered leadership in a nutshell. May God bless you and help you to become a spirit-empowered leader that the world desperately needs as you cultivate these vital ingredients of supernatural leadership in your life as a leader

LEADERSHIP – A DIVINE DUTY

## LEADERSHIP WISDOM – WORD'S GREATEST NEED

---

*"The greatest need of this century is developing authentic, wise, courageous and compassionate leaders. Leadership wisdom is the ability and capacity to lead wisely, morally, courageously and compassionately." -- Dr. C. K Ekeke*

I wish all a happy and blessed 2007. My prayer is that you will have a great and blessed year. Like me, most of you may have set some goals and made resolutions for 2007. For instance, one of my resolutions this year is to offer through my writing ideas and opinions that might help you to become a better leader. As you know, our country Nigeria is suffering from chronic and epileptic leadership mindset and behavior. As the nation prepares to hold national elections in a few months, I am amazed as well as amused the manipulations and maneuvering being made by people aspiring to be in power. Some of these people do not even understand what leadership is all about but they have got money to throw around to get elected. Unfortunately, those who may have the right qualifications, competence and capacity to lead don't get elected because they do not have millions of Naira to throw around or know someone at the top. We must reverse this trend if we must move forward as a nation, achieve greatness and fulfill the purpose for which God has ordained Nigeria as a nation. While those who put us together as a nation meant it for their political and economic gains, God allowed it in order to fulfill his purposes in Africa through Nigeria. This means that, we must work together to establish core-values, fair and equitable system that will enable us to live together as a nation in order to fulfill our purposes on planet earth.

My last article on this forum entitled: "Emulate the Life and Leadership Style of Jesus Christ" generated quite a few positive comments and negative criticisms. Some criticized me of promoting Christian leadership while others warned me to separate biblical leadership from secular leadership. I have said this before and I repeat; I understand that Nigeria is a pluralist and multi-religious society and therefore no religion should be promoted more than others. However, as a biblical scholar, I write from biblical perspective. I have no doubt in my mind that the principles of leadership found in the pages of the Bible if embraced and applied can help Nigerian leaders or those aspiring to lead in any fashion to be better leaders. I also appreciate those who give constructive criticism such as keep the article short and brief and those who lavished on me beautiful praises. I thank all of you. However, let me make this statement which I sent to some of you individually: "Our political culture is now democracy and the beauty of democracy is the freedom to dialogue and disagree without resorting to abuse words, insults, and anger, hatred or death threats." I have received such from some of you and I do forgive all of you. I also pray that God will forgive us all.

This year, I will begin writing on leadership wisdom, offering biblical perspectives for true, pure, honest, wise courageous and compassionate leadership. I believe with all my heart that authentic and compassionate leadership is the most urgent need of our society today. For Africa, it is a desperate need. That leads me to make this bold statement that the greatest need of the 21$^{st}$ century will not only be stem cell scientists, miracle doctors, visionary

270

MBA's, brilliant lawyers, caring educationists, technology and computer whiz kids, genuine religious gurus, hard-working farmers, transparent and honest accountants, heroic sport men and women or even charming and sensual entertainers but authentic leaders. The greatest need of this century will not only be developing oil and gas alternative, finding a cure for AIDS or cancer but developing pure, true, genuine and authentic leaders. There are no doubt the professionals and careers mentioned above have made significant contribution to our society and continues to make. However, the greatest need of our society today is finding courageous and compassionate people who are capable of bringing lasting solution to the myriad of leadership problems facing the peoples of this planet earth.

The plethora of problems facing our world today especially the continent of Africa is not just economic, social, moral, environmental, or political issues but lack of real and genuine leaders. Today more than ever, we live in a world that is insecure and full of uncertainty. For instance, while the Western rich nations are threatened by nuclear weapons, terrorism, natural disasters, social apathy and moral degradation, the continent of Africa is ravaged by poverty, greed, corruption, lawlessness, crime, injustice, political instability, spiritual bankruptcy, religious and ethnic hatred, violence, killings, tribal wars, and pandemic diseases. There is no security or respect for the sanctity of human life anymore. Anywhere you turn to in Africa, people are dying like chicken. In a nutshell, Africa is undergoing a terrible waste of human potential and therefore in desperate need of competent and visionary individuals to help bring relief and end to the sufferings in our blessed continent.

Barely six years into this century, we have seen an unprecedented catastrophic event of unimaginable proportions. Many of us still have vivid memories of the unprecedented disasters and rash of tragedies that have occurred since 2001, the dastardly terrorist attacks in New York city, the ethnic, religious, economic and political wars that decimated most of the population in Senegal, Afghanistan, Iraq, hurricane Ivan that destroyed the coastlines of Florida; the tsunami that devastated more than six countries in the continent of Asia and Africa and drowned thousands; the massive earthquakes that killed hundreds in Japan; plane crashes in Soviet Union, Nigeria and other countries, the unforgettable catastrophic hurricane Katrina that ravaged the U.S. Gulf Coast killing and displacing thousands in Alabama, Louisiana, and Mississippi and leaving nearly half a million fleeing to other part of the States for shelter, food, sanitation and medical needs. Not to mention the just concluded war between Israel and Hamas of Lebanon, the continued US war in Iraq against al-Qaeda, Taliban's, and terrorist groups from Iran and Syria, the recent Ethiopian and U.S insurgency against the Somali Hornets Nest, the so-called Talibans of Africa, the threat of nuclear weapons by Iran and North Korea and lastly the hanging and execution of one of world's brutal dictators, Saddam Hussein.

As I ponder over the horrendous times in which we live, the Spirit of God revealed to me that lack of God empowered leadership is the root cause of all societal problems. Lack of authentic, wise, moral and visionary leadership is the primary cause for poverty and the travails of our society. Our planet does not lack men and women with natural abilities to lead; what we lack is the failure to lead from godly perspective. King Solomon realized the need for godly wisdom for leadership despite his natural attributes when he prayed in 1 Kings 3:7-9 for wisdom and discerning heart to govern the people of Israel. Most of the leaders who made impact in our society have been those who led wisely, courageously and compassionately. In a nutshell, leadership wisdom is lacking today.

What is leadership wisdom? Leadership wisdom is the ability and capacity to lead wisely, morally, courageously and compassionately. It is a gift from God. It is wise, visionary, compassionate and spirit-empowered leadership. It is leadership that involves divine initiation and less of human intervention. It is leadership that is inspired and empowered by God. Leadership wisdom is the ability to create an enviable environment in which followers can thrive, prosper and reach their fullest potential. It is about being an excellent steward of God's human and natural resources. If you are called to lead, God wants to instill in you wisdom or divine ingredients for leadership. These ingredients if carefully cultivated and developed will turn you into great and admirable leader.

Leadership is hard work and our world is in desperate need for leaders who have the vision, character, courage, capacity, charisma and compassion to bring peaceful solutions to the peoples of this blessed planet. Imagine starting now to retrain your leadership mind or begin to sow into the future generation the seed of authentic leadership. Imagine starting now to teach them the skills necessary for great leadership, skills such as the art and power of listening, motivation, service, stewardship and accountability. Imagine helping them to learn how to build character develop courage, and compassion for different peoples and cultures that inhabit the world. Imagine training and teaching the young ones how to lead courageously and compassionately. Imagine inspiring your children to become the best in what they do. Imagine providing our children the enabling environment necessary to help them fulfill their God-given potential. That is what authentic and great leadership is all about.

Leadership wisdom is the greatest need of our time. It will be perhaps the most important need of the 21st century. God kind of leadership is the only leadership that can lead our societies into a real and genuine change.

## LEADERSHIP, A DIVINE DUTY

October 2006 will be remembered for long time in our nation's history not only because Nigeria turned 46 years old and old enough to be a grand-nation but because of the myriad of events that occurred in the month of October 2006. The nations Independence Day celebration was low-key despite the fact that THISDAY organized a Mega Music Festival in which most of the superstar singers from United States including the beautiful, brilliant and sensual Beyonce visited Nigeria. I read that some of the senators and high government officials were choked up trying to see Beyonce on the stage. The widespread gossip is that after Beyonce perfectly sang the Nigerian National Anthem, President Obasanjo awarded her Nigerian citizenship and now many wants her to run for the nations presidential elections in 2007. Honestly I welcome the idea or the gossip about Beyonce running for Nigeria's presidential election rather than the dumb idea and initiative of Mr. Mo Ibrahim to give the sum of 5 million US Dollars to good African leaders who leave after serving their term.

In addition to the visit of America's mega stars, the week following, billionaire Bill and his beautiful and brilliant

wife, Melinda Gates visited Nigeria to meet with President
Obasanjo at Otta farms. Personally, I see Mr. and Mrs.
Gates visit to Nigeria and other African nations as divine
and great potential for Africa's jobless youth. Bill and
Melinda Gates are the richest couple on planet earth.
Moreover, they are compassionate and charismatic couple.
I was not surprised when I received InformationWeek of
June 19, 2006 and read that Bill was leaving after 30 years
of leading Microsoft. Now, he wants to team up with his
lovely wife to carry out their divine mission, which is to
alleviate poverty and promote education. When the Gates
met with President Obasanjo in Otta farms, they did not
promise the president that they would give their money to
African leaders who govern well and leave office. I mean
the Gates are 100 times richer than Mo Ibrahim and yet
they were wise enough to donate their riches to eradicating
poverty, disease and promoting education in Africa. Even
though Bill Gates is gradually relinquishing his technical
leadership at Microsoft Corporation, a multi trillion U.S
dollar corporation that he founded with his Harvard
roommate, classmate and friend, during their second year,
he's still an influential figure in its day-to-day business
decision and activities.

Today, Microsoft is still surveying lucrative markets and
potential areas for technical skills to open its plants. With
the soon release of VISTA operating system and myriad of
business applications application being developed
according to Craig Mundies, the chief research and strategy
officer and Ray Ozzie, chief software architect, Microsoft
is yet to reach its potential in Information technology world
market. . India one of the early beneficiaries of Microsoft
plants, now provides thousands of jobs every year to
India's burgeoning youth. In addition to Microsoft, many
US technology and IT services companies including IBM,
Oracle and Accenture have made their home in India. No

wonder India today provides one-third of all Information Technology and technical skills worldwide.

How did they do it?  Because they had visionary leadership and the minister of Science & technology saw that the future of India wealth creation lies in technology about 40 years ago.  Today they are reaping the benefits of that vision.  Nigeria could become the next target for Information technology and technical knowledge skills.  The question is whether our government has the vision to tap into a man that has blessed humanity through his technical knowledge and marketing genius - or whether they will continue to depend on oil and gas revenue which according to many experts may be less needed 30-50 years from now.  With the oil prices skyrocketing, America's top physicists, Derek May and Melvin Prueitt are teaming up with other solar and nuclear scientist as well as entrepreneurs to unveil alternative energy technologies.  Even the Texas oilman President George W. Bush, Governor Schwarzenegger of California and other leaders are offering tax incentives and multibillion-dollar initiatives to support solar technologies.  According to entrepreneurs at the forefront of this initiative, "the cost of solar power cells has been decreasing, so the economics are becoming more favorable.

The President and Congress have also realized that energy independence is vital to national security and the only way to achieve energy independence is through alternative energy like solar energy. In a recent speech, President Bush declared, "our nation is on the threshold of new energy technology that I think will startle the American people...."We're on the edge of some amazing breakthroughs – breakthroughs all aimed at enhancing our national security and our economic security and the quality of life the folks who live here in the United States."

Nigeria does not lack men and women who can provide such visionary leadership, what we do misunderstand are the divine obligations of leadership. Nigeria can boast of men and women who have the education, qualification, impressive resume, and technical know-but what we lack are the character and courage to provide positive and good leadership. Nigeria's socio-political problems are not due to lack of human potential or natural resources, these are in abundance. Nigeria's epileptic infrastructure at all levels is due to the fact that the men and women at the affairs of our local government, state and national government have not truly understood the divine purposes, tasks and obligations of leadership. Nigeria does not lack people and resources to turn around the deteriorating economic situation, create jobs, provide good public healthcare sound and competitive education, revive and rebuild debilitating infrastructure, restore order, confidence and hope for its citizens. What we do lack is the will power, courage and moral authority to truly transform our nation to be one of the best in the world. Unfortunately what we have today, as leaders are people driven by greed, corruption, jealousy and hatred.

No wonder we have seen to many corruption, violence and political motivated killings in the last seven and half years. And this month of October has been the worst especially after EFCC charged 31 out of 36 governors with financial mishandling, money laundering and corruption. We also learned that the past military leaders squandered over 380 billion US dollars in the last 40 years. The World Bank and other international organizations have also reported that Nigeria risks collapse and disintegration if the current looting, corruption, killings and criminality do not stop. In addition to all this, we also witnessed the accusations between President Obasanjo and his vice, Atiku. Here is a classical case of leadership disloyalty and admittance of guilty. Now, we have so-called impeachment saga and declaration of state of emergency rule that are heating up the polity unlike before. Governor Fayose in Ekiti State has been impeached and Governor Peter Obi in Anambra State is going through the same ordeal. If the situation in Anambra State is not resolved amicably, the president may be compelled to impose emergency rule in Anambra state as well. This is a state that has produced the most brilliant minds in Nigeria and since this democratic dispensation the State has not seen any order, peace and security. In the last seven and half years ago, four governors have impeached and state of emergency declared in three states. It makes one wonder if Nigeria is really ready for this borrowed system of Government or if she has sit down with all the kingmakers and design a system of government that will fit its multi-cultural and religious society. More than its pluralistic nature, I think that that poverty, illiteracy, ignorance, incompetent educational system and lack of middle class have contributed to make democracy very impracticable in Nigeria. What we have in our nation today is reckless abuse of power, a desecration of the position leadership and a lack of quality stewardship and transparent leadership. In a nutshell, Nigeria current leadership is driven by greed, envy, jealousy, corruption, use of threat and innuendos to achieve political power, authority and influence.

**What is leadership?**
Leadership is a divine duty. It is a great sacrifice and service to humanity. It is a sacred task and it was originated and designed by God. Leadership is hard work. Leadership requires wisdom and courage that can only come from the originator. Jesus, the greatest leader ever known to mankind made this statement more than 2000 years ago, "Whoever wants to become great (leader) among you must be your servant, and whoever wants to be first (leader) must be your slave (servant) just as the Son of Man

278

did not come to be served, but to give his life as a ransom" (Matthew 20:26-28). I do not want to go into the biblical and theological exegesis of this statement, but in a nutshell, Jesus said that to be a leader in any capacity, you must be willing to serve, be a slave and ready to die - that is what genuine, pure and godly leadership is all about. What we see today in Nigeria and in many cases in the world is not leadership. Today's leaders want to be served rather than serve. None of the world leaders today want to die for their followers in the sense of working for the people rather they want the people to work for their selfish interest. They do not have the interested of the people at heart at all. Most of them are rather driven by greed, corruption, jealousy and hatred. And any criticism of their leadership style is a threat to their satanic power, authority and influence. May God have mercy upon you all?

**Who is a leader?**
As a student of biblical leaders and leadership styles, I read so many definitions of leadership. However, the one that truly fulfills all the ingredients of genuine and pure leadership is the definition that was developed in one of my leadership classes which states that, "A leader is one who is called by God, people or circumstances to possess virtuous character and who effectively motivates, mobilizes resources and directs people toward the fulfillment of a joint embraced vision from God. Leadership is the ability to set goals in accordance with God's purpose for the future and to communicate those goals to others in such a way that they voluntarily and harmoniously work together to accomplish those goals for the glory of God. Any thing outside this definition and practice is satanic leadership and that what unfortunately prevails in our world today. God has blessed our planet earth that there is no need for people of this planet to suffer poverty, hunger, lack which

279

naturally leads to crime, corruption, hatred, violence, war and death.

Seeking to be a leader no matter the level of leadership position is an honorable ambition and a noble task. The Apostle Paul, one of the great church leaders of the first century wrote to his prodigy, Timothy, "If any sets his heart on being an overseer (leader), he desires a noble task." That noble task however requires wisdom, character, integrity and vision in order to lead others. King Solomon, the wisest and richest the world has ever know realized the need for wisdom, discernment and anointing (power) from God despite his charisma and wealthy heritage, when he asked for godly wisdom and discerning heart to govern the children of Israel (1 Kings 3:7-9).
What is the divine obligation of leadership?
The greatest duty of any leader, a father, a mother, a CEO, State Governor, local government chairman/chairlady, or nation's president is to provide security. Stability, safety and security are the golden obligation of any leader. The Bible says that God ordained government in order that His people might have peace and order (Romans 13). Peace, order and stability will in turn create an enabling environment in which people can be mobilized, motivated and inspired to achieve their God given potential. The greatest obligation of any leader is to properly harness the resources within his or her disposal so that the people can flourish and fulfill the talents and skills that reside inside them. A good father will not only provide food for his children and wife but will make it his utmost duty to protect them from harm and danger. A lovely mother will not only nurse her baby but also protect him or her from germs and danger. A visionary company CEO will always want his employers to excel and his customers to be safe and protected. Likewise a good nation's president will always want his or her people to live in peace and security.

When the people under your leadership only enjoy bread and butter and lack peace, order and security, that leader has failed.

Nigerians have not enjoyed bread, butter, order, peace or security. I cannot remember in my lifetime the period in which the people of Nigeria lived in peace and security. It has always being ethnic and tribal clashes, cultural and religious conflicts, corruption, violence and war. In addition poverty, hunger, diseases, illiteracy and death continue to prevail abundantly in one of the richest nations in the world. Last month, 13 generals and senior army officials perished in a military plan crash. It took a young lad playing around the village bush to notice the incident and then reported it to his father. As I write, a plane crash was reported this morning that claimed the life of Sultan of Sokoto and other highly placed individuals in the country. This is a curse that needs to be revised at all cost. God's people cannot continue to die and perish in vain. History will not judge us well. The situation in Nigeria and Africa demands for leadership with integrity and character and divinely called and appointed by God to deliver its people from the current satanic and demonic leadership oppression all over the continent. To achieve this goal, good African leaders must work together as one people of faith. They must be a people who understand the issues and how to build godly and strong value system and develop a continental passion that will inspire others to action. By so doing, they will salvage our generation that is being wasted and then motivate people to embrace good change, to live their fullest potential, and thereby create and enhance credible future leadership reservoir.

My friends, effective and excellent leadership requires the understanding of divine nature of leadership. It requires courage, character and wisdom that can only be bestowed by God Himself. It requires a call, a commission and competence (preparation). Today, many want to lead without praying for these divine ingredients of leadership. To be a leader over people requires more than being likeable, charismatic, educated or have money. It requires a definite call from God, or from people or by divine circumstances. However, one must be prepared and ask God for wisdom, direction and power to lead other human beings. In Numbers 27:18-23; The LORD told Moses to commission Joshua, a man in whom is the spirit. Then Moses laid his hands on him before all the assembly of Israel and before the high priest Eleazer and commissioned Joshua as the LORD instructed. Also in the book of Deuteronomy 31:14 and 34:9, Joshua was filled with the spirit of wisdom as Moses laid his hands on him. Joshua was then presented as the successor of Moses at the Tent of Meeting before all the children of Israel and they listened to his wisdom.

As 2007 draws near and Nigerians prepare to go to pooling booths again, let us elect those who have the character, courage and capacity to lead one of the most powerful nations in Africa. Let us elect those who are ready to serve the people rather than expect to be served. Let us elect those who are willing to sacrifice and work hard for the common people. Let us elect those who will provide peaceful environment for the people of Nigeria to prosper and fulfill their God given life. Let us elect those who are willing to become slaves rather than being a slave master. Let us elect those who will provide order, peace and security for all Nigerians. Let us elect those who are willing to give their lives as ransom in order to serve. My brothers and sisters, let us elect those who truly understand the divine duty of leadership – that's those who are willing to die first in order to provide pure, genuine, excellent and godly leadership. This is my life long cry, a cry for supernatural leaders, God empowered and spirit led leaders.

May the souls of those who perished in ADC Boeing 737 flight from Abuja to Sokoto rest in peace! May the LORD dry the tears of family members that are left behind and fill them and the entire people of Nigeria with His peace and strength during this time of sorrow, sadness and mourning? Be encouraged Nigeria.

A CALL FOR MORAL AND COMPASSIONATE
LEADERSHIP

## A NATION OF FALSE PROPHETS, MURDERERS, AND UNGODLY LEADERS

---

*"The prophets prophesy falsely, and the priests rule by their own power; and my people love to have it so" (Jeremiah 5:31).*

*In addition to the numerous challenges facing African countries, I believe without any shadow of doubt that false prophets and bad political leadership are the two major, serious and damaging challenges facing many African nations. -Rev. Dr. C. K. Ekeke*

Let me use this opportunity to thank all of you who have written to me in the last few months wanting to know if all is well with me and also to inquire why my articles are not being published on nigeriaworld.com. In fact many of you managed to get my number and called to ask about my well being and expressed the joy of reading my articles. On few occasions, I unashamedly told some of you that I am not a trained writer or journalist. I write because that's one way I participate in the discourse of nation building through constructive criticisms while proffering ideas to address major social and moral issues confronting our country Nigeria. I have also met some of you who reside in this great city of Atlanta who applauded and encouraged me to continue to offer my voice through writing. Some of you passionately encouraged me to put my ideas into a book. I sincerely appreciate all of you.

However despite the applause, joy and encouragement, I have also received threats from many including the security personnel at high places in our land. At one engaged and prolonged follow-up with SSS personnel, I was told and warned: UNLESS YOUR LEG WILL NOT TOUCH NIGERIA AGAIN. YOU STAY IN AMERICA AND WRITE RUBBISH. Frankly this is not the reason why I refused to send any more articles. Despite several other engagements, I defended my doctoral dissertation this month. I also had a few other writing opportunities that really made it terrible difficult for my freelance on Nigeriaworld.com. I want to assure you that with God's help you will continue to hear from me especially on issues that touch my sympathy with God and compassion for His creatures.

In the last few months, so much have happened and I followed as much as I can, the death of Third Term Agenda and the mischievous political killings as the nation prepares for 2007 national elections. However, what necessitated me to write this particular article were the prophetic utterances published by Daily Sun on Tuesday, August 15th, 2006 in which one Prophet Dr. Olagunroye Faleyimu claimed that God told him that Buhari would be Nigeria's president in 2007. When I read that report I meditated for about thirty minutes and then angrily began to ask God many questions.

Some of the questions I asked were:

1. Is Dr. Olagunroye Faleyimu truly God's prophet?
2. Why are you (God) choosing Buhari, a military dictator to rule us again?
3. Is Buhari in the right party to win the presidency or will the Nigerian establishment foists Buhari on us?
4. Is there no other genuine, courageous, compassionate and godly leader among the millions of Nigerian people that you can choose and raise up to deliver the Nigerian nation from our present state of darkness and death?

I must have asked twenty or more questions to God during this moody state of mind and spiritual anger. When I finally finished asking my questions, God began to speak to me. One of the clearest statements from Him was: BEWARE OF FALSE PROPHETS! Then He referred me to Mark 13:22, "False Christ's and false prophets will rise and show signs and wonders to deceive many."

**Who is a Prophet?**

God does not do any thing on planet earth without revealing it first to His true prophets. Why, because God is intimately involved in all of our lives. God cares and loves us too much. This incomprehensible quality of God, theologians call "Divine Pathos" which simply means divine passion. Despite His self-sufficiency, God passionately seeks and desires a relationship with His creatures and mankind is the most loved of all God's creation. That is why He sent His Son, Jesus Christ to suffer agony; pain and excruciating death on the Cross in-order to repair the damaged relationship caused by Adam's sin. God is the same yesterday, today and forever. He continues to speak to His people through His prophets. He continues to find willing hearts to deliver His prophetic messages to mankind. His compassion, love and faithfulness for His people have not ceased.

Therefore, since the beginning of redemptive history, God has always sought for a man or woman to deliver His message of care and love to His creatures. Theologians call this mouthpiece of God - Prophet. It is derived from two Hebrew Words: (1) Ro'eh - which is translated "Seer" in English. It indicates a special ability to see in the spiritual realm and foresee future events as given by God through dreams, visions, revelations or spoken words. The second Hebrew Word is: (2) Nabi - which is translated Prophet. It literally means to prophesy, to put forth words abundantly from God's minds and by God's spirit. A Nabi is a spokesperson that poured out words under the impelling power of God's spirit. And so throughout human history such men and women have arisen and spoken courageously and compassionately the Words of God to His people. In addition to being the mouthpiece that reveals the message of God, a prophet is also a preacher, a poet, a patriot, a diplomat, a moralist and a social critic and reformer. He is a political being who speaks to the social, political, religious and moral issues of the day. Therefore he is sort of an advisor and consultant on moral and social issues to society at large.

**What are Prophetic Messages?**

Prophetic messages are not only central to our faith and beliefs system but also to our personal life, social life, business life, and political life as well. Throughout biblical history, the men and women who God towered spiritually to speak on His behalf such as Moses, Deborah, Samuel, Elijah, Isaiah, Daniel, Hosea, Amos, Jeremiah, Jesus just to mention a few received divine knowledge and spoke courageously the messages of God These prophets spoke not only in religious places but also in every area of people's lives. They spoke against sin, idolatry, immorality, and all kinds of evil in the society. They warned against corruption, greed, unrighteousness and injustice especially in the lives of Kings and Priests. They warned people of God's judgment and therefore called them to change and follow God's instruction. They encouraged people to remain faithful to God and his covenant. The prophets loved people, cared for them and sought the highest good for them. The prophets were in a nutshell social and moral activists in their era. Since God is the source of prophetic messages, people are called to obey the words spoken by the prophets. Even in recent times, we are reminded of the prophetic messages of Mandela, Gandhi, Mother Teresa, and John Paul II and off course Rev. Dr. Martin Luther King. Their prophetic words and insights have saved mankind from slavery, apartheid, destruction and death. Today, we need such prophets to arise and speak to the monumental challenges facing our planet earth.

**The Rise of False Prophets**

As the prophets gain a place of influence in their ministry and success in society, counterfeits and imposters disguised themselves and began to act as God ministers and ambassadors of righteousness. Satan, who before the fall was an Angel of Light and now number one and chief enemy of God, began to plant false prophets in the church and society. These prophets who claim to speak on behalf of God quickly began to enjoy some degree of popularity, influence and success among the people. While their lives are full of hypocrisy, wickedness, lust, immorality, adultery, greed and self-centered indulgence, they manipulated the people with their ability and charisma.

In Oliver Discourse, Jesus warned, "Take heed that no one deceives you. For many will come in my name. And will deceive many" (Matthew 24:4-5). Jesus answering the disciple's question: what will be the sign of your coming and of the end of age - gives the signs that will characterize the whole course of the last days that will intensify as the end draws nearer. The first major sign, he gives in an answer to the disciples question, was that age of religious deception will be rampant on earth. False prophets and religious establishments within the visible church will increase and deceive many (Matthew 24:4-5, 11). Today we are witnesses of the increase of church planting and establishment of ungodly religious organizations in the world. In the United States alone, there are about thirteen thousand satanic churches. Today the Nigerian society is rapidly being engulfed by all kinds of churches and ungodly religious leaders. The headlines are full of sad news of atrocities, rape and murder being committed by these so-called prophets and pastors against those who have been entrusted into spiritual care, while murder, killings, sorcery, rituals and witchcraft have not abated at all.

The second sign, Jesus tells his disciples is the increase of wars, famines and earthquakes will be the beginning of birth pains of the new Messianic age (vs. 6-8). Since the beginning of this century, there has been an unprecedented catastrophic event of unimaginable proportions. Many of us have vivid memories of the unprecedented disasters and rash of tragedies that have occurred since 2001, natural disasters, ethnic strife; religious wars, nuclear threat and violence have been more frequent than ever. In addition to many conflicts and challenges going in our planet, the United Nations is currently working day and night to enforce cease-fire between Israel and Hezbollah - Lebanon. Many have prayed that it does not erupt and escalate into Holy War. Let me not forget to mention that Nigerian reporters and journalists have failed to report about this one-month war between Israel and Hezbollah because of fear of Islamic fundamentalism. Nigerian society has now become a safe haven for Taliban and Al Qaeda who are eager to kill whenever they get angry. We must all learn to live in peace on earth now otherwise heaven will not contain us.

Jesus went on to tell the disciples that as the end draws nearer, the persecution of God's people will become more severe and many will forsake their loyalty to Christ (vs. 9-10). Today, our society is saturated with these kinds of people Jesus talked about. We have now all kinds of churches and religious superstars who preach unsound and biblical messages that lead people to death rather than teach the abundant life that Jesus came to give to mankind. What we have in this dispensation is unholy, unrighteous and Christ counterfeits that have arisen to perform witchcraft as

290

signs, miracles and wonders in-order to deceive the people including even the very elect - Just watch the Nigerian movie: Church Business, where Pastor Jimmy entered into unholy alliance with the princess of Sea in order to have power and wealth. Such unholy alliances are abundant in our society today.

Jesus gives the fourth and final sign that violence, crime and disregard for God's law will increase rapidly, and natural love and family affection will decrease. However in-spite of this intensification of trouble, the gospel will be preached in the whole world. The saved will be those who stand in their faith through all the end-time distress. The faithful, as they see the intensification of these signs, will know that the day of the Lord's return for them is approaching (vs. 12-13).

Years later, Apostle John before he closed his eyes, warned his readers that "many deceivers have gone out into the world" (2 John 7). He admonished all believers, "Beloved, do not believe every spirit, but test the spirits, whether they are of God; because many false prophets have gone out in the world (1 John 4:1). The prophets of Old, New and even in our modern times have always wrestled with false prophets and teachers because what they preach and teach does not match with the Word and wisdom of God.

Frankly speaking, I have a problem when I see abundant darkness in midst of light. If there is light in any place, there shouldn't be too much darkness there. Jesus said that we are the "light of the world" (Matthew 5:14). In a place of darkness, if there is someone with a touch light, others should be able to see some light. Two or more blind people cannot lead themselves - one or more who can see even if it is with one eye can only lead them. For instance, about 65% of Nigerian population claim to be Christians, attend mass every Sunday and mid-week church activities and yet rituals, divination, astrology, sorcery, witchcraft, magic, and all manners of evil and satanic worship abound among the people. Greed, hatred, corruption, idolatry, jealousy and envy continue to be rampant among our people yet we have Evangelists, Bishops, Priests, Pastors and Prophets who claim to speak for God. They claim to be God ambassadors and representative of Christ on planet earth and yet the very people that God has entrusted into their spiritual leadership are dying and perishing in darkness and ignorance. They are only interested in gathering milk, honey and wealth from the people and then deceive them with satanic tongues and pronouncements.

Some of these religious leaders cannot claim to be genuine and true messengers of God because if they boldly preach and teach the Word of God, ungodliness cannot have room for fetish acts in their presence. The Word of God is His presence and where there is presence of God, evil and ungodliness cannot stand without being destroyed. I have preached in churches where people practicing witchcraft and voodoo have stood up and left the sanctuary because they couldn't stand the Word of God being taught. On more than one occasion, I have been told to stop preaching fear and preach love. I replied that I am not preaching fear; I am preaching deliverance. There cannot be genuine love without repentance and deliverance. "For God so loved the world that He gave His one and only Son, that whoever believes in him shall not perish but have eternal life" (John 3:16). When I truly love you, I cannot allow you to continue in darkness and ignorance. Ignorance, envy, jealousy and greed are venomous vices. However ignorance is my worst enemy. And I have seen a lot of it among my people.

## Responding to Dr. Olagunroye Faleyimu

Let me briefly address the prophecy of Dr. Olagunroye Faleyimu. I am not here to criticize a prophet of God but if my biblical study is correct, I read many places in the Bible where false prophets who arose among the people to deceive them were confronted. If the prophecies of Dr. Dr. Olagunroye Faleyimu are from God, I cannot wait to see Buhari become president in 2007. Moreover, I also pray that I live long to see him become the Elijah, the anointed and the chosen one of God from Ondo state to rule Nigeria in future. The fact is that the Nigerian establishment is evil and satanic. Many of you will agree with me that all the past leaders who have ruled Nigeria since after the civil war were insinuated on Nigerians. Either they took power by force through military coups or the Nigerian power brokers met and decided on who will be loyal to the establishment. Otherwise how could a second grade teacher become Nigeria's president in 1979? That person will be imposed upon the Nigerian people and against their will.

President Obasanjo was one of such leaders in this dispensation. However, he has been a disappointment to those who appointed him. If he has achieved nothing, his war against corruption has yielded some results even though he has not really gone against the so-called big boys. We also have to understand that as the nation agitate over whose turn the presidency will shift to, the power brokers are in serious and secret talks how to continue to manage the Nation to avoid disintegration. Even though I do not subscribe to rotational presidency, however I think that that it is the best solution for Nigeria multi-ethnic society. For personal reasons, I have refused to write about Igbo leadership, let me humbly and respectfully say that the power brokers of Nigeria are not yet ready to allow an Igbo man to rule until they can find a suitable Igbo person they can trust with Nigeria evil establishment. They will rather reach a consensus with South-South rather than South East in this dispensation of our nation's history. It is not that the South East doesn't have able men and women that can rule Nigeria. They know that the Southeast have perhaps better and qualified men and women who can change the destiny of Nigeria for good but they want someone who will be willing to submit to the evil establishment of Nigeria dark powers. The Ohanaeze Ndi-Igbo and other Igbo social groups will have to work it out with them. The youthful and exuberant Governor Orji Kalu has played his cards so well with his massive business investments in the North and his friendship with the Northern Emirs but he fell out of favor with President Obasanjo. Moreover, his outburst and immaturity makes it very difficult for him even with the Northern Oligarchy. Moreover, this is a governor like the rest of them who have managed to siphon the revenues of his state through his million businesses and associates around the world.

So if you run through the list of those who have ruled Nigeria since 1993 as prophesied by Dr. Olagunroye Faleyimu, you will notice that those leaders were imposed upon and against the will of the people. All I am trying to say here that the person who becomes the president of Nigeria in 2007 will not be chosen by God or the people but will be imposed upon the people by the evil establishment. If God wants to speak to Nigerians at this time, it will be for us to repent, forsake our atrocities, forgive one other and reconcile with each other. There is too much sin, immorality, darkness and death in the land. Why would anyone plan and murder his or her political opponent? Who gave them the right to take someone's life? If God were speaking to any true prophet about the affairs of Nigeria, it would be for us to repent and seek his face. The message cannot be that Buhari; a military dictator will be Nigeria's president in 2007. This is a man who ruled with the worst decree during his military era and killed hundreds of innocent people who opposed his brutal regime. What has he done to show and demonstrate that he has repented of his atrocities and wickedness toward Nigerian people? If he becomes Nigeria's president in 2007 that means that he has agreed to play by the rules of the Nigeria power oligarchy and off-course the people will continue to suffer the consequences if they allow it.

## Discerning and Responding to False Prophets

False prophets have been around since the beginning of redemptive history (Deuteronomy 13:1-5), and they always find ways to get their human words out to the society at large. Jesus warned, Beware of false prophets, who come to you in sheep's clothing, but inwardly they are ravenous wolves (Matthew 7:15). Saint Jude, in his brief letter to believers, warned against false prophets and told us how to respond to them by keeping ourselves in the love of God (Jude 21). Therefore, I have every right to question the prophetic utterances of Prophet Dr. Olagunroye Faleyimu. I read that most of his prophecies in the past have become history. The questions I asked therefore, how do we know that he actually prophesied those things? If those prophecies were from God, why are we in such a bad shape we are now? When the children of Israel rejected Prophet Samuel and demanded for a king like other nations. God told Samuel to anoint King David from the house of Jesse but the people wanted King Saul because he was tall, handsome and a warrior. Human beings have always chosen whom to lead them by these outward appearances rather than inward qualities. Even in our modern times, money and cultic associations have been become necessary requirements to be a leader rather character and good virtues.

In the teachings and writings of Jesus, Apostle Paul, Peter, John and even Saint Jude, we are also encouraged to confront false prophets and their followers, doing so with a special dependence on the Lord and being careful not to get contaminated by their false teachings. The most dangerous characteristics of false prophets are that they claim to be from God and to speak for Him. False prophets always appear to be pleasant and positive. They like to be with Christians and they know how to talk and act like believers - Pharisees and Sadducees for example. False prophets usually exude sincerity and thereby more easily deceive others. False prophets serve mostly their own interest rather than the ministry and mission. False prophets are not content with basic needs of life and ministry, but make excessive appeal for many. False prophets do not practice what they teach. They teach one thing and practice another. False prophets ignore and have problems with fundamental and controversial biblical truth. Their teachings are heretical.

The Didache, one of the earliest Christian writings after the New Testament, gives several guidelines for discerning false prophets.

1. Discern Character. Do they have diligent prayer lives and do they show a sincere and pure devotion to God. Do they manifest the fruit of the Spirit such as love, kindness, do they love righteousness, hate wickedness and cry out against sin and wickedness.
2. Discern Motives. Do they honor Christ, lead the ministry and church in holiness and sanctifications, save the lost, proclaim and defend the gospel of Christ.
3. Discern their Teachings. This is a key issue. Do they teach, believe and submit to the un-adulterated Word of God?
4. Discern Integrity. Do they handle Lord's money and ministry finances with integrity and responsibility? Do they seek to promote God's work in ways that are consistent with fiscal laws of their country?

False teachers and prophets have been around since the history of mankind. They are in our churches and society at large and they are hard to be detected until God determines to expose them for what they are. However, the Bible warns us to have a discerning spirit and learn how to respond to them. God's plan is too precious and His purpose too powerful to be wasted because of our childish behaviors. We really need to get serious and sincere in this country; otherwise we will die to face God's wrath and justice. One fine day, we will appear before the judgment seat of Christ and account for what we have done in this brief earthly life. Let those who ears, hear the Word of the Lord!

## A PROPHETIC CALL FOR MORAL LEADERSHIP

Today, we live in a world that is insecure and full of uncertainties. While, the Western rich nations are threatened with terrorism, chemical, biological, and nuclear weapons, the continent of Africa is ravaged with poverty, ethnic hatred, tribal wars, disease, greed, corruption, political instability and spiritual bankruptcy. Our children, the future human resources for Africa are dying in thousands of AIDS in South Africa and Central parts of Africa and with the recent threat of SARS reaching the shores of Africa, the continent of human origin risks to be extirpated or obliterated if African leadership remains unconcerned and immobilized.

Recently while communicating with God in prayer concerning the above issues, the spirit of God quickened me to understand that the plethora of problems facing our world and especially the continent of Africa today is not merely economic, social, environmental, or even political issues but lack of strong, courageous and moral leadership. God ordained government for divine plan and purpose but those who are placed in power and positions of authority have intentionally or unintentionally ignored the divine privileges for leadership. God has ordained leadership in order to bring about His Will on earth but those placed to rule and reign are negligent, ungodly and seeks only for their own selfish desires.

God established government to bring about peace and order as well as to provide opportunities for His human creation to discover and fulfill their God given desires and dreams through those who are placed in position of authority. Rather people who occupy leadership positions today in government, business entities, families and even our churches and mosques seem not comprehend the divine obligations of leadership. They appear to forget that the greatest task of the leader is to inspire, motivate and to help those under their power and influence to become all they can be. They do not understand that the primary goal of leadership must be to inspire people to live rightly and to enable them to accomplish their God-given purpose and mission on earth.

African leaders do not seem to embrace the fact that leadership is all about the people and servant-hood. Africa leaders in this contemporary time must be willing to mobilize, motivate and inspire people to achieve, succeed and reach their fullest potential. That is the greatest task of leadership. The job of any leader is to make sure that the people under his or her influence and authority discover and fulfill the potential that lies inside them.

Oliver Wendel Holmes, an American poet and philosopher said, "What lies behind us and what lies before us are tiny matters, compared to what lies within." The Apostle John said it best when he wrote, "You are God, little children, and have overcome them, because He who is in you is greater than he who is in the world (1 John 4:4). Even the Apostle Paul reminded us that, "We are Gods workmanship, created to do good works, which God prepared in advance for us to do (Eph. 2:10)." This means that when you are privileged to be a leader over people, you must be willing to make resources available by inspiring people to use their God given talents and skills to fulfill their potentials.

Africa does not obviously lack courageous men and women who can lead nor does she lack the resources, manpower, skills, talents, natural and physical resources to turn around deteriorating economic situation, create jobs, provide good healthcare, and sound education for its citizens, develop and build infrastructure, restore order, confidence and hope. What is lacking is a strong, courageous and moral leadership that is transparent in its private, domestic, public and foreign responsibilities.

Dr. Joseph Nanven Garba said it best in his book: Fractured History, Elite Shifts and Policy Changes in Nigeria, "Nigeria, to my mind, does not lack real men and women. The ingredients for creating a formidable nation exist. What is lacking is leadership with the political will and the selfless dedication to galvanize the entire nation." Africa's problem is not economic, political, social, cultural or even moral but a leadership crisis. Chinua Achebe in his book entitled: The Trouble with Nigeria, writes, "The trouble with Nigeria is simply and squarely a failure of leadership." Other noted Nigerians and Africans at motherland and abroad have also blamed the dramatic poverty, ignorance and moral decadence in Africa to leadership corruption.

For instance, Nigeria as a nation has not enjoyed any genuine political peace and national economic prosperity since after the civil war despite enormous blessings that

God has endowed upon her. In fact immediately after the civil war in 1970, Nigeria began to deteriorate rapidly following corrupt political leadership and military dictatorship that denied its citizen any sense of security and God given destiny. So far Nigeria has had only political and military hypocrisy, idolatrous religious system, extravagantly indulgent with corrupt judicial system and oppression of the poor. In short, Nigeria's leadership at all levels has failed to fulfill its divine obligations.

Many African leaders lack insight, wisdom, vision and as a result the continent of Africa is ravaged with many problems such as poverty, ignorance, religious violence, killings, prejudice, injustice, AIDS and recently SARS. Despite enormous and huge houses of worship and church planting at every corner of our cities and towns, religious conflict, ignorance, intolerance, armed robbery, witchcraft and occultism are still rampant. There is no order or security in our continent today and yet people want to be leaders. The policemen or any armed personnel cannot be trusted for safety. In fact African leaders at all levels have failed the people because they have not fulfilled any of the responsibilities of leadership.

What Africa needs today is not carnal, prejudiced and murderous leaders who are destiny destroyers but servant, strong, courageous and compassionate leaders? It was not my purpose to express my intense sorrow and emotional pain over African leadership failure and drastic deprivation of its citizen of their God given blessing and destiny. My real objective for writing this article is to personally and prophetically remind African leaders of the divine responsibilities and obligation of leadership and to warm of them of the judgment and consequences reserved for those who are called to be leaders. Biblical history and world events prove this fact clearly. It does not matter whether you believe in God or not because the only thing that is real and true is the existence of a creator whom all of us will come to face and make account of how and what we did with the life, resources, opportunities and privileges that He gave us.

Seeking to be a leader no matter the level of leadership position is an honorable ambition and a noble task. In First Timothy 3:1, the Apostle Paul writes to his prodigy Timothy, "If any sets his heart on being an overseer, he desires a noble task."

However, it requires wisdom, discernment, character, integrity, and vision to lead others. King Solomon realized the need for wisdom and anointing from God despite his charisma, heritage and riches, when he prayed in First Kings 3:7-9 for wisdom and discerning heart to govern the people of Israel.

Moral and courageous leadership also requires calling, commissioning and competence. Today, a lot of our people want to be leaders without character, calling, commissioning and competence. In Numbers 27:18-23; we read how the LORD told Moses to commission Joshua, a man in whom is the spirit. Then Moses laid hands on him before all the assembly of Israel and before the high priest Eleazer and commissioned Joshua as the LORD instructed. And also in Deuteronomy 31:14 and 34:9, Joshua was filled with the spirit of wisdom as Moses laid hands on him. Joshua was then presented as the successor of Moses at the Tent of meeting before all the children of Israel and they listened to him.

Today, God is calling for servant as well as transformational and transparent leaders. African leaders want to be great and acquire enormous wealth without service. They want to be honored, praised and embellish their material blessings in disdain of those who placed them in power. Jesus said to His disciples, "Whoever wants to become great among must be your servant, and whoever wants to be first must be your slave just as the Son of Man did not come to be served, but to serve and to give his life as a ransom"(Matthew 20: 26-28). The word slave in Greek and Aramaic literally means servant. God is looking for servant leaders who will become servants before they become masters, those who will serve before they become great.

God is looking for leaders who will simply serve and serve so well that the people put him or her on their shoulders and elevate him or her to that honorable position. God will honor leaders who show character, integrity, faith and dependence upon Him. God is calling African leaders to be strong and courageous (Joshua 1:6) and faithfully depend upon Him while humbly facing their leadership responsibilities without compromise. Moses and Joshua in the Old Testament were that kind of leaders (Exodus 3:11; Deuteronomy 8:2, 15; Joshua 1.8).

African leaders must also be men of great vision and mission - a vision that is embraced by all and a mission that is broad as well as brief and strategic with a strong value system that will drive the nation's priorities not personal priorities. African leadership must establish core value system that will dictate every decision and determine the nations' priorities. More than this, African leaders must have strategy and develop plans with formidable team to carry out the vision and mission for Africa and its citizens. African leaders must not ignore or neglect the skills, resources and potential of its citizens no matter where they live or reside. If African leaders want to make a difference, they must be willing to have the best of the best in their team and not their best friends, families, or tribal folks. It is time that African leaders stand up and makes a difference. Our people are tired of status quo and mediocrity. If they fail to do so, history will tell and judge but more than any thing else, God will judge them also.

The situation in Africa demands for leadership with integrity and character and divinely called and appointed by God to deliver its people from the current satanic and demonic leadership oppression all over the continent. To achieve this goal, good African leaders must work together as one people of faith. They must be a people who understand the issues and how to build godly and strong value system and develop a continental passion that will inspire others to action. By so doing, they will salvage our generation that is being marginalized and wasted and then motivate people to embrace good change, to live their fullest potential, and thereby create and enhance credible future leadership reservoir.

The Apostle Paul wrote this statement towards the end of his life of leadership and ministry to both Gentiles and Jews, "However, I consider my life worth nothing to me, if only I may finish the race and complete the task of the Lord Jesus has given to me - the task of testifying to the gospel of God's grace" (Acts 20:24). African leaders can rightly share this statement with the Apostle Paul. God has not appointed leaders to rule to disappoint Him. God has ordained the office of leadership for a purpose. I prophetically make this clarion call to all African leaders and especially the Nigerian leadership to lead with vision, integrity, character and competence. In everything remain courageous and strong. The Lord will honor and so the people.

In conclusion, permit me to tell a Nigeria proverb that says, "All we do on earth, we will account for kneeling in heaven."

I pray that African leaders will grow in the grace and knowledge of our Lord and Savior Jesus Christ and to have spiritual insight, understanding and wisdom of the seed of leadership that God has placed in them and called them to exercise?

TIME FOR CAPABLE, COURAGEOUS, AND
COMPASSIONATE LEADERS


TIME TO PRAY FOR THE PRESIDENT NOT TO
ENGAGE IN TRIBAL AND DIRTY POLITCS

---

*"If my people, who are called by my name, will humble
themselves and pray and seek my face and turn from their
wicked ways, then will I hear from heaven and will forgive
their sins and will heal their land." 2 Chronicles 7:14*

*"For I know how many are your offences and how great your
sins. You oppress the righteous and take bribes and you deprive
the poor of justice in the courts." Amos 5:12*

*"I urge, then, first of all, that requests, prayers, intercession
and thanksgiving be made for everyone - for kings and all
those in authority, that we may live peaceful and quiet lives in
all godliness and holiness" (1 Timothy 2:1-2).*

I like to take this opportunity to personally pray for
President Umaru Yar'Adua. I pray that Almighty God -
Jehovah "Rapha" – the LORD who heals to forgive all of
his sins and heal all of his diseases. I release and send the
Word of God to heal and rescue President Yar'Adua at the
King Faisal hospital in Jeddah, Saudi Arabia, where he is
currently hospitalized and under medical care. I cry out to
the LORD on his behalf and on this day of uncertainty for

Almighty God to save him and rescue him from this heart aliment. I call upon God of Abraham, Isaac, and Jacob, creator of the universe in this time of distress to deliver our President and our nation from trouble (Exodus 15:26; Psalm 50:15; 103:2-3; 107:13, 20).

I also invite every Nigerian - Christians, Muslims, and all the litany of religious leaders in Nigeria and worldwide - The Most Reverend, Pastors, Priests, Bishops, Primates, Prelates, Evangelists, Apostles, Prophets, etc. to humbly pray for President Yar'Adua.

Having offered prayer to God on behalf of the president, I am compelled by the spirit of God to say that this is not the time to play tribal politics. It is a shameful thing that Nigeria's President was flown from Abuja to Jeddah in Saudi Arabia for an emergency medical treatment. It was a close family member, a healthcare professional, who first notified me of the news about the emergency hospitalization of President Yar'Adua. She asked me to check the news. When I finally found time to read some of the news about President Yar'Adua's heart ailment, I informed her about the President's emergency evacuation to Saudi Arabia for a heart medical condition. She was saddened that a country of nearly 150 million, the so-called Giant of Africa, will transport the President to Saudi Arabia for a chronic heart condition, which can be treated by Nigerian doctors. She is also explained what pericarditis is and the possible causes of pericarditis heart aliment. She further told me that perhaps the President's pericarditis ailment may be in acute stage otherwise there is no need to fly the president of Nigeria to another third world country for such a medical emergency.

Her explanation raised many questions about Nigeria as a nation, the knowledge and the ability of various medical staff of the president. I have no doubt that the Presidency has a team of doctors – probably specialized in various medical fields. Why would these medical staff around him not able to offer the president of Nigeria treatment for such a medical condition that's not a serious emergency heart condition here in the West? Where was his medical staff trained? Does the president's medical staff even understand medically what pericarditis is all about? I have read a few reporters trying to explain the Pericarditis ailment – mostly taken from WebMD and other medical resources which are available online. Why would the chief surgeon or the spokesperson for Aso Rock not able to explain to the Nigerian people what the president is suffering from and what the president's medical team is doing to take care of him? Why would the president of the largest black nation in the world be flown to another third world country for medical emergency when there are thousands of qualified Nigerian doctors?

Here in the U.S., there is no hospital or medical facility in the major cities you will walk-in without seeing a Nigerian medical professional working there or even heading that medical facility. Thousands of Nigerian doctors with various medical expertises are scattered across the globe offering such noble services to other people while such services are lacking in their homeland. In fact the few qualified doctors in Nigeria are running away to foreign countries where they can find employment, better living conditions and be treated like human beings. Yet, people at their homeland are dying each day in thousands for common treatable illnesses. In fact Nigerian professionals – educationists, scientists, medical doctors, writers, etc are leaving the shores of Nigeria to other countries due to insecurity, injustice, corruption and lack of basic life needs which is supposed to be the basic responsibilities of government.

Four years ago, Nigerians woke up one morning to read about the sudden death of Mrs. Stella Obasanjo, wife of former President Olusegun Obasanjo who died at a Spanish hospital where she had gone for cosmetic surgery. During that time, many writers including this writer wrote about the urgent need to invest in developing medical facilities in the major cities of Nigeria. Nigeria has the financial resources and qualified doctors that can make this happen if we are sincere with our selves and for Nigeria's future. Since then, it has not occurred to the presidency, the health minister or even chief surgeon of the president to establish such a laudable venture. Currently, we know that the Nigeria's former First Lady Maryam Babangida, the wife of another former dictator, General Ibrahim Babangida is receiving chemotherapy at UCLA's Jonsson Comprehensive Cancer Center in Los Angeles after her ovarian cancer surgery. Why would Nigerian politicians and people in government tend to go abroad for their medical needs while millions of Nigerians are suffering medically, psychologically, and emotionally? Healthcare is a moral right and should be one of the top priorities of government. Instead of Nigerian leaders to invest in healthcare system at home, they are stashing Nigeria's revenue to foreign banks where it is invested to enrich the host nations. When will we extricate ourselves from colonial mentality? When will Nigerian leaders stop this nonsense?

The more I reflect on the political consequences of President's health condition and the political maneuvering of some political prostitutes and enemies of democracy, progress and unity of Nigeria who are already angling themselves for political power by trying to compel Dr. Goodluck Jonathan to resign, I could not but stop to blame the former President Obasanjo for it. President Yar'Adua is Obasanjo's legacy. One of the key legacies of great leadership is the joyful transfer of power and authority to a healthy, courageous, compassionate, trustworthy, and honest individual. Former President Obasanjo did not do that. He knew about Yar'Adua has health issues. We knew that when he was governor, yet Obasanjo imposed him on the Nigeria people. I do not have anything against President Yar'adua; in fact I pray sincerely that he recovers and humbly hands over power to his VP, if he cannot finish his term.

But the former President Obasanjo has had the tendency and history to impose incapable people into leadership position after his term. In 1978, after his robust not exceptional military government, he handed over to the first democratic elected president, Alhaji Shehu Shagari, a primary school teacher who was then handpicked by the king makers to lead Nigeria. Shehu Shagari's government was so corrupt that the army guys patiently waited for the

310

end of first term to take over the affairs of governance from the inept and visionless government. That period led to the dictatorial, brutal and murderous military regimes of Buhari, Babangida and Abacha. Again, at the end of his two terms as civilian president, he made the same very mistake to hand over to Governor Yar'Adua, who until one month before the PDP primaries was not even considered a candidate. So much was written about Yar'Adua, his selection and his health. This writer also wrote a piece entitled "Vicious Circle", where I questioned Yar'Adua's health, his capacity, courage, boldness and vision to lead a diverse country like Nigeria enumerating serious domestic issues threatening the nation then such as Nigeria's unity, crime and security of life, constitutional amendment, religious bigotry and violence, economy & job creation, health care crisis & infrastructure, power supply, clean water, good road, corruption & injustice, national reconciliation, moral and social decadence, climate change & environment challenges: These did not even include serious regional and international challenges as well.

However, I am profoundly amazed that there are certain political elements the so-called Kaduna Mafia under the guardianship of Ibrahim Babangida who are asking Dr. Goodluck Jonathan to resign so that David Mark, the senate president could take over to make sure that the power remains in the North as agreed within PDP caucus. What about those who are also insinuating that the President's wife, First Lady Turai Yar'Adua should take over. When did we become a monarchy? This is ridiculous and insane. How foolish and nonsensical thinking to ask the VP to resign. This goes to explain Nigeria's flawed establishment.

When will these power hungry politicians grow up? When will these political nonentities realize that that we are in a democracy and that the constitution overrides party policies? Why would these politicians want to cause anarchy and trouble in Nigeria again? What type of childish politics is this? Do these politicians know that we have a Vice President who has been in the position as VP for more than two years now? Why would these cabals force the VP to resign when he is certainly capable of finishing the one and half years of the current presidential term? And people should stop asking who's in charge now. There is no question about who's in charge. The VP should be in charge in the absence of the President of Nigeria. Any other arrangement is crude, uncivilized and can led to anarchy.

I believe the VP has the capacity, skill and knowledge to run the country for the remainder of this current political dispensation. The country needs a man of wisdom, courage, strength, compassion, and discernment who understands the plight of Nigerians and the need to do what's right for the suffering masses. Nigeria does not need superficial, cryptic, unqualified and incompetent group of leaders; a leadership cult that is crippling and wasting enormous human potentials. Nigeria does not need a group of leaders that is only after their own personal profit, power and influence. Nigeria does not need greedy, incompetent and pre-mature political figures who abuse power for their personal gain and pleasure, who extort, levy heavy taxes on poor citizens, take bribery and loot the state treasury, who lie, compromise, harass, threaten and even resort to violence and murder in order to attain and solidify their temporal influence, superficial charm and evil power.

The Nigerian constitution is so clear on this matter that if the president is unable to continue, the VP should naturally take over the affairs of the nation. Only when both the president and VP are incapacitated, should it fall into the hands of the senate president? The constitutional experts, the upper and lower House should not allow this democrazy to happen to the people of Nigeria. Nigerians had tolerated a similar situation before when Ibrahim Babangida canceled the 1992 democratic elections in which Chief Moshood Abiola clearly won. The Nigerian people should not allow this to happen again otherwise, we will be a laughing stock to the entire world. The constitution is clear that if the president is unable to continue in office due to ill health, death, or any other incapacitated condition, the VP should take over the affairs of running the country as president. The policies and arrangements of PDP have no moral justification over the constitution of the Federal Republic of Nigeria.

Even the mindset and thinking of this insanity hinges on the flawed establishment called Nigeria. I have written in the past about how the eminent nationalist leaders who fought for Nigeria's freedom and independence against the British Empire bequeathed us a nation so frazzled and fragmented. If our forefathers in the likes of late Dr. Nnamdi Azikiwe, Chief Obafemi Awolowo, Alhaji Abubakar Tafawa Belwa, Alhaji Ahmadu Bello, Ernest Ikoli, H. O. Davis, Chief S. L. Akintola, Dr. M. I. Okpara, Solanke and Eyo Ita among many other nationalists who fought for Nigeria's independence had worked together to give the Nigerian state a suitable constitution that embraced the aspirations of every Nigerian citizen, we would not come at this point of our history to even talk about power shift between North and South. Nigeria needs a man or a woman who has wisdom, courage, compassion and vision to lead a multi-ethnic and resourceful people of Nigeria. It does not matter where the president comes from provided every Nigerian is considered a true and patriotic citizen. What Nigeria needs at this juncture considering the geo-political division; multi-ethnic, tribal and religious differences is just two political parties and no more. And it should not be Northern or Southern party but two political parties that portray national census.

Staying on this issue of constitution, as I have written again and again, Nigeria's first constitution was put together by the British people in 1922. These are people who do not understand our culture or social systems. How do you think our colonial and slave masters will give us a document that is capable of creating a peaceful and prosperous society. Since then, our constitution has been revised few times yet the constitutional experts could not come up with a constitution to accommodate the social, cultural, religious and tribal norms of all the variant groups that make up Nigeria. The fundamental rights as defined in our constitution today are not the same as a well defined set of core values such as character, honesty, genuine integrity, discipline, trust, truth, commitment, dedication, patriotism just to mention a few that that will enhance credible leadership, spur nation's building, promote good business culture and inspire people to embrace good change in-order to reach their potential. I was disappointed that CONFAB conference was called by President Obasanjo to determine how to divide, distribute and allocate oil revenue rather than how to establish basic core and patriotic values that will help unite the nation.

The most recent constitution of 1988 was put together by some foreign commission assembled by a military and murderous dictator, General Abacha. It is absolute ridiculous that a country like Nigeria with so many trained lawyers and constitutional experts at home and abroad cannot come up with a constitution that embodies and embraces the common aspirations of every Nigerian citizen. And yet, these military dictators' tuned politicians continue to play dirty and tribal politics to the detriment of the entire Nigerian people. I am convinced that in order to build a respectable and prosperous Nigerian nation that we aspire and dream to have, there must be first of all a set of well-defined core values or code of conduct that will help to create an environment in which government, businesses, investment and people can thrive and prosper.

Therefore, the ongoing political squabble instead of praying for the President is an opportunity for Nigerians to address ethnic and tribal politics within the polity. It is a well known fact that before the white men came as missionary workers with pretense to colonize the territory known today as Nigeria; the various inhabitants of that vast area lived in peace and traded with each other. To subjugate and dominate this vast area for their economic and political purposes, these variant groups of people with profound linguistic, cultural, religious and even political differences were coerced to amalgamate into one country. A name was chosen for the people without due consultations. Since then this marriage of inconvenience has been very problematic and difficult to manage especially after they were granted freedom and independence to live together and govern them selves. The marriage became more turbulent following the 1960's political crisis, tribal and religious killings that led to unforgettable genocidal civil war of 1967-70 in which more than three million lives were lost. The civil war created such a wound among the peoples of Nigeria. Even the end of war slogan "No Victor No Vanquished" could not bury the tumultuous and fractured history of a people that has been traumatized and dehumanized. Today, for the various groups of Nigerians to live peacefully and to trust each other has become a very challenging problem.

Many in the past had written on the economic and political amalgamation of Nigeria. The late visionary leader, Chief Obafemi Awolowo once observed that Nigeria is not a nation, but merely a geographical expression. Other notable visionaries and leaders of thought have also referred the Nigerian nation as merely a political expression for the economic and political interest of the colonial master - Britain. The amalgamation of Nigeria as a nation is an issue that must be addressed if we truly desire to live in peace. I believe that without genuine forgiveness and reconciliation, there cannot be order, unity and peace in our country. We cannot move forward as a nation and fulfill our common purpose and destiny if ethnicity, tribalism, corruption and injustice are not addressed in our country. We truly need a national identity that harbors ethnicity and discourages tribal identity. Without righteousness and justice no nation can flourish; or have order, peace, security and prosperity. Justice should be a major concern of any credible and courageous leader who loves and cares for all Nigerian citizens equally. But that has not been the case in Nigeria as far as I can remember. Ours has been a society barricaded by injustice, an openly conspicuous in the manner in which the nation's revenue are shared, award of business contracts, infrastructural development and appointment of political positions. Instead of our leaders to administer justice, they mete injustice on the poor, children, elderly, widows and minorities. No nation can truly flourish if she treats her people that way. Injustice is sin before Almighty God and He hates it with a passion. The injustices in our system must be eradicated otherwise; we cannot truly flourish as a nation. The negative effects of injustice will always hunt and prevent us from reaching our potential as a nation. Corruption and Injustice must be eradicated.

Those who truly love Nigeria must get angry in order to stop this vicious circle of corrupt and inept leaders. Nigerians must resist and refuse men and women who are intoxicated with power, wealth, and fame. We must reject visionless leaders. We must search out for Nigerians who are humble, credible, and qualified to serve the people with courage and compassion. We must look out for men and women with wisdom, courage, and integrity as leaders. This tribal politics must stop for Nigeria to move forward.

I wish the President speedy recovery, and to his family peace and strength during this difficult time.

# TIME FOR THE JOSHUA GENERATION

*"Be strong and courageous, because you will lead these people to inherit the land I swore to their forefathers to give them. Be strong and very courageous...Have I not commanded you? Be strong and courageous. Do not be terrified; do not be discouraged, for the LORD your God will be with you wherever you go."(Joshua 1:6, 9)*

*"Courage is resistance to and mastery of fear, not the absence of fear." Leaders without this virtue will fail to make fair and right tough decisions" – Dr. Myles Munroe.*

*Courage is not absence of fear but to act – Former Senate President, Ken Nnamani*

The title of my article: Time to pray for the President not to play Tribal and dirty politics, generated many negative comments from my readers and critics. The title was called outrageous, senseless, etc. Others questioned why they should pray for the president only while there are millions of Nigerians who are suffering from all kinds of debilitating diseases. Others questioned which god to pray to - God or Allah. Believe it or not, a good number of critics warned me to leave God out of Nigerian politics. It has not been my practice to publish my readers' feedback, comments or viewpoints on a public domain; however, I could not believe the level of frustration, anger, and outright condemnation of the title rather than the content of the article.

I also received a few good comments. One particular writer wrote, "It should have been better to pray for capable, courageous and strong leaders." This is why I

318

chose the title for this piece, which is by the way an excellent ensue to my previous article. I thank all of my readers and critics for their generous comments and feedback.

My intention in this article is not to answer my critics publicly, but to make this point that the idea or mentality to remove Almighty God from the affairs of any nation is a myth and a subtle deception of Satan, because God is the source of all power including political power. Study the biblical prophecy of End Times and discover how world events are clearly and carefully being fulfilled in our very eyes. God is a politician. He uses people, events or circumstances and every available channel to establish His purposes over nations. King David wrote, "For the Kingdom is the Lord's; and He is governor among the nations" (Psalm 22:28). Jesus said to Pilate, "you have no power over me except it is given to you from above" (John 19:11). That means Pilate's authority and power as king was from heaven not earthily. God controls the rise and fall of leaders. He sets up kings and removes kings.

I agree that we ought to pray for capable, courageous and strong leaders to emerge in our nation. It ought to be our moral duty as citizens to offer such prayers to God or to Allah or to any other god in which faith is expressed. Personally, I do not believe for a moment that capable, courageous and strong leaders are lacking in Nigeria. God has blessed every nation and gifted every human being with indescribable talents, abilities and potential. Nigeria does not lack the manpower or talented people who have the capacity, vision and strategy to turn the tide of national decline, infrastructure deterioration, and moral decadence in our country currently. I believe there are skillful politicians in our country today who are competent and have the capacity to deal with the wrenching problems facing the nation.  I believe that the ingredients of good governance such as character, honesty, integrity, vision, dedication, discipline, commitment, sense of justice, trust, loyalty, patriotism, accountability, compassion, and ability to serve selflessly exist within the polity.

Dr. Joseph Nanven Garba in his brilliant book: Fractured History, Elite Shifts and Policy Changes in Nigeria, wrote,

*"Nigeria, to my mind, does not lack real men and women. The ingredients for creating a formidable nation exist. What is lacking is leadership with the political will and the selfless dedication to galvanize the entire nation."*

Good leaders exist inside and outside the shores of Nigeria. What is missing is the political will – godly courage and selfless dedication – passion and divine strength to galvanize the Nigerian masses.

Godly Courage is one of the sterling ingredients of great leadership.  No one can change anything or become a great leader without godly courage and divine strength.  One of the great examples of biblical leaders with godly courage and divine strength is the biblical account of Israel's leader Joshua and how he faced a daunting task of taking the nomadic troops of Israelites into battle against the fortified cities of Canaan.   After the death of the great Jewish leader Moses, Joshua, his protégé was overwhelmed with the enormity of the task of taking more than 3 million Israelites into the fortified cities of Canaan, a land flowing with milk and honey.  God had to command Joshua to be strong and courageous because he will lead the children of Israel into the land of Canaan (Joshua 1: 6-8). God promised to give the Israelites victory despite the overwhelming odds against them.

In Deuteronomy 31:7-8, "Moses summoned Joshua and said to him in the presence f all Israel, "Be strong and courageous, for you must go with this people into he land that the LORD swore to their fore-fathers to give them, and you must divide it among them as their inheritance. The LORD himself goes before you and will be with you; he will never leave you nor forsake you. Do not be afraid; do not be discouraged." Then Moses laid his hands on Joshua before all the assembly of Israel and before the High Priest Eleazer and commissioned Joshua as the LORD instructed. In Deuteronomy 31:14 and 354:9, Joshua was filled with the spirit of wisdom as Moses laid hands on him. Joshua was then presented as the successor of Moses at the tenth of Meeting before all the children of Israel and they listened to him. Joshua courageously led the Israelites into the Promised Land. Moses and Joshua were the epitome of courageous leadership.

The most admired virtues in a leader are character and integrity; however people trust leaders that exhibit godly strength and courage. A strong leader is a secure leader in God as well as before the people. Such leaders are always courageous, compassionate, and competent individuals. Great leaders know how to confront crisis and challenges with courage and compassion. Also we noticed the leadership transition from Moses to Joshua, we can observe how Moses mentored Joshua and before his death, formally presented Joshua to the people and publicly charged him to be strong and courageous (Deuteronomy 31:1-8). His personal preparation and public recognition of his successor made the leadership transition smooth and unambiguous. Leadership transfer doesn't have to be your son, daughter, and family member or friend. A leader must be chosen based on preparation, training, ability, integrity and especially by the guidance and direction of God. The true measure of leadership success is when a leader joyfully transfers leadership responsibilities to a well trained, groomed and developed leader. What we are witnessing in our nation today is a crude, wrongful and premature leadership succession that is capable of throwing the entire nation in a political muddle.

Courage is also the virtue and ability that enables a leader to make wise decisions and take tough actions. According to Dr. Myles Munroe, an expert on leadership development and potential, writes, "Courage is resistance to and mastery of fear, not the absence of fear. Leaders without this virtue will fail to make fair and tough decisions." Leaders need courage to make tough and right decisions. Leading is hard work and our nation is in dire need of leaders who have the godly courage and divine strength to lead the people out of economic, social, cultural, political, religious, and moral darkness. We have been in this captivity and darkness for too long.

Throughout history, leaders who have made impact are those who have led with divine strength and great courage. The father of the American nation, Abraham Lincoln did not only abolish slave trade through the Emancipation Proclamation of 1863, but he was courageous enough to unite a nation and preserved the Union through a policy of reconciliation despite the apposition from his party. The British Prime Minster, Sir Winston Church and his American counterpart, Franklin Roosevelt provided courageous leadership that led to the defeat of German Adolph Hitler. Their decisive leadership helped rebuild Europe and restored the world from economic crisis and world war. Rev. Dr. Martin Luther King Jr. prophetically and courageously inspired the United States of America and the world to judge people by the content of their character and not by the color of their skin. His powerful oratory and courageous leadership freed an entire nation from hate, bigotry and self-destruction and gave millions freedom and hope around the world.

Nelson Mandela an anti-apartheid activist and international icon of freedom defeated the apartheid regime of South Africa because of his courage, strength and personal integrity. Mandela courageously stood against apartheid and won an insurmountable war against apartheid and discrimination. The late American president, Ronald Reagan challenged his Russian counterpart, Mikhail Gorbaceov to tear down the walls of Germany otherwise the two countries will meet in the woods. Recently Barack Obama with an unbridled faith and audacity of courage against all odds shocked the world when he became elected the first black president of the United States of America. These leaders and more that I cannot list here epitomized the true essence of transformational, courageous and great leadership.

During Nigeria's independence struggle, our nationalist leaders showed such courage against the British imperialist regime to achieve Nigeria's independence and freedom from Britain. A few years ago, the former Senate President, Chief Ken Nnamani averted what could have been another horrible dark time in Nigeria when he and some of his colleagues at the Hollowed Chambers said NO and voted against the Third Term Agenda, which was the main ingredient of the 1999 Constitution Amendment. That heroic act and vision on the part of Senator Ken Nnamani saved the nation from plunging into abyss of civil war and put Nigeria's fledging democracy to a genuine path of political freedom. Chief Ken Nnamani exhibited great courage and divine strength despite the inducement with millions of Naira and perhaps possible threat to his life, family and career, rather he chose to do what is right and just no matter the consequences. Assuming the Third Term Agenda had succeeded, it would have probably led to another civil unrest with an incalculable loss of human lives. Senator Ken Nnamani did not derelict on his constitutional duties. His heroic act saved the soul of Nigeria. I believe he is one guy who is capable of leading the nation today.

Former Senate President Ken Nnamani and other courageous leaders have also spoken out concerning the vacuum in Aso Rock and the brazen neglect of the Nigerian constitution since President Yar'Adua became sick. Yet, it has not occurred to David Mark, the current Senate president to review the constitution concerning the absence of the head of a country who has been away for over two weeks now and whether President Yar'Adua followed proper protocol and procedure in abdicating his official duties for medical treatment in Saudi Arabia. We know that he is sick and we wish him well, but the affairs of the nation must go on. He is not the owner of Nigeria. I read where the president's wife, and his sisters, in-laws and wishy-washy friends are saying that those who called for Yar'Adua's resignation are "enemies of democracy." Nigeria is an interesting nation.

Frankly the President's continued hospitalization in Saudi Arabia and the vacuum it has created in the federal government is another sobering reminder of the vicious cycle of Nigeria's tumultuous leadership history. Where is the moral conscience of Nigerian politicians especially those who support the status quo and vacuum in Aso Rock today? There is a serious crisis of conscience in the hearts of these men and women in power today. How can a country go on with the critical affairs of government without a president or a delegated leader? It is utterly despicable that a nation of over 140 million with enormous human potential will tolerate this kind of autocratic and tyrannical leadership.

Leadership is a divine and a sacred duty and our society is desperately in need for courageous and strong leaders. Leadership is hard work that requires divine strength, godly wisdom and great courage that can only be given by God. Leading involves great sacrifice and selfless service to the people. Jesus Christ, the greatest leader of all time made this powerful statement, "whoever wants to become great (leader) among must be your servant, and whoever wants to be first (leader) must be your slave (servant) juts as the Son of Man did not come to be served, but to give his life as a ransom" (Matthew 20:26-28). Jesus profoundly made it clear that if one desires to serve in any position of authority and power that one must be willing to serve, be a slave and ready to die. This is what genuine, pure and godly leadership is all about. President Yar'Adua is an advocate of servant leadership and rule of law and now he can't uphold what he advocates.

What we see and read in the media today about Nigeria is not leadership but dictatorship. Today leaders want to be served rather than serve the people. Today's leaders do not seem to have the interest and the welfare of the people at heart. Most of today's leaders are rather driven by ego, pride arrogance, greed and self-importance. We cannot truly experience any genuine peace, progress and prosperity until men and women of abiding faith and believe in the principles of freedom, equality, peace, security, right to life and pursuit of happiness for all are enthroned in position of power; men and women who have the wisdom, courage, and compassion to lead.

The problem with Nigeria is that the game of politics has become the quickest and easiest way for instant wealth. No wonder, Transparency International came out recently with a report in which they stated that Nigerian politicians are the highest paid in world, which is not true anyway. We know how they get paid and I know that TI knows it too well also. Even in rich countries, that is not the case. In the U.S, for instance, the CEO of a medium size company makes more money than the president of the United States of America. Imagine what most CEO's of fortune 1000, 500, 100 or 50 companies in America make. Those CEO's will not for a minute accept to be president of this country. Can you imagine asking Bill Gates to vie for the presidency of the United States? He will not even think about it. Even if he does, he will ask not to be paid. This is a man who is currently giving his money away through his foundation to support education and health programs. Most Americans get involve in politics after they are retired as millionaires. Arnold Schwarzenegger makes just one dollar as the governor of California, the largest and the richest state in the Union. The young folks, who join politics start making money after their political career. When they leave politics, they write books, give speeches, teach at reputable universities or head foundations – profit or non-profit. Complete opposite of what is obtainable in Nigeria. What we have in Nigeria is a recycle of politicians because that's only what they know to do. It is a shame.

Another problem I see in Nigeria is the premature exposure to power and leadership and perhaps one of the major roots of Nigerian leadership failure and the archenemy of peace, progress and stability of democracy and civil rule in Nigeria and in most of Africa. Our history is strewn with many examples of people coming into power overnight without knowing how to handle the pressures and weighty issues of governance. The premature exposure to power and positions of authority always creates strife, agitation, and chaos. It also undermines justice, which results in all forms of political ruffians, unrest, violence and crisis. People with great talents, abilities and potentials have been destroyed due to premature exposure to position of power and authority.

Today, we see all kinds of people with great political aspiration joining the game of politics without adequate training, education and public accountability. As a result, we have witnessed, and still witnessing some of the worst forms of anarchy, dictatorship, and tyranny. The result has been abuse, vandalism, embezzlement or intoxication under the influence of power even to the point of insanity. Nigerians have suffered unimaginable pain throughout history because of premature involvement in various positions of power and authority. In their insatiable lust for power some will do anything and will not desist from using the most savage, crude, barbaric, unethical, and inhumane ways to achieve their ends. The overall impact has been indescribable sufferings and seemingly incurable wounds inflicted on countless lives.

The nation and her citizens need national healing and reconciliation, which can only come through forgiveness and by the power of God. There cannot be healing without justice and justice requires punishment. Without forgiveness, justice and righteousness no nation can flourish; or enjoy any order, peace, security and prosperity. God's mercy, love and compassion always precede justice. Justice should be a major concern of any credible and courageous leader who loves and cares for all Nigerian citizens equally. Nigerians must enthrone strong, capable, competent and credible people in position of leadership and power. The Nigerian people must say now "Enough is enough." Men and women of conscience, courage, strength, and compassion who truly love this country must stand up now to save the sole and unity Nigeria before it is too late.

Unity is strength and a vital leadership obligation. Great and quality leadership produces unity and wise leaders are willing to sacrifice in order to sustain unity. Unity produces treasured memories and enduring relationships. To have a prosperous nation, every Nigerian must pursue unity and peace. We must learn how to create, instill and appreciate unity. We must put aside the sycophants and those who create disunity among us. A wise leader does all he or she can to build unity. Unity means so much for the development and progress of any nation. It is a pre-requisite to progress and sustained success. Unity rarely happens. Unity is essential. It has to be sought and taught. Jesus said a house dividend against it couldn't stand. He spoke a truth that is applicable to every human endeavors and situations. As a nation we should not be afraid to standup against agents of disunity within the polity. This is also an absolute responsibility of truly genuine and authentic leaders.

The Joshua generation must stand up now to finish the work of national reconciliation and nation building. When Joshua was faced with the daunting task of taking the children of Israelites into battle against the fortified cities of Canaan, he was overwhelmed. But the Lord commanded Joshua not to fear. He told him, "Be strong and have courage, for I am with you wherever you go." The Nigerian masses must be strong and courageous to confront the great enemy of the Nigerian state. We must be strong and have godly courage to confront the enemies of democracy, progress and prosperity. We must be strong and courageous in face of oppression and repression from the autocratic and tyrannical leadership. We must say NO

328

to bad leaders, tribal and ethnic hatred, , injustice, greed, corruption, abuse and looting of public treasury, embezzlement , tax evasion, political godfathers and kidnappings, ignorance, poverty, , idolatry, jealousy, envy, satanic anger , religious intolerance and hypocrisy, moral bankruptcy, evil rituals, divination, sorcery, witchcraft, voodoo, and satanic worship.

We must be strong and have the godly courage to take back our nation from the giants and enemies of progress and civil society.

Long Live Nigeria!

## PROF. (MRS.) DORA NKEM AKUNYILI REBELS AGAINST LAWLESSNESS, WEAK LEADERSHIP, AND A FAILING NATION

*Therefore hear the word of the LORD, you scoffers who rule this people in Jerusalem. You boast, "We have entered into a covenant with death, with the grave we have made an agreement. When an overwhelming scourge sweeps by, it cannot touch us, for we have made a lie our refuge and falsehood our hiding place." (Isaiah 28:14-15)*

*"For I know how many are your offense and how great your sins. You oppress the righteous and take bribes and you deprive the poor justice in the courts." (Amos 5:12)*

*"Courage is resistance to and mastery of fear, not the absence of fear." Leaders without this virtue will fail to make fair and right tough decisions" – Dr. Myles Munroe.*

*"Courage is not absence of fear but to act." – Former Senate
President, Ken Nnamani*

Now that Anambra State governor's election is behind us
and according to my estimation, it was a transparent and
fair election. The right candidate, the incumbent Governor,
Mr. Peter Obi has been peacefully re-elected. Despite fears
of political thuggery, violence, missing ballots, etc that mar
the governor's reelection in Ekiti last year, which was
feared could happen in Anambra State governor's election,
INEC Chairman, Prof. Maurice Iwu, proved all wrong and
has shown that he can conduct organized and peaceful
election. I salute him and encourage him to use the same
strategies employed in Anambra State in the national
elections next year. I also give my kudos to the
Anambrarians for voting for the right candidate.

The Anambra State governor's election will be a topic for
another time, but for now let us focus on the president's
handover saga, memo and indomitable spirit of Prof.
Akunyili against the lawlessness in the Federal Executive
Council (FEC). Since President Yar'Adua's illness became
publicly known due to his absence and protracted
hospitalization in Saudi Arabia, the nation has been thrown
into a constitutional crisis mainly on the modality to hand
over power temporarily to the Vice President Dr. Goodluck
Jonathan so that he could function with executive powers
pending on the return and recovery of President Musa
Yar'Adua.

Even though the 1999 constitution was not explicit on the
process of power transfer from presidency to VP,

nevertheless, section 146(1) states clearly that, "the vice-president shall hold the office of president if the office of president becomes vacant by reason of death or resignation, impeachment, permanent incapacity or the removal of the president from office for any other reason in accordance with Section 143 of this constitution." You don't have to be a constitutional law expert to notice five specific reasons listed in the section 146(1) of the 1999 constitution for power transfer. Furthermore, section 145 requires the President of the Federal Republic of Nigeria to notify the Senate President and the Speaker of the House of Representatives in writing whenever he or she is out of the country for vacation or medical treatment so that the vice-president can assume presidential powers and run the country while the president is away.

Presumably the ailing president has not transmitted this letter to the Senate and House of Representatives or that his close aides are just playing kangaroo politics with 150 million citizens of Nigeria. The handover saga that is on-going to the third month tells me that something is fundamentally wrong with Nigerian leaders and that Nigeria is not yet one nation. For sure, it is a nation founded on lies, falsehood, and hypocrisy with overwhelming and unimaginable scourge. There is no structure for justice, righteousness and compassion and the Nigerian people especially the nations' leaders are evil, wicked and rebellious people.

Among those are the president's chief Physician and medical team, who lied to the Nigerian people about Yar'Adua's illness, but it does not take divine revelation to know that the president's long time hospitalization and absence were ominous signs of serious health problems.

331

Now we know that the President has failing lungs, liver problems, some form of skin cancer and acute pericarditis. These are serious health conditions. How on earth can the president suffer from these serious medical conditions and still function as the president of the largest and most complex black nation on the planet? I believe that the president's wife and the president's aides are bunch of hypocrites, who do not care about the people of Nigeria but rather their own egoistic and personal agenda.

I also believe that the continued political theater and handover saga was compounded by the lies and falsehood of the presidents' cabinet ministers, whose ambition is to capitalize on his illness and his medical absence to control power and abuse the system. The chief among them is Mr. Michael Aondoakaa, the Attorney General of the Federation and Minister of Justice, who declared that a vacuum has not been created in the Presidency as a result of the ailing condition of Alhaji Umaru Musa Yar'Adua since the presidential system of government allows the president to exercise his powers anywhere in the world. He stated then that President Yar'Adua could rule Nigerian from anywhere.

This is a very serious and mischievous statement. The AGF, a Chief Law enforcement officer, an expert in matters of law and letters, should be working to defend the Nigerian constitution and the people of Nigeria and not work against her. He preferred to breach the constitution of Nigerian by defending his boss. Chief Michael Aondoakaa breached the Nigerian constitution, which he supposed to uphold. He committed an act of treason against the Federal Republic of Nigeria, which is punishable by imprisonment. The AGF did not realize that there is a great danger playing such falsehood to defend the president in matters that are so clear and explicit. He does not have any political wisdom at all.

By the way, Mr. Michael Aondoakaa was brought in by President Yar'Adua to do exactly what he is doing. He has been the brainchild and force behind the removal of Prof. Charles Soludo as CBN governor, and Mallam Nuhu Ribadu, head of Economic Financial Crime Commission (EFCC). He has been working tirelessly to free most of the corrupt governors such as Ayo fayose, Joshua Dariye, Orji kalu, Peter Odili, Borde George, and other government officials from the EFCC charges of money laundering and corruption. Remember, Chief Borde George was the main sponsor of Yar'Adua's presidency. So, the AGF is playing the card that he was appointed to do. As one writer clearly stated, he is the leader of the new Benue TIV mafia in Nigerian politics. No wonder, his cousin, also a Benue man is now the Chief Justice of the Federation among other Benue personalities in the Federal Government.

Another important personality in the handover saga is off-course the President's wife, First Lady Turai Yar'Adua, who should not be exonerated either from the bunch of sycophants that lied and deceived the Nigerian people about President's illness. She insisted that her husband is capable to rule Nigeria and even rained curses on eminent Nigerian leaders, including Arewa elders and called them enemies of democracy when they called for her husband to handover power to his vice. At the early stages of the president's handover saga, some political prostitutes even insinuated that the First Lady should take over as President of Nigeria as she did in Katsina State as governor during her husband's long absence from office due to medical treatment overseas. Unfortunately, Nigeria is not Katsina.

Nigeria is a 36- state federation with Abuja as capital city. It is a much bigger and larger political landscape than Katsina and with serious national issues and international matters to deal with. Those who insinuated such ideas and plans are egoistic politicians, who think that we are in a monarchial system of government. Later, First lady Turai opted for VP, should Dr. Goodluck Jonathan be elevated to the office of the president. I just think that Mrs. Turai Yar'Adua is power drunk and a dreamer. What we have read and seen so far about this handover saga and lawlessness is just a complete charade of democratic government that could lead to anarchy and breakup of an already fractured nation.

Then, we have the "dishonorable" lawmakers of both Lower and Upper House, The Federal Executive Council (FEC), the Cabinet Ministers, the Governors Forum, and PDP leadership, all of whom insisted at one time or another that there is no vacancy in Aso Rock. Despite the public outrage and consistent call by former Nigerian leaders, eminent Elders Group, eminent Nigerians, G53, G31, 3G, North Central governors, Anti Military and Pro-Democracy Groups, Human Right Organizations, Civil Liberties Organization, Religious leaders, Socio-Cultural and Political Groups, protests led by indomitable Prof. Wole Soyinka and Spiritual leader, Pastor Tunde Bakare, democracy marches held in U.S., U.K and several other places, and among other public outcry, the FEC dismissed calls for Yar'Adua's exit .

The Governors Forum, after a late night meeting in Abuja early last month refused to back-down against President

334

Umaru Musa Yar'Adua but rather dismissed those calling for his resignation as traitors and betrayers of democracy. Both the Senate and the House of Representatives also rejected the motion to handover to the vice-president, Dr. Goodluck Jonathan. In fact, most of the members of the FEC, Cabinets' Ministers, Governors Forum, Senate and House of Representative members lacked courage and political will to do what is right for the nation. Their attitude and behavior show that they are not working for the Nigerian people but rather for their personal agenda and selfish interests. Both leaders at the Senate and House of Representatives lacked honor and moral integrity.

While the political saga public and outcry was going on, the AGF orchestrated the swearing-in of his cousin as the new Chief Justice of the Federation by the outgoing Chief Justice, which is the first time this has happened in the history of Nigeria. This is usually a ceremony that is performed by the President or in the absence of the president, the vice president. To make the matter worse, Mr. Michael Aondoakaa in cohort with close aide's of the president forged and signed into law the 2009 supplementary budget in order to prevent Vice President from assuming the position of acting President in the absence of President Yar'Adua. There is no debate that the people involved in forging the president's signature on the 2009 supplementary budget breached the Nigerian constitution and therefore committed an act of treason against the Federal Republic of Nigeria, which is punishable by imprisonment.

One cannot also exonerate the former president Olusegun Obasanjo, for imposing Alhaji Umaru Musa Yar'Adua on Nigerians. President Yar'Adua current saga will be a major part of Obasanjo's legacy and bully leadership. Now we are reading that Yar'Adua knew one year ahead of time, that Olusegun Obasanjo, considered tipping him to be his successor in order to pay back to his family for his friendship with General Shehu Musa Yar'Adua, who was Chief of Staff, Supreme Headquarters during the Murtala/Obasanjo military regime (1976 – 1979). Yet, OBJ recently lied at a 7th Trust Annual Dialogue, last week Thursday in Abuja, that he never considered governor Yar'Adua in his choices for his successor and even called upon God to punish him, if he knew that he was so sick and could not govern Nigeria.

Even though Nigerians are forgetful people, it was just a little over two years ago, that we learned a new election buzzword when former president Obasanjo vowed that the 2007 election is '**do or die for him**' while campaigning for Musa Yar'Adua. He told the mammoth crowd in Aba few weeks before the presidential election in 2007, that he would not hand over power to crooks and criminals. In fact, he campaigned more for Governor Yar'Adua than he did during his 1999 and 2003 presidential campaigns. Former president Obasanjo talking about honor and morality at 7th Trust Annual Dialogue exposed his falsehood and lies. How can he open his mouth to ask God to punish him for an act that was carefully orchestrated and carried out to give favor to his family friend and off-course the Northern Oligarchy for the promise that was not only agreed within PDP but also a way to pay back for the murder of Chief M. K. O Abiola. Where is the honor and moral integrity of today's leaders?

By the way, Chief Olusegun Obasanjo has not been very successful in transferring power to his successor. He has the tendency to enthrone incapable people to succeed him each time. In 1978, after his robust though not exceptional military government, he handed over to the first democratic elected president of Alhaji Shehu Shagari, a primary school teacher who was then handpicked by the Northern king makers to lead Nigeria. Shehu Shari's government was so corrupt that the military waited patiently for the end of the first term to take over the affairs of governance from the inept and visionless government of Alhaji Shehu Shagari. That period led to the dictatorial military government of Buhari, IBB, and Abacha and in 1999 the presidential democratic election of Chief Olusegun Obasanjo. Again, at the end of his two terms, he has made the same very mistake to hand over to Alhaji Musa Yar'dua, who was not a candidate until one month to PDP presidential primaries. At that time, so much was said and written about Yar'Adua's selection and his health. Many of us questioned Governor Yar'dua's ability, strength, courage and boldness to deal with the many challenges facing a complex nation called Nigeria.

Nevertheless, President Yar'Adua came into the office in May 2007 with such high hopes that he would continue the struggle against corruption. He was reputed as a man of character, integrity, transparency, rule of law, due process, and most especially a servant leader, which he popularized among the Nigerian masses. He also said that he would be

337

a listener and lead with fear of God. During his presidential campaign tours, he promised that he would continue the policies and economic reforms of ex-president Obasanjo. President Yar'Adua admitted that Nigerians are going through hell and promised to create 40 million jobs within 10 years. He promised to boast economic growth and empower all Nigerians to become small business owners rather than meddling into politics of greed, violence and corruption.

He stated that he would have zero tolerance for public officials who steal and embezzle pubic funds. Yet he has reversed most of policies of his predecessor and even sacked Mallam Nuhu Ribadu, the anti corruption czar. Today President Yar'Adua is hospitalized in Saudi Arabia for acute pericarditis ailment with other serious medical conditions for well over two months while his VP, Dr. Goodluck Jonathan has not been officially delegated to carry on the presidential duties.

At the meantime, the president's wife, his closet aides and dishonorable lawmakers are toying with the millions of Nigeria and off-course the nation's unity. The Niger Delta militancy has resumed despite the little progress that was made. Ethno-religious crises have also resumed in the Northern States with religious riots, which has claimed many lives and destroyed properties and church buildings. Also clashes have erupted between Muslims and Christians in Jos and Bauchi State, in which many people have lost their precious lives. Religious extremism, violence and killings of Christians in Northern Nigeria and the militancy in the Niger Delta are ominous signs of overwhelming scourge of a nation that is not yet one nation. Meanwhile, the nation is still saddled with other serious challenges such as unemployment, poverty, diseases, lack of drinkable water, lack of good roads, lack of power supply, bribery and corruption, injustice, political assassination, armed robbery and kidnapping, lawlessness, ethnic & tribal hatred, false religious leaders and prophets, murderers, and ungodly leaders, among many other issues.

Internationally, Nigeria's image has been rubbished further after the failed 2009 Christmas bombing attack by a Nigerian, which Prof. Dora is desperately fighting to re-brand. Nigerians are still looked upon as crooks and criminals, drug peddlers, credit card forgers, child trafficking, '419' tycoons and now as terrorists, thanks to the young Nigerian Umar Farouk Abdul Mutallab. The Senate and Information & Communication Minister have condemned the US action for enlisting Nigeria as a terrorist nation, but the damage is already done.

Despite the re-branding efforts of Prof. Akunyili, nothing seemed to be working. I think it is based on these issues that gave her the moral anger, strength and courage to rebel against the lawlessness and abuse of power in Nigerian government today. And so last week Wednesday, when Professor Dora Akunyili, at the Federal Executive Council, presented a memorandum on the need for the President to transmit a letter to the National Assembly to enable the vice -president to act as 'Acting President.' The members of FEC were taken by surprise and they shouted at her to follow proper procedure and order.

It is intriguing that it will be Prof. Akunyili, the only woman in FEC to make such a moral call and condemn the lawlessness, lies, falsehood and satanic conspiracy of the members of FEC, Cabinet Ministers, Governors forum, Senate and House of Representatives, the Northern Oligarchy and family members of Yar'Adua. Her memo, no doubt was succinct and bold. She has earned my admiration just like former Minister of Finance, Mrs. (Dr) Ngozi Okonjo-Iweala, who refused weak leadership, falsehood and the callousness of men in position of power and authority. Her courage to face the consequences reminds me also of another hero, former Senate President, Chief Ken Nnamani, who averted what could have been a horrible time in Nigeria when he and some of his colleagues at the Hollowed Chambers said NO and voted against the Third Term Agenda, which was the main ingredient of the 1999 Constitution Amendment.

Prof. Dora Nkem Akunyili, before her appointment as Information and Communication Minister in President Yar'Adua's cabinet, was the former Director General of National Agency for Food and Drug Administration and Control (NAFDAC), during former president Olusegun Obasanjo's regime. At NAFDAC, she was the indomitable spirit and lioness who fought against pharmaceutical drug barons and tycoons for manufacturing illicit and importing illegal medical drugs into the country that was killing people rather curing them. Despite death threats toward her and her family, she fought like a lion and helped Obasanjo's government to remedy the satanically conspiracy of illicit medical drug manufacturing and trafficking in Nigerian especially in Southeast region.

Prof. Akunyili is a fair and honest human being. She is a strong and focused leader, a visionary and courageous leader. Is she the woman president that Nigeria is yet to have?  Frankly, her courage, personal integrity and vision qualify her to such a high position and honor if Nigeria is a nation that recognizes leadership skills, vision and ability. Professor Akunyili is also a virtuous woman.  As a mother of six and a grand mother, she is intelligent, elegant, confident, dedicated, and tenacious.  She is also kind, courageous, and compassionate woman of great strength and with heart of a warrior.  She is unlike her colleagues in FEC, who have used their position of influence, power, prominence and authority to enrich themselves and amass millions of dollars for their children and great grand children.  She is a genuine, true, pure, courageous, and super lady.  Her memo and courage to condemn lawlessness especially during this political theater, handover saga, lawlessness and constitutional crisis, is very admirable.  She has left a remarkable, legendary leadership and lasting legacy for our country and the whole world.

In a nutshell, Prof. Dora Nkem Akunyili is a woman of wisdom, courage and compassionate leader.  She was willing to sacrifice her life in order to save Nigeria and serve Nigerians.  She has earned my admiration and truly exemplified my long life call and cry for courageous leadership.  The heroic act and vision of Prof. Dora will save the nation from plunging into chaos and put Nigeria's fledging democracy back to genuine political democracy. Prof. Akunyili has exhibited great courage and divine strength despite the consequences and perhaps possible threat to her life, family and career.  She chose to do what is moral and right no matter the consequences.  Her heroic act will save Nigeria from the brink of collapse and from the peevish plans of Yar'Adua close aides, whenever Dr.

Goodluck Jonathan is elevated to become the president of Nigeria.

May the LORD bless you, Mrs. Dora Nkem Akunyili and keep you; May the LORD make His face shine upon you and be gracious to you; May the LORD turn His face toward you and give you peace" (Numbers 6:24). Amen.

GODLY WISDOM FOR LEADERS

## OUR LEADERS NEED GODLY WISDOM - PART I

In my last essay: "Leadership Wisdom - World's Greatest Need", I stated that leadership wisdom is the greatest need for leaders of this century. I also defined leadership wisdom as the ability and capacity to lead wisely, morally, courageously and compassionately. In that article I also concluded by saying that God kind of leadership is the only leadership that can lead our societies into real and genuine change, which includes social, economic, political, moral and spiritual prosperity. Because of the divine nature of leadership, no one can effectively lead another fellow human being(s) without the gift of godly wisdom. In this article, I like to examine wisdom, the source of wisdom and how to receive the gift of wisdom, which is one of the most precious gifts for genuine, pure and great leadership.

In Nigeria today, many who aspire to the honorable duty of service do not show any form of wisdom - human or heavenly wisdom. They do not even consider wisdom as an important ingredient of leadership. Today's leaders do not think about wisdom as a character trait that needs to be carefully cultivated for leadership. And this is why there are so much misery, poverty, hunger, disease, pain, and desperation in the richest continent of the world. The desperation in our country today led a nineteen year Iwuchukwu Amara Tochi, who supposed to be attending college with promises and hope of a bright and prosperous future to risk it all by carrying 700 grams of heroin to Singapore, a country that has harsh laws for drug

343

trafficking and does not tolerate such illegality and criminality. Despite the intervention of President Obasanjo and United Nations, Singaporean authorities still went ahead to hang a 21 year old to death after he had served about two years in jail.

The sad end of Tochi is one among many untold and unreported deaths being suffered by Nigerian youths in their quest and desperation to leave Nigeria. I have never seen or been to a country where its citizens young and old queue at foreign embassies from 2 AM in the morning with all kinds of papers and documents soliciting and begging for any kind of visa to leave their country. There are many young Nigerians who continue to loose their lives in their quest and desperation to get out of Nigeria through road transport and seas. Recently, the world was shocked about the Tanzanian who in his desperation to come to America hid himself inside the baggage wind of the Aircraft. Off-course without being told, there was no way, he would survive because he is a living being not inanimate object like luggages. Many of these kinds of stories paint a picture of a continent that continues to deny her people life and destiny due to inept and corrupt leadership. Many Africans who successfully make it to America, Europe or Asia are being constantly humiliated and subjugated to do menial jobs despite that many of them are skilled and have quality education. However, I will not also negate the fact that many Nigerians as well as other Africans have contributed immensely and continue to add value socially, economically, politically and morally to their host and new found countries. Tochi's hanging in Singapore is a sad story that clearly reveals the pain and suffering in Nigeria today and exposes the inept and visionless leadership that has hijacked the affairs of the nation. The Word of God clearly teaches that when the righteous (wise) rule, the people rejoice but when the unrighteous (unwise or wicked) rule, the people suffer. When the wise govern, peace, wealth, favor, happiness, justice, power, safety, protection, prosperity will come and nations will listen to her. But when the wicked and unwise rule, war, poverty, bitterness, anger, insecurity will come and nations will not listen but laugh and make mockery of her (1 Kings 10:23-25; Ezra 7:25).

Let me return to my subject. Apart from the indescribable gift of life, there is no other gift that is more important than wisdom. For leaders, it is even more precious than any inherent leadership ability or learned leadership skills that a leader may have. King Solomon realized the need for godly wisdom for leadership despite his natural attributes and family heritage when he prayed in First Kings 3:7-9 for wisdom and discerning heart to govern the people of Israel. No wonder, he wrote in the Book of Proverbs some 6500 years ago, "Wisdom is the principal thing; therefore get wisdom; and with all thy getting get understanding (Proverbs 4:7). Here King Solomon makes it abundantly clear that godly wisdom is a very important ingredient of leadership as well as a key element for supernatural living. The Apostle James wrote to the Saints at the Church in Jerusalem, "If any of you lacks wisdom, he should ask God, who gives generously to all without finding fault, and it will be given to him (James 1:5). If you are called in any fashion to lead people, you must pray and ask for godly wisdom. It is impossible to lead effectively, efficiently, genuinely and compassionately without godly wisdom.

**What is Wisdom?** - The Merriam-Webster dictionary defines wisdom as:

1. The accumulated philosophic or scientific learning;
2. Knowledge - the ability to discern inner qualities and relationships;
3. Insight - a good sense;
4. Judgment - generally accepted belief.

Basically, wisdom is wise attitude, belief, or course of action. It is teachings of the ancient wise men. Wisdom is knowledge of what is true or right coupled with good judgment. It is a scholarly knowledge or learning. Wisdom is the noun form of the word wise, which is the ability to judge properly what is true or right, showing or based on good judgment, learned or erudite, discerning, judicious, prudent, crafty, cunning, sage and sensible. These definitions are not far fetched from biblical meaning of wisdom. The Bible teaches that when a person demonstrates exceptional ability in a craft or art, that person is said to have what the Hebrew language calls HOKOMA, which is translated in English as "skill," However, the wisdom that is used mostly in the Bible especially in the New Testament writings of the Apostles Paul and James, refer to the quality and capacity that enables one to live an outstanding, exceptional and excellent life. Biblical wisdom therefore relates to prudence, understanding, discernment, instruction, insight, knowledge, guidance, sound judgment, faithfulness, humility, justice, diligence, trust, servant-hood and reliance upon God. Biblical wisdom relates to eternal perspectives on life, purpose and destiny.

In the writings of James, the Apostle makes a clear distinction between wisdom of men and wisdom of God. He writes,

*"Who is wise and understanding among you? Let him show it by his good life, by deeds done in the humility that comes from*

*wisdom. But if you harbor bitter envy and selfish ambition in your hearts, do not boast about it or deny the truth. Such wisdom does not come down from heaven but is earthly, unspiritual, of the devil. For where you have envy and selfish ambition, there you find disorder and every evil practice. But the wisdom that comes from heaven is first of all pure; then peace loving, considerate, submissive, full of mercy and good fruit, impartial and sincere" (James 3:13-17).*

In the above passage, James tells us that there are two kinds of wisdom:

1. First, we have wisdom of men, or wisdom of the world, or earthly wisdom, human wisdom, unspiritual wisdom and devilish wisdom. Earthly wisdom is full of bitter envy, selfish ambition, disorder and every evil practices. The Apostle Paul sums up human wisdom as foolishness to God (1 Corinthians 2:4; 13; 2:20-25; 3:19).
2. Second, there is wisdom of God, or heavenly wisdom, or spiritual wisdom, or divine wisdom. Heavenly wisdom is pure, peaceful, loving, considerate, submissive, full of mercy, impartial and sincere. The Apostle Paul calls it superior or divine wisdom and this wisdom is foolishness to man (1 Corinthians 2:4-5; Proverbs 18:2; Isaiah 55:8-9).

Here we see that there are two distinct kinds of wisdom - the wisdom of God and wisdom of the world and we must not confuse the two. James also tells us some of the characteristics of these two kinds of wisdom. We shall examine them next time and see the merits (benefits) and demerits of these two kinds of wisdom.

**Source of True Wisdom**

The source of true wisdom comes from the Fatherhood of God or what theologians call Trinity. Only God is the source of leadership wisdom and His wisdom is evident in the beauty, splendor, variety, order and intricacies of His creation. His wisdom is also evident in the persons, powers and authority that He has ordained for mankind.

First, the Bible teaches that wisdom is a gift from God. The Bible also makes it abundantly clear that people are called to leadership first and foremost by God, second by people and finally through circumstances. Then the leader is anointed, commissioned and empowered for leadership. Leaders are not appointed or elected as the case of many leaders in our society today. In God's economy and system, leaders are selected. Therefore, God is the true source of wisdom and a genuine call to leadership. The great Patriarch Job asked the question, but where can wisdom be found? Where does understanding dwell? Where does wisdom come from? (Job 28:12, 20) He answered those same questions in verse 28; the fear of the LORD is wisdom and to shun evil is understanding. To God belong wisdom and power, counsel and understanding (Job 12:13). King Solomon wrote in Proverbs 2:6, For the LORD gives wisdom, from his mouth come knowledge and understanding. The fear of the LORD is the beginning of wisdom (Proverbs 9:10). King David in Psalms 119:98-100 writes that the law and statues of God make us wiser and gives us understanding.

Second, the Apostle Paul writes in First Corinthians 12:24 and Colossians 2:3, that Christ is the wisdom of God in whom are hidden all the treasures of wisdom and knowledge. Jesus Christ is the supreme manifestation of the wisdom of God (1 Corinthians 1:30). Jesus is the wisdom of God. The wisdom of Jesus is greater than the Wisdom of Solomon and any other prophet who had lived. Jesus Christ is the epitome and embodiment of pure and true wisdom. This wisdom is available to those who desire and earnestly seek for it (Proverbs 1:20-33; 8:1-36).

Third and finally godly wisdom comes from the Holy Spirit, who unleashes gifts, talents and skills to people who desire him. (Exodus 31:1-4; 36:1; Daniel 1:4). Wisdom is the one of the gifts the Holy Spirit can give to you as a leader (1 Corinthians 12). Even though the Holy Spirit is the invisible person of the Trinity, yet we know, fell, hear, recognize and worship his presence

There is no doubt that godly wisdom is the most important element for genuine, strong, courageous, compassionate and great leadership. The Bible teaches that wisdom is more precious than rubies and nothing you desire compare with her, "How much better to gain wisdom that gold; to choose understanding rather than silver (Proverbs 8:11). As a leader, you must treasure godly wisdom far more than silver, gold and precious jewels. Leadership wisdom is the application of knowledge in a right way. It is a wise, visionary, compassionate and spirit-empowered leadership. It is the spiritual capacity to see and conduct life from God's point of view (Proverbs 1:2). Leadership wisdom involves making right choices and doing what is right according to God's will as revealed in His Word and the leading of the Holy Spirit (Romans 8:4-7). It is leadership that involves divine initiation and less of human intervention. It is the ability to create an enviable environment in which followers can thrive, prosper and reach their fullest potential. It is leadership that is inspired and empowered by God. It is about being an excellent steward of God's human and natural resources. Any leadership apart from the above is worldly, foolish and satanic. If you are called to lead, God wants to instill in you divine wisdom for leadership. This divine ingredient if carefully cultivated and developed will turn you into a great and admirable leader.

Today, our leaders are in dire need of godly wisdom. Only God empowered and Spirit led leadership or what I called supernatural leadership can deliver the peoples of Africa from hunger, poverty, penury, misery, pain, diseases and war. African nations have not made any significant progress since they gained independence from their colonial masters some 45-50 years ago. Rather the most blessed continent on the face of this earth is frazzled in violence, war, poverty, diseases and waste of human potential. In the case of Nigeria, the so-called Giant of Africa, the opportunities for greatness were continually wasted due to foolish and selfish rivalries among our leaders. For instance Nigeria's prominent politicians and eminent leaders during the colonial days who courageously fought for the nation's independence instead of utilizing their learning, skills, talents, charisma, and vision to give the people of Nigeria hope, future and great leadership, they wasted the opportunities and their energies fighting against one another. Even at the dawn of the civil war, our leaders then had the opportunity to mend matters but because of greed, envy, pride, arrogance and lack of godly wisdom, they led the country into a three year civil war that claimed more than three million lives and created the animosity, bitterness and lack of trust that exist today among the variant groups that make up Nigeria. Nigeria leaders allow their ego, pride, personal and political vendetta, selfish ambition and envy to prevail against the wishes and welfare of the peoples of Nigeria. This is sad and unfortunate to be persistently denied of basic human, constitutional and divine rights.

Even today, we can see the same selfish tendencies being played out among our high-ranking leaders. For example the feud and rivalry currently going on between the president and his vice is potentially risky and can be a dangerous situation as the nations prepares for national elections in a few months. These prideful behaviors always impart negatively on the people and society at large. Even the U.S and world community have spoken out against the feud and disloyalty in the office of the presidency and the consequences it may cause as the nation prepares for national election in April. Not to mention the irrational behavior and corruption in the local and state government agencies. For instance, tell me if it made any sense whatever that a governor of a state is arrested overseas for money laundering while government workers in his state have not received any pay for several months. Most of the senators and governors have been involved in some form of bribery, corruption or money laundering while the vast majority of people in their states lack basic livelihood such as food, water, electivity and health care. And yet these men and women consider themselves leaders. These kinds of irrational leadership behavior and attitude are always due to pride, ego, selfish ambition, arrogance and lack of godly wisdom. It is worldly, foolish and devilish leadership.

The mentality of most of our leaders today in Nigeria and in many African countries amazes me. Sometimes, I am compelled to ask whether African leaders have any sense at all. What makes them behave so irrationally and senselessly? The mere fact that some of them may be crafty, shrewd, well informed and highly educated does not make them good leaders. Otherwise how can someone justify the inept and corrupt leadership that is so prevalent everywhere in Africa today? Bad and visionless leaders have hindered and denied the people and countries of Africa from making any significant step toward progress. African leaders aspire to service for their own selfish interest, which is far from the basic obligations of leadership. To aspire to leadership is not a bad thing; rather it is an honorable ambition and a noble task. The Word of God says, "If any sets his heart on being an overseer (leader), he desires a noble task (1Timothy 3:1)."

Seeking to be a leader is an honorable ambition and a noble task. However, it requires wisdom, character, integrity, prayer, perseverance, passion, shared vision and strategy in order to lead others. Prayer is perhaps the key ingredient that holds all leadership together. Without persistent and passionate prayer life, you cannot be an effective leader. Time alone and team prayer is necessary for successful leadership. Certainly, prayer is important as you look toward the inevitable difficulties you will face as a leader. The times of personal and team prayer will strengthen and sustain your leadership. As a leader, you must make prayer the first act and true mark of your leadership. Prayer is the key to dynamic faith, strength, power, success and victory. It is a noble act and a divine habit that must cultivated in your life as a leader. Fervent prayer of godly leaders will accomplish the will of God on earth. As a leader, you must pray and seek for wisdom, discernment, understanding, knowledge, counsel and most of all delight in the fear of the LORD. That is my prayer and my long life cry for leaders of our beloved country Nigeria.

## OUR LEADERS NEED GODLY WISDOM - POLITICAL BENEFITS - PART II

In part one; I dealt with wisdom, the kinds of wisdom and the source of true wisdom. In this part two, I will examine the benefits of godly wisdom focusing primarily in this piece on the political benefit of godly wisdom.

Barely two months before the national election, the EFFC selected list, INEC signs of incompetence and the political maneuvering in Nigeria begs to ask the question whether there will be any genuine national elections in April 2007. The election atmosphere does not portray any seriousness at all, rather a situation of harassment, manipulation, violence and disorder. The candidates for various offices are not holding any visible campaigns to articulate their agenda and strategies to accomplish them. There are no plans to conduct any debates among the candidates especially those running for high offices such as senatorial, governorship and presidency. Rather the whole political climate is in disarray because of EFFC list, which its main purpose is to cause confusion.

Even though EFFC list is admirable, because many names in that list are justified; however it does not contain certain names of people well know by many Nigerians for their financial crimes such as money laundering, fraud and embezzlement. Mr. Ribadu has done a good job so far but this list reveals the weakness of EFFC and clearly shows that it is not entirely an independent commission but a creation of President Obasanjo to threaten the little dogs and those in his bad book. The April election is at risk as well as the security and unity of Nigeria. As I wrote in the past, President Obasanjo's legacy will be measured by the manner in which he transitions the next civil government after May 29. His popularity among the Western powers today was earned because of his courageous effort to transfer power from the military to civilian government in 1979. He still has time to redeem himself of any mistakes before May 29. I hope he avoids the terrible mistake made by his friend General Babangida. Today, people do not even remember the billions IBB stole from the national treasury anymore, Nigerians tag him today for his unwise and undemocratic decision to cancel the presidential election won by Alhaji M. K. O. Abiola, who happens to be his good friend also. I am afraid that the same trick and tendency are being staged out in this dispensation as well. Third term agenda is still alive and well. The people of Nigerian must reclaim their destiny through this election. After all in democracy, the real power belongs to the people not the government.

What is then the problem with our leaders? Does it mean that our politicians are incapable of governing? Do I want to agree with the National Association of Resident Doctors (NARD) that has recommended psychiatric tests for politicians jostling for public offices in our country? The problem with that recommendation is the culture of corruption that is so rampant in our society today. A two-year-old child cannot even be trusted nowadays in Nigeria. The psychiatrists can take huge bribe from the candidates and certify them as mentally competent. Unless, we have to use foreign psychiatrists but that will be a slap to well trained and qualified Nigerian psychiatrists. Or do I want to agree with Mr. Temple Chima Ubochi who seems to suggest in his article: Nnamdi Azikiwe International Airport, Abuja: A beauty in the Savannah whether we should invite foreigners to govern us again. That will also be a big insult to the capable and qualified Nigerians at home and abroad as well as those who fought for our independence 47 years ago. And what shall we call that: post -colonialism or what. Already, we are in neocolonialism since we can't think for ourselves and the biased policies of the Western powers continue to exert its influence over major social, moral, economic and political life of the people of Nigeria.

I do not believe that Nigeria lacks men and women, who can lead. We have many of them. What we lack is the character and wisdom to lead morally, courageously and compassionately. Mr. Akintokunbo A. Adejumo, in his powerful and passionate article: Corruption and the Nigerian mentality boldly and truthfully stated that Nigerian leaders hate Nigeria and Nigerian people. He is right. We do not like ourselves. And the primary reason is because our leaders do not have any reverence for God. Nigerian politicians do not understand the divine dimension of leadership. They do not understand that leadership is a divine duty. They do not understand that God is the ultimate authority and that one-day they will give account of their stewardship before Him. Our leaders have refused to understand this; that one day they will give an account before God of the atrocities they committed against those entrusted in their care. Secondly we are greedy, corrupt, afraid and selfish. In a nutshell, our leaders do not have godly wisdom.

I have written in the past about the need for national core values. Nigeria as a nation does not have any value system primarily because of our history and the variant groups that make us up. Nigeria is not as diverse and complex society as the U.S that has over 191 nationals and hundreds of ethnic, cultural and tribal peoples that makeup the United States of America. Yet, everyone of them adhere to the core-values such as the right to life, work, family, faith, justice etc that enables the citizens and residents alike to build character, integrity, civility, godliness, responsibility, accountability, stewardship, hard work and patriotism. That does not mean that every one in the U.S is a saint. There is no saint anywhere as Dr. Femi Ajayi used to say. I can only vouch for one, the late mother Teresa. However, lawlessness do not go unpunished in any civilized society unlike in Nigeria, where an attorney general of the Federal Republic was murdered in his home few years ago and up till now, no one has been convicted for the crime. Not to mention situations where some individuals have terrorized an entire state and commit all manners of atrocities and still walk freely in our society. Something is wrong in our country or that we are just a lawless people. Educated and civilized society cannot continue to live this way especially in this 21st century. Even the animals are getting better organized and sophisticated in their kingdoms and political life than some of us in the so-called third world countries. Enough is enough. The urgency to create a fair and equitable system or whatever you want to call it is now otherwise; the unity of Nigeria is at stake. For those who play presidential parrot for this government and claim that everything is peaceful and serene should check their history records and also read the United States intelligence report on Africa and especially on Nigeria.

Why do our people, politicians and those in leadership positions behave irrational and awkward? The answer is found in God's Word for mankind. Listen to the Apostle Paul as he writes, "For the message of the cross is foolishness to those who are perishing, but to us who are being saved it is the power of God. For it is written: "I will destroy the wisdom of the wise; the intelligence of the intelligent I will frustrate." Where is the wise man? Where is the scholar? Where is the philosopher of this age? Has not God made foolish the wisdom of the world? For since in the wisdom of God the world through its wisdom did not know him, God was pleased through the foolishness of what was preached to save those who believe. Jews demand miraculous signs and Greeks look for wisdom, but we preach Christ crucified: a stumbling block to Jews and foolishness to Gentiles, but to those whom God has called, both Jews and Greeks, Christ the power of God and the wisdom of God. For the foolishness of God is wiser than man's wisdom, and the weakness of God is stronger than man's strength (1 Corinthians 1:18-25).

In this prophetic passage, the Apostle Paul informs us that the message of the good news not only involves the truth, wisdom but also the active power of God to transform lives and redeem people from the power and bondage of sin. Sin is the root cause for poor behavior, selfish lifestyle, corrupt, and inept leadership today. However, the Apostle goes on to say that the wisdom of the world is a wisdom that excludes God, emphasizes human self-sufficiency, makes humanity the highest authority instead of God and refuses to recognize God. The Jews looked for miraculous signs and yet because of their blindness, they could not see Jesus. The Greeks looked for human wisdom and undermined the wisdom of Christ. Their human wisdom God calls foolishness, for through it human beings have failed to find the truth, peace, order, happiness, and genuine prosperity. In verses 25-29, The Apostle Paul emphasizes that God's standard and values are different from those accepted by this world. God is now showing the world and their leaders that their wisdom and standards are not working through the monumental hopelessness, poverty, diseases, hatred, and violence, social, moral and political problems beseeching mankind in this universe.

I cannot totally ignore or negate worldly wisdom. Human wisdom has some merit in leadership; however, to lead wisely, courageously and compassionately, leaders must rely heavily on God. To lead people is the highest and purest form of leadership. Leading people is more than being a CEO or president of a country. It goes beyond that. As a leader, you are entrusted with people lives, aspirations, hopes, dreams, and desires. A leader is not only required to empower people, but a leader also manages the enormous talents, skills, and abilities in them. Essentially, we are talking about people's spiritual abilities and natural talents. It will take a visionary and godly person to lead wisely in order to harness the enormous potential that lies in every human being. It would take godly wisdom, passion, courage, compassion, character and emotional intelligence to lead, influence and develop the enormous talents that lie within each and every person. It does not mean that a leader wouldn't make mistakes. Great leaders always do however, one thing is certain; they always lead people to achieve success if not their fullest potential. Great and wise leaders will always work hard to minimize and possibly eliminate poverty, hardship, suffering, pain, corruption, violence, wars and death under their leadership. Wise leaders always work hard to provide an environment in which people subject to their influence can flourish and fulfill their God given potential. That is what great leadership is all about and it is going take godly wisdom and character. In our country today, it is not the case rather millions are hopeless and thousand die each day from starvation, disease, poverty, crime, violence, ethnic and tribal hatred, witchcraft, and most especially because of corrupt and poor leadership.

**Benefits of Wisdom**

What is then the benefit of godly wisdom in leadership? People must understand that God is interested in every nation within the earthly realm. The earthly kingdom is the Lord's and He is governor among the nations (Psalms 22:28). God has plans, purposes and blueprints for every nation and peoples of this planet. The Word of God according to the writings of King Solomon, Prophets Isaiah, Ezra and others teach us that godly wisdom in leadership brings Peace, Favor, Wealth, Happiness, Good Justice, Power, Safety, Protection, Blessing, Prosperity, and Respect to people and nations. Therefore, there are social, moral, economic and political benefits of godly wisdom.

Let us examine first the political benefit of godly wisdom in leadership. In First Kings 10:23-25, the Bible tells us that King Solomon was greater in riches and wisdom than all the other kings of the earth. The whole world sought audience with King Solomon to hear the wisdom God had put in his heart. Year after year, everyone who came brought a gift - articles of silver and gold, robes, weapons and spices, and horses and mules (1 Kings 10:23-25). In that same chapter, we read that the powerful Queen of Sheba of Ethiopia when she heard of the fame of King Solomon and his relation to the name of the LORD, she came to test him with hard questions. Arriving at Jerusalem with a very great caravan - with camels carrying spices, large quantities of gold, and precious stones - she came to Solomon and talked with him about all that she had on her mind. Solomon answered all her questions; nothing was too hard for the King to explain to her When the Queen of Sheba saw all the wisdom of Solomon and the palace he built, the food on his table, the seating of his officials, the attending servants in their robes, his cupbearers, and the burnt offerings he made at the temple of the LORD, she was overwhelmed. She said to the King, "The report I heard in my own country about your achievements and your wisdom is true (1 Kings 10:1-6).

For those who are quick to write this off as a six thousand years old event, please understand that these kinds of visits are still relevant today and happen all the time. In fact one of the major duties of any nation's president is to receive other heads of states for talks on economic, trade, defense and political concerns. In our modern time, the White House receives more heads of states than any other government house in this world today. The question that we can ask ourselves: why do most world leaders and government officials come to Washington DC all the time to seek for helps and answers to their political problems?

Does it mean that the man at the White House is smarter than them? Not necessarily but we will answer that question later and cite examples using great American presidents such as Abraham Lincoln, Ronald Reagan, Bill Clinton or even the current president now for their various and respective contributions to the American society and world at large.

The passage above is loaded with political insights that doing detailed exegesis may take up few more pages. Rather let me briefly examine the highlight and significance of the Queen's visit. We read that when Solomon became the King of Israel at the age of 20, one of the things he did despite his family heritage and wealth was to ask God for wisdom to govern the people of Israel (1 Kings 3:7-9). Because of his humble request, God gave him what he requested and also added riches and honor to enable him govern the children of Israel effectively, efficiently and excellently. In chapters three and following, we read of King Solomon's demonstration of wisdom in his skillful leadership, cabinet of administrators, administration of justice, choosing of district governors, advisers and the construction of the Temple and Palace which was the highlight of his reign as King. His reign was so glorious that rulers came from all over the world to see his kingdom and seek his wisdom. One of those was the Queen of Sheba of Ethiopia. Her primary purpose in visiting King Solomon was to observe his wisdom and wealth. But she also came to seek answers for her questions and to discuss about trade and defense for her kingdom. She came to seek for political alliance, defense, trade and economic relationship. After the meeting and exchange of gifts, which is also common today, the Queen was highly impressed with Solomon's wisdom especially the adornment of the Kings Palace, services and the brilliance of his officials.

As I said earlier, such visits are common today and many of such visits occur at government houses around the world. And today the White House receives more world leaders than any other nation in our known world. It is on record that the four presidents named above have recorded more visits at the White House than any American president. Even though Abraham Lincoln served only one term from 1861 to 1865 and was assassinated in 1865 before his re-election, yet he remained the greatest of all the American presidents till date. He is comparable to King Solomon in many ways. First he was a devout man of God, who challenged the American people to read the Bible. In fact he always said and argued strongly that mere reading the entire Bible can give more knowledge than someone who obtained a bachelors degree from a university. He was a skillful leader who appointed godly officials in his administration, opposed slave trade, which he abolished in 1863, and fought for the unification of a divided country through his generous and compassionate reconciliation policies against the wishes of his republican party. He left a lasting influence on U.S. political values by redefining republican values and promoting nationalism and patriotism. During his time, many leaders of the world came to America, which opened up the massive migration of people to the U.S, which has continued till today. Also during his presidency the United States snatched from Britain and France their glory, which has remained until today.

Queen of Sheba went to Jerusalem about six thousand years ago because she needed answers for the social, economic and political problems confronting her kingdom. She returned home fully impressed and satisfied. Today many leaders who come to White House come not only to observe the riches, wealth and brilliant presidential advisers but many return to their country with fabulous financial, economic and trade packages.

Why is the situation in our country different? How many world leaders does ASO Rock receive? Frankly speaking, world leaders don't come because we can't give them anything. We cannot advise them because our advisers are ungodly, visionless and people of questionable character. And we cannot give them food because millions of Nigerians go to bed hungry every night. We cannot give them financial assistance because average Nigerian earns less than 130 Naira per day, which is equivalent to one U.S dollar. The ones that are coming now for instance the Chinese are buying up Nigeria and our leaders are getting huge benefits out of it.

King Solomon, President Abraham Lincoln and many other great leaders surrounded themselves with godly and wise advisers. The political benefits a nation gains when a president surrounds himself or herself by people with godly wisdom, character and courage cannot be overemphasized. The story and successes of Joseph and Daniel in Old Testament Scriptures clearly illustrates the political benefits of godly wisdom. Today's leaders must surround themselves by wise people not shrewd and crafty individuals but godly and compassionate human beings. Great leadership cannot occur when crooks, criminals and self-seekers cluster around the leader. Most of the men especially around our president today behave and talk like parrots. They are not advisers or ministers but presidential parrots who are quick to speak and most of the time they speak from the wrong side of the mouth. Their words are quick, hurried and harsh and most especially lack truth and wisdom.

It is my firm belief that every nation's president should surround himself of herself by genuine people of faith and wisdom. Any serious leader must seek for spiritual and religious advisers who have the capacity to tap into the mind and heart of God because to move in line with God's plans, purposes and political agenda for nations, one must know the mind of God. Today's politicians should seek advice from religious leaders who understand history and have prophetic insights about world events. Today's leaders must seek advice from spiritual leaders who have the capacity to tap into the glorious and powerful presence of God. They must seek guidance and protection from God through the special abilities of godly people who know how to access on timely basis into the heart of God not false religious and spiritual leaders who are self-seekers and who sacrifice their calling, mission and privileges for riches and worldly affluence. God wants to bless us politically. He reveals His plans, purposes and Will for peoples and nations through His servants (Amos 3:7). Let's not separate God from our political life.

## OUR LEADERS NEED GODLY WISDOM -PART III

In part one and two of this essay series; I dealt with wisdom, kinds of wisdom, source of true wisdom and the political benefits of wisdom. In this concluding portion, I will examine how to receive godly wisdom for leadership as well as pointing out some of the moral, social and economic benefits of godly wisdom.

But before, I will like to say that I found myself the last few weeks reflecting, cogitating, meditating, questioning and praying over the dark times in which we live. These are critical times for Nigeria, Africa and rest of the world. When I hear, read and see the sort of unimaginable events happening in the continent of Africa, I am compelled to ask what is wrong with Africa. Is this a curse, disobedience, ignorance or lack of wisdom? When I listen to Chief Adebibu's interview on Oyo politics and the Nigerian political history, watch as Alhaji Yar'Adua is flown to Germany to treat shortness of breath, read about Atiku's medical emergency to Britain to treat knee dislocation, listen to the feud between the president and his deputy, national treasury and PTDF looting, EFCC bulldog actions, the double standards of INEC not to mention the pandemic poverty, diseases, violence, conflicts, witchcraft, stannic worship and cultic association that prevail in our society today, I am forced to enter into this spiritual agony and serious dialogue with God the creator.

It is a proven fact that the continent of Africa was the point of origin for civilization including science and religion. It is also true that Africa is the motherland of all the people of color in this world. In fact it is often said though not proven that among every five black people around, one person is directly or indirectly a Nigerian. Therefore black people in every country on this planet earth expect Africa and especially Nigeria because of its size and massive natural and human resources she is endowed with to assume responsibility and provide leadership to a continent that desperately needs it. Instead, the continent that gave birth to civilization is now stagnated by poverty, hunger, starving children, refugees, and hopelessness, regional and religious conflicts.

The new Secretary-General of the UN, Mr. Ban Ki-Moon in his recent interview with BBC correspondent, Kwaku

Akyi-Addo said Africa would be his focus. "Two-Thirds of issues discussed in the Security Council are about Africa. Africa needs to overcome poverty, pandemic diseases and many regional conflicts, he said. He is right. Despite the billions and billions of U.S dollars that the world invest in the continent, Africa continues to lack basic necessities of life such as clean water, electricity, food, and drivable roads. Poverty, hunger, diseases, violence, destruction and death loom everywhere. Basic infrastructures are practically non-existent due to greed, corrupt and chaotic government leaders. In-fact most African leaders are not just autocratic, dictatorial, and tyrannical but still have colonial mentality. If not how would a forty-six year independent country like Nigeria justify for the medical emergency of Vice president Atiku to Great Britain to treat knee dislocation or that of governor Yar 'dua and a contender in the next presidential election being flown to Germany to treat shortness of breath. These events and many others reveal the sad truth about a people that is still not de-colonialized and a nation that has no trust or confidence in its hospitals, doctors and other infrastructures.

So for me, it is a terrible time of sadness, sorrow and of serious dialogue with the LORD. Like Prophet Habakkuk in the Book of Habakkuk Chapter 1:2-4, I have been asking God the following questions; "What and how long will it take to salvage the continent of Africa starting with Nigeria?" When will God do something about the evil, wickedness, poverty, diseases, hunger, violence, destruction, and injustice that are so prevalent in Nigeria today? Why does God allow these atrocities to go on unpunished or wait until the last minute of life to punish man's wickedness? Why does God allow the innocent, the voiceless, the women, the children and the righteous ones to suffer in the hands of wicked and corrupt leaders? After these series of questions, God answered by encouraging me to trust His wisdom and live by faith in His ways, regardless of the circumstances. He assured me that evil and wickedness must surely be punished. My justice is coming soon says God Almighty. If my people will repent and confess their heinous atrocities, I will heal the land and give them a new heart. I will also enthrone the righteous ones to lead the land. These righteous leaders will obey me and I will cause peace, prosperity and joy to come to millions of Nigerians again. The image, purpose, dignity and destiny of the nation will be restored around the world again says the LORD Almighty.

There is no doubt that godly wisdom can help the peoples of this world especially the black race to eradicate illiteracy, alleviate poverty and ultimately overcome other monumental burdens such as moral, social, religious and political problems. This wisdom can be received in the following ways:

By Asking. According to the Apostle James, the best way to receive godly wisdom is to ask God for it. The Apostle James commanded and encouraged every one aspiring to lead to pray for godly wisdom. He writes, "If any of you lacks wisdom, he should ask God who gives generously to all without finding fault, and it will be given to him (James 1:5). The Apostle James himself earned reputation for his great wisdom, insight, integrity, compassion and godliness as a respected leader in the early church and bishop of the church in Jerusalem. In fact during the Jerusalem Council debate in A.D. 49 in which a certain Jewish sect called Judaizers tried to destroy the church with their teachings which was contrary to the teachings and sound doctrine of the gospel message, it was the Apostle James who proposed a resolution that ended the debate and restored the unity, dignity and honor of the early church.

King Solomon realized the need for godly wisdom for leadership despite his physical attributes and family heritage when he asked God for wisdom, knowledge and discerning heart to lead the people of Israel (1 Kings 3:7-9; 2 Chronicles 1:10-12) In First Kings 5:12, we read that God gave Solomon wisdom just as he had promised him. He gave Solomon wisdom and very great insight, and a breath of understanding as measureless as the sand on the seashores. Solomon's wisdom was greater than the wisdom of all the men of the East, and greater than all the wisdom of Egypt... Men of all nations came to listen to Solomon's wisdom, sent by all the kings of the world, who had heard of his wisdom (1 Kings 4:29-34). During his reign as king every nation under the sun came to King Solomon for political, economic and strategic alliances. In the Book of Proverbs, which he authored, he wrote, "Wisdom is the principal thing; therefore get wisdom; and with all thy getting get understanding (Proverbs 4:7)." Here King Solomon makes it abundantly clear that godly wisdom is a very important ingredient of leadership as well as a key element for supernatural living. King Solomon applied godly wisdom to the economic and political benefits for his people; however he failed to apply the same wisdom in his personal life.

It is significant to note also that many great leaders of the past demonstrated that godly wisdom is the secret to great and purposeful leadership. The father of the American nation, Abraham Lincoln did not only abolish slave trade through the Emancipation Proclamation of 1863, but he applied his God-given wisdom to unite a nation and preserved the Union through a policy of reconciliation despite the apposition from his party. Rev. Dr. Martin Luther King Jr. inspired the United States of America and the world with his non-violent civil right activities and the famous "I have a Dream" speech, which electrified the entire nation to rethink of its segregation and enslavement laws. His powerful oratory and wise leadership freed an entire nation from hate, bigotry and self-destruction and gave millions freedom and hope around the world. Nelson Mandela an anti-apartheid activist and international icon of freedom defeated the apartheid regime of South Africa with wisdom and patience. He became the leader of African National Congress (ANC) while in prison where he quietly and patiently served unjustly for more than quarter of a century. He won the hearts of millions of people across the globe, which eventually led to the defeat of apartheid and dethronement of the racist regime of South Africa. Nelson Mandel became the first black president of free and rich South Africa. Within four years of his presidency, he introduced policies of reconciliation that led to the multi-racial democracy and prosperity that South Africa enjoys today. He is truly a global icon and great leader.

Many world leaders and thinkers who made significant impact and contributed immensely to world peace and prosperity like Franklin Roosevelt, George Washington, Theodore Roosevelt, Harry Truman, Albert Einstein, Winston Churchill, Charles De Gaulle, John F. Kennedy, Margaret Thatcher, Ronald Reagan, Pope John Paul II, Billy Graham, John Wesley, Watchman Nee, Mother Teresa, Mahatma Gandhi, Marcus Garvey, Toussaint Louverture, Nkwame Nkrumah, Bill Clinton etc were men and women of great insight and wise leadership. Even though some of them made personal mistakes, nevertheless, they lead with wisdom, discernment, compassion and courage. Their leadership inspired nations and produced social, moral, economic and political prosperity not only to their respective nations but also to the entire world. Most of these political and spiritual leaders and thinkers in their autobiographies claimed that it was that higher power that encouraged and empowered them to inspire nations and to serve humanity so richly.

Anyone aspiring to be a great leader must ask for godly wisdom in order to lead purposeful and successfully. Godly wisdom is the most precious gift that a leader can possess. Apart from prayer, wisdom is the most important ingredient of leadership. No one can lead effectively, efficiently, genuinely and compassionately without godly wisdom. As a leader, you can receive godly wisdom and leadership anointing simply by asking God in faith.

Another way to receive godly wisdom is by Fear of the LORD. As the writer of Proverbs extols, "The fear of the LORD is the beginning of wisdom, and knowledge of the Holy One is understanding (Proverbs 9:10)." To fear the LORD does not mean to be afraid or scared of God. It means to reverence Him and to have an attitude of awe before Him. It means to nurture a sense of humility before Him and to walk in obedience to His perfect Will and purpose for your life and leadership. To fear the LORD is to understand your divine responsibilities as a leader; to understand that leadership is a divine call, a duty and an enormous service, stewardship and sacrifice to humanity. To fear God means to realize that you are under a divine and higher authority knowing that one-day, you will give an account before Him. Such fear is based on the acknowledgement that God is a holy God, whose very nature causes Him to judge sin and wickedness. To fear the LORD is to regard Him with holy awe and reverence and to honor Him in everything because of His great glory, holiness, love, mercy majesty, justice and power. King David, in his reflections on God as creator and wise God explicitly stated, "Let all the earth fear the LORD; let all the people of the world revere Him. For He spoke, and it came to be, He commanded and it stood firm (Psalm 33:8-9).

True fear of the LORD will cause leaders to place their faith, trust, decisions, and actions in Him alone. Moses the greatest leader of the Jewish people experienced this aspect of the fear of God when he spent forty days and nights in prayer on behalf of the sinful Israelites. "I feared the anger and wrath of the LORD, for He was angry enough with you to destroy you (Deuteronomy 9:19). Daniel, one of the three Hebrew children taken in captivity in Babylon became the special adviser and the most trusted prophet to the Kings of Babylon and Persian empires. Daniel rose to become a great leader and statesman in a hostile culture because of his fear (reverence), commitment and faith in God. His wise advice and leadership caused King Nebuchadnezzar to become the most powerful kings at his time. Babylonian empire reached its zenith and became the center of world power and influence because of Daniel's great advice and wisdom.

Another powerful way to receive godly wisdom for leadership is by Favor of the LORD. Joseph, King Solomon, Daniel just to mention a few received knowledge and understanding of all kinds of literature and learning. Daniel and Joseph could understand visions and dreams of all kinds. In Daniel 2:23, Daniel thanks and praises God for giving him wisdom and power. Because of his godly wisdom, he became the spiritual adviser to King Nebuchadnezzar. King Solomon was gifted with extraordinary wisdom for leadership. However, the biblical character that stands tall in this area was Joseph the eleventh son of Jacob. Genesis 37:3, 4 teach that Jacob loved and favored Joseph more than all his children. Because of that his brothers hated him and looked for ways to deal with him. When they found an opportunity they sold him into slavery. The Medennites later sold Joseph as a slave to Portipher, an arm bearer of King Pharaoh. In all of Joseph's travails, the Bible says that God was with him. Joseph was later thrown into prison for an offense he did not commit. Joseph was a genuine man of integrity and would not sin against God. While in prison, God was still with Joseph. God was with Joseph in everything that He did (Genesis 37:21). To make the story short, Joseph went from being a slave and a prisoner to become the prime minister of Egypt and counselor to King Pharaoh. Joseph's sequence of life events from being a salve to prisoner and then prime minister of the most powerful nation then is an extraordinary event of divine nature, timing and perfect demonstration of God's favor on Joseph.

Examples of such people are many in our society today. But most of them have failed to acknowledge the hand of God upon their lives. Our current president is a beneficiary of enormous favor of God but I am afraid he trusts in man rather than God for his leadership obligations.

Godly wisdom for leadership can also be gained by impartation. Impartation can occur in several ways: by lying of hands, by prayer of blessing, by public acknowledgement and presentation before the people etc. Before Joshua became the leader of the children of Israel, Moses had personally prepared and trained him to become his successor. When Moses climbed Mount Nebo in the plains of Moab to meet with God in his final hour, he publicly charged Joshua to be strong and courageous. In Deuteronomy 31: 7-8, "Moses summoned Joshua and said to him in the presence of all Israel, "Be strong and courageous, for you must go with this people into the land that the LORD swore to their fore-fathers to give them, and you must divide it among them as their inheritance. The LORD himself goes before you and will be with you; he will never leave you nor forsake you. Do not be afraid; do not be discouraged." Now Joshua the son of Nun was filled with the spirit of wisdom because Moses had laid his hands on him. So the Israelites listened to him and did what the LORD had commanded Moses. (Deuteronomy 31:7-8; 34:9).

This personal and public act of affirmation of Joshua before the people made the leadership transition smooth and unambiguous. Joshua was encouraged and empowered to face the daunting task of conquering the giants in the land of Canaan and settling more than three thousand Israeli families in the land of Canaan where they lived in peace and prosperity. Joshua was a powerful leader because Moses mentored him. But most importantly he was a powerful leader because he was a godly man. When faced with risky business decision, the godly leader must look to God in prayer and courage to make the right choice. A joyful and peaceful transition of leadership will encourage, empower and challenge the new leader to perform well. Leadership transfer doesn't have to be your son, daughter or family members. A leader must be chosen based on preparation, training, ability, integrity and especially by the guidance and direction of the Holy Spirit of God. Wisdom can be tangible in that genuine prophets of God can impart wisdom by laying of hands on the leader. The same sources of courage and wisdom that empowered Joshua are available today for any leader who will accept them.

Studying and meditating on the Law of God is another way to gain godly wisdom. Joshua had been an intimate and faithful assistant to Moses during the forty years desert wandering. As one filled with the Holy Spirit, he has been commissioned as Moses successor. But immediately after the death of Moses, Joshua did not ascend the throne as someone who had worked with Moses for forty years and more. He wanted God's assurance and empowerment. In Joshua 1:1-9, the Lord basically assures Joshua that He will be him as He was with Moses. He told Joshua, "be strong and very courageous. Be careful to obey all the laws my servant Moses gave to you; do not turn from it to the right or to the left, that you may be successful wherever you go. Do not let this Book of the Law depart from your mouth; mediate on it day and night, so that you may be careful to do everything written in it. Then you will be prosperous a successful. Have I not commanded you? Be strong and courageous. Do not be terrified; do not be discouraged; for the LORD your God will be with you wherever you go (Joshua 1:5b, 6-9)." Here is a classical passage that gives the secret to successful life and great leadership. We have to remember that Joshua was one of the twelve spies sent to survey the land of Canaan. Despite the giants he saw in the land of Canaan, he came back with good report and confidence that the Israelites will defeat those giants.

The Bible is the Word of God. It is our infallible authority on life and leadership. It contains the mind of God, the plans, purposes and destiny of God for mankind. It is our guide to life and our road map to experience genuine joy, prosperity, happiness, success and life everlasting. Spiritual instruction must be critical to any leadership learning and development. Devotion to the LORD should not be an option but a necessary requirement for leaders of today. The prophet Ezra devoted himself to the study and observance of the Law of the LORD, and to teaching its decree and laws in Israel (Ezra 7:10). In verse 25, "And you Ezra in accordance with the wisdom of your God, which you possess, appoint magistrates and judges to administer justice to all the people of Trans-Euphrates, all who know the laws of your God. And you are to teach any who do not know them. As leader, I encourage and challenge you to read it slowly, frequently and prayerfully, because those who truly study the Scriptures and law of God will be successful, prosperous and successful for they will possess the wisdom to live righteously and achieve God's goal for their lives and leadership.

To conclude, most leadership authors and experts agree that wisdom is a key ingredient for leadership success. Both secular and spiritual leaders also agree that wisdom is perhaps one of the greatest leadership qualities. And the wisdom I am talking about is not human wisdom but godly wisdom. It is divine wisdom, which deals more with obedience rather than ideas. I believe that wisdom for leadership is a great leadership trait perhaps more valuable than competence, charisma and even compassion. It is comparable to character, honesty and integrity. This wisdom is a container of prudence, understanding, discernment, discipline, insight, knowledge, discretion, guidance, instruction, faithfulness, sound judgment, humility, justice, and diligence. Leadership decisions must be made based on carefully thought and reliance on God. Decisions and issues that impart our corporate existence cannot be made based personal feelings, ideas or with biased minds. It must be made with complete dependency on God. God's plan, purpose and Will for all us are always good. His idea and strategies are always good and successful. Jesus showed us that godly wisdom is an essential ingredient of great leadership. He was a man of wisdom and discernment.

Anyone aspiring to lead in any fashion must ask for higher wisdom. Divine wisdom is the most precious gift that a leader can possess. The spirit of wisdom and anointing are necessary ingredients in order to maximize the leadership potential that lies inside each and every one of us. We must exhibit keen insight and foresight about decisions that impact life and destiny. As leaders, we must thought things carefully and consult God regularly in prayer before making important decisions. We must pray regularly to God especially when confronted with tough decisions. We must show extreme caution in all of our decisions, activities and actions. Wisdom is the sustained application of skilled thinking to life. No one can be wise without thinking carefully and thoroughly. God requires us to think and reason carefully. We cannot achieve any genuine peace, joy and true prosperity in this world without godly wisdom. Effective leadership, wise leadership, godly leadership requires careful thought and reliance on God. As a leader, you must pray and seek godly wisdom and most importantly delight in God. That is my prayer and my long life cry for leaders of our blessed country Nigeria.

## REBRANDING NIGERIA – ELEVEN KEYS FOR RESTORING NIGERIA'S IMAGE

Paper Presented at the Symposium organized by Alliance of Nigerian Organizations in Georgia (ANOG) to mark Nigeria's 46th Independence Anniversary

*"Nevertheless, I will bring health and healing to it; I will heal my people and will let them enjoy abundant peace and security. I will bring Judah and Israel back from captivity and will rebuild them as they were before. I will cleanse them from all the sin they have committed against me and will forgive all their sins of rebellion against me. Then this city will bring me renown, joy, praise and honor before all nations on earth that hear of all the good things I do for it; and they will be in awe and will tremble at the abundant prosperity and peace I provide for it.'"*
*(Jeremiah 33:6-9).*

*"If my people, who are called by my name, will humble themselves and pray and seek my face and turn from their wicked ways, then will I hear from heaven and will forgive their sin and will heal their land" (2 Chronicles 7:14).*

### GREETINGS AND INTRODUCTION

Your Excellency, coordinator, moderators, fellow panelists, distinguished ladies and gentlemen, let me begin by thanking God, our heavenly Father who has made it possible for all of us to be here this very morning. I want to salute and welcome His Excellency, Dr. George Obiozor to the United States of America. I pray that you will enjoy your service in this great nation. I thank Dr. Femi Ajayi and the organizers of this special symposium. Dr. Ajayi, your commitment, service, sacrifice, dedication and desire to see Nigerians in Diaspora rise up to the challenge of nation building is unprecedented. I also like to thank my fellow panelists. I feel specially honored to participate in this important dialogue with all of you. And thank you distinguished guests for coming.

## PRESENT SITUATION IN THE WORLD

Paul Marshall, a victim of his own rage, wrote many years ago, "We live in a world of cynicism, cruelty and corruption. We live in a world that is insecure and full of uncertainties. While, the Western rich nations are threatened with terrorism, chemical, biological, and nuclear weapons, social and moral degradation; the continent of Africa is ravaged with poverty, ethnic hatred and strife, tribal and religious wars, crime, cultism, violence, social apathy and moral insanity, poverty, corruption, greed, lawlessness, injustice, political instability, spiritual bankruptcy and immoral sexual act and transmitted diseases that have left thousands of children, young women and men dead and yet Nigerian politicians remained immobilized and unconcerned.

Today, most of you if not all will agree with me that the situation in Nigeria is not fun. What we are reading, hearing, seeing and experiencing in our lovely nation today is sad, sordid and shameful. It is not only a national disgrace but also an international embarrassment. So we are gathered here this morning to have a dialogue:

Restoring Nigerian Image to mark the 46<sup>th</sup> independence anniversary of Nigeria and to welcome His Excellency, Ambassador Dr. George Obiozor to the United States of America. There is no that Nigerians need a dialogue like this one even in the national and international setting. Nigerians in Diaspora must come together and have a dialogue about the future of our country. We must have the courage to look each other in the eye and honestly decide what kind of country we want. We must make a decision whether we want to live as one people or separately. We must decide whether we are courageous enough to pursue God's ordained destiny together like ants do or separately like wolves. We must stand up as one people and refuse these carnal, cruel, idolatrous, ruthless, visionless, malicious and murderous people over the affairs of our lovely nation – Nigeria. We must muster courage, standup against this brutal, ruthless and murderous leadership that have taken control of the destiny of God's children. We must stand up and refuse and reject this visionless and satanic leadership.

Nigeria does not obviously lack courageous men and women who can lead nor does she lack the resources, manpower, skills, talents, natural and physical resources to turn around deteriorating economic situation, create jobs, provide good healthcare, and sound education for its citizens, develop and build infrastructure, restore order, confidence and hope. What is lacking is a strong, courageous and moral leadership that is transparent in its private, domestic, public and foreign responsibilities. Dr. Joseph Nanven Garba said it best in his book: Fractured History, Elite Shifts and Policy Changes in Nigeria,

"Nigeria, to my mind, does not lack real men and women. The ingredients for creating a formidable nation exist. What is lacking is leadership with the political will and the selfless dedication to galvanize the entire nation." Africa's problem is not economic, political, social, cultural or even moral but a leadership crisis. Chinua Achebe in his book entitled: The Trouble with Nigeria, writes, "The trouble with Nigeria is simply and squarely a failure of leadership." Other noted Nigerians and Africans at motherland and abroad have also blamed the dramatic poverty, ignorance and moral decadence in Nigeria to leadership corruption.

I would never forget in 1996, when I had the opportunity to meet with Mrs. King at the Kings Center. When she noticed my accent, she asked me, young man where do you come from? Once I told her that I am a Nigerian, she told me how she admired the struggle, courage and leadership qualities of Nelson Mandela, Rev. Desmond Tutu and a few others. She also told me how she respected African leaders of the colonial era and how they challenged colonialism fighting for freedom to be independent. However, she wondered why Africa has not risen to its potential and why there is still enormous poverty despite abundance of human, mineral and material resources.

For instance, Nigeria as a nation has not enjoyed any genuine political peace and national economic prosperity since after the civil war despite enormous blessings that God has endowed upon her. In fact immediately after the civil war in 1970, Nigeria began to deteriorate rapidly following corrupt political leadership and military dictatorship that denied its citizen any sense of security and God given destiny. So far Nigeria has had only political and military hypocrisy, idolatrous religious system, extravagantly indulgent with corrupt judicial system and oppression of the poor. In short, Nigeria's leadership at all levels has failed to fulfill its divine obligations.

So the question today is how and what do we do especially Nigerians in Diaspora to restore our country's image?

## RESTORING NIGERIAN IMAGE
What does the phrase "Restore Nigerian Image" means?

First, let us examine the word: "Restore." (1) It means to bring back into existence or use. (2) To bring back to a former or normal state. (3) To bring back to health or strength. (4) To put back to a former place or rank. (5) To give back.

Second, the word image means picture, copy, likeness, and reflection. The Bible teaches that God made us in His image (Genesis 2: 26-27). However, in this context it simply means "the impression that a country or corporation creates or tries to create through the mass media. When you put these two words together, we can conveniently say that "restoring Nigerian Image" simply means to bring Nigerian back to its former or predestined likeness, place, position, rank or even glory among comity of nations. The image that Nigeria presents today are not what God intended it to be. Our people are being denied of their dreams, desires and destiny.

We cannot talk about restoring Nigerian image without mentioning the other 'R's – repair, recover, rebuild, re-establish, renovate, return, renew, reinstall, return, reinstate, revive, rehabilitate.

**From a political perspective**, we are essentially talking about how to re-engineer and reform our systems thinking. Moses, Nehemiah, Reagan, Winston Churchill, Ronald Reagan, John Paul II, Gorbachov all reformed the systems thinking of their people.

**From a social perspective**, we are talking about rebuilding and reconstruction of nation building and infrastructure. Nehemiah rebuilt the walls of Jerusalem. The USA rebuilt the economy and social infrastructure of Europe after second war.

**From a religious and spiritual** point of view, we are truly talking about the root of restoration. We are in essence talking about regeneration, redemption, revival, reconciliation, and righteousness. Restoring Nigerian image cannot effectively take place without regeneration, redemption and revival of the soul of Nigeria and Nigerians. Genuine restoration of our nation cannot happen without repentance, forgiveness, justice and reconciliation, which come from God through His Son Jesus Christ. Revival must come and righteousness from God must rain on us for His divine mercy, grace and love to be bestowed upon all of us again like how Jonah was asked and sent to bring revival to the sinful city of Nineveh.

**Reconciliation** may be seen as part of a process of restoring a relationship gone awry, typically as the result of one party causing a rift. Theologically, it is righteousness from God and refers to God's redemptive activity in the sphere of human sin by which He in a just way puts us in a right relationship with Himself liberating us from the power of evil. The righteousness from God refers to His character as a righteous God and His activity in salvation. The righteousness from God comes to us through faith in Jesus Christ. God took the initiative to reconcile us to Himself by Jesus Christ. He delivered us from law, wrath, sin, and death – the tyrannies that hold humanity in check and brought us by faith in Christ into a peaceful relationship with Himself (2 Corinthians 5:18, 19; Romans 3:21; 5:10).

**Redemption** (Romans 3:24) is ransom by the payment of a price. The expression denotes the means by which salvation is procured namely by the payment of a ransom. Redemption denotes deliverance or emancipation. Redemption is a concept of a thing being redeemed, or restored in terms of its value. It typically refers to salvation, meaning an escape from ways of sinfulness, by paying a price (atonement), and acceptance of spiritual goodness.

**Regeneration** is the process by which men are given new hearts; that is, the process by which they are "born again", experiencing a "new birth". It refers to a radical change in which God brings individual from a condition of spiritual defeat and death to a renewed condition of holiness and life. God is the only one who makes this change possible.

Prophet Jeremiah and King David prayed and asked God to give them a new heart (Jeremiah 31; Psalm 55). After the great confession of King David in Psalm 51, God cleansed him and chose him as king of Israel and a man after His own heart. In Jeremiah 33, God gave the weeping Prophet "Promise of Restoration – (Jeremiah 33). Prophet Ezekiel challenged the house of Israel to: "Rid yourselves of all the offenses you have committed, and get a new heart and a new spirit. Why will you die, O house of Israel"? (Ezekiel 18:31) and in Ezekiel 36:26: God told the prophet that He will give you a new heart and put a new spirit in you; I will remove from you your heart of stone and give you a heart of flesh." God must give Nigerians new heart so that we can love God and obey Him. We must receive this divine heart so that we can have the ability and capacity to love each other and ourselves.

There must be a social, economic, political, religious and spiritual revival. We Nigerians must renew our covenant with God so that God can write His laws and decree in our hearts. As Moses received the law and entered into covenant relationship with God on behalf of the children of Israel, we must be willing to be sensitive to the Spirit of God for such a covenant relationship. God will not do anything without first revealing it to His servants and prophets (Amos 3:7). God is interested in all nations, "for the kingdom is the Lord's and He is governor among the nations (Psalm 22:28). God has blueprint for the politics and leadership challenges of every nation, tribe, tongue, kindred and people. Moses was not only a priest and prophet of God but a great politician and spiritual leader who brought the law, which formed the foundation of civil and criminal law in many countries today. He was used by God to bring the children of Israel out of captivity in Egypt. Moses led the children of Israel out of bondage, slavery and captivity from Egypt into the Promised Land.

# ELEVEN THINGS THAT WE MUST DO TO RESTORE NIGERIAN IMAGE

## 1. Restore the Honor and Dignity of the Family Institution

The family is the first and most important institution that God gave to mankind after creation (Genesis 2:24). The family is the most important institution on planet earth and yet it is taken for granted. The family is the foundation and bedrock of any society. It is the moral fiber of any civil society and that's why Satan is out to destroy it. Today, the family at war with anti-family and feminist movement groups who want to redefine the institution of marriage and family by advocating sex-same marriages. In United States, Canada and many European countries, anti-family agenda is strong, active and fighting hard to destroy the most important institution that exist in the entire universe. The same liberal agenda is also reaching Third World countries. Recently, we were all astonished when the Changing Attitude Nigeria (CAN), which is unfortunately, an Anglican gay movement, protested and were seeking for freedom to express openly. God forbid. They were also asking for sex marriage recognition like their counterparts here in the West. Thanks to Almighty God, Obasanjo's government stood firm against their request, which is an aberration and abomination before God. If nothing, God will reward him for his courageous leadership against this nonsense sex-marriage request by CAN. Imagine if they had succeeded to have their way and then allure the jobless

384

youth into this unholy life style, managing the consequences of illegal sexual lifestyle and other kinds of sexual transmitted diseases and illnesses would have been monumental.

Why is the family under attack and continuously being assaulted by these propagandistic movements? What are some of the causes of this satanic assault against the family? Why is the family, God's most important institution for a moral and civil society is ravaged by sin, violence, idolatry and sexual immorality? The major reason is the lack of strong, courageous and authentic fathers. As our society erodes into social and moral degradation, honest, wise and godly fathers are hard to find. When God created Adam and later gave him Eve as wife and companion, He consecrated them as a family, blessed them and empowered them to multiply. They were to bring glory to God by fulfilling the divine purpose for their creation, which is to build strong homes and raise godly children. But they sinned and the consequences of that sin on humanity are still felt today.

For instance today, we see that fathers have abdicated their place as the spiritual head and leader of the home. There is no doubt that while mothers have leadership influence over their children, fathers are called to exercise leadership authority in the home. In-addition, fathers have ceased to be the spiritual leader in the home. Many fathers have unbelief and unwavering faith in God who gave man the gift of fatherhood and divinely appointed him to be the priest of his home. Husbands are also treating their wives as possessions rather than persons to love, serve, protect and provide for their needs. We have neglected and taken our wives and children for granted in order to pursue material wealth, political powers and cultural relevance. Fathers as well as mothers wrestle against sinful tendencies and selfish desires. A lot of fathers nowadays compete with their wives in leading the home and making money and as a result many marriages end in divorce. These kinds of cases are becoming rampant among African families here in USA even though it is not our culture and pattern of life. We must revise this trend and restore the purpose and dignity of the family.

## 2.  Restore the Glory and Power of Religious Institutions

What we have in the church today is spiritual capitalism. Despite the challenges of social apathy, moral degradation and spiritual ignorance, the church of Jesus Christ has remained powerless and inactive while people perish everyday. Christianity must restore its credibility. Today, church leaders are building million dollar buildings and temples where the presence of God is lacking. Satan himself inhabits most of these buildings. Where there is presence and glory of God, there should be His power and His power will destroy sin, wickedness, witchcraft and all manners evil. Church leaders must restore their confidence, trust and credibility.

Spirituality is the act of attaining wisdom, grace and presence of God within us. But what we have today in most of our churches is religious teachings that are totally inconsistent with the Word of God. What we have today is pragmatic psychological philosophies and metaphysical powers to attaining success or solving spiritual problems rather than a sound exposition of God's Word. Religious hypocrisy, rituals, divination, astrology, sorcery, witchcraft, magic, and all manners of evil and satanic worship abound among the people. Greed, hatred, corruption, idolatry, jealousy and envy continue to be rampant among our people yet we have Evangelists, Bishops, Priests, Pastors and Prophets who claim to speak for God. They claim to be God ambassadors and representative of Christ on planet earth and yet the very people that God has entrusted into their spiritual leadership are dying and perishing in darkness and ignorance. They are only interested in gathering milk, honey and wealth from the people and then deceive them with satanic tongues and pronouncements.

Nigerian communities need a spiritual environment where our children can learn in order to grow morally, socially, economically, physically and most importantly spiritually. Our effort must be designed to lead them to have a personal relationship with Jesus as savior, to challenge them with the truth of God's Word, to help them to have a biblical world view that speak to their culture, to motivate them to have a kingdom vision, and to help them to grow in God's wisdom, knowledge, and discernment so that they can become all that God has created and called them to be."

I have also noticed that Christian and religious leaders shy away from public life and then stay on the side and complain. We cannot separate the church from community. Socially, economically, politically, there is no difference between the two. The only difference between Christians and non-Christians is the miraculous. Religious leaders must get involved in public. God did not only call to be an ambassador of good news but also to engage in the social, economic and political issues that affect His people. You are not only called to be a pastor, priest, prophet, bishop and what have you but to be patriotic and political. Moses was a priest and powerful leaders of the people. Samuel was a priest, Judge and King at the same time.

Katherine Harris, a US representative who is running for senate as in Florida said this recently, "If you are electing Christians, then in essence you are going to legislate sin,"

### 3. Restore the Responsibility of Civil and Governmental Institutions

What Nigeria need is a set of institutions that would enable them to effectively demand the very modest conditions the people deserve and subject all officials to full responsibility and accountability. However, given the levels of ignorance, ethics, loyalties, poverty, disillusionment and despair, absence of strong nationalistic, patriotic attitudes, and poor leadership, creating such conditions would be impossible. We must hold our politicians at levels of government accountable and responsible for their actions.

### 4. Restore the Vision of Governance, Transparent and Compassionate Leadership

Nigeria is in desperate need for genuine leaders, compassionate and courageous people to work together in order to salvage the horrendous unrest and poverty in the black continent. The challenge of leadership is to be strong but not rude; be kind but not weak; be bold but not bully; be thoughtful but not lazy; be humble but not timid; be proud but not arrogant; have humor but not without folly,"

– Jim Rahn, American author & businessman

## 5. Pursue and Restore Peace, Security and Stability through Genuine Repentance, Forgiveness ands Reconciliation

The greatest task of any government is to provide security. A president or leader of any nation will always want his or her people to live in peace and security. When the people do not enjoy security, leadership has failed at all levels - such social issues such as corruption, safety, order, security, ethnic and religious hatred. Nigerians must demand the federal government to introduce and implement policies to stop religious fundamentalism, violence and atrocities?

## 6. Restore the Beauty and Strength of our Diversity, Cultural, Ethnic, and Tribal Differences through a National Core Value System.

Our societal value today is unforgiving, conditional and self-centered. It focuses on desire, self-pleasure and lust, the very opposite of God's perfect way of life. Our way of life is Satan's pervasion. Societal change can only come by changing the way people think. We must demand leaders with great vision and mission - a vision that is embraced by all and a mission that is broad as well as brief and strategic with a strong value system that will drive the nations' priorities not personal priorities. Nigerians in Diaspora must establish core value system that will dictate every decision and determine the nations' priorities. More than this, we must have strategy and develop plans with formidable team to carry out the vision and mission for its citizens. Nigerians must not ignore or neglect the skills, resources and potential of its citizens no matter where they live or reside. If Nigerians in Diaspora want to make a difference, they must be willing to have the best of the best in their team and not their best friends, families, or tribal folks. It is time that we stand up and makes a difference. Our people are tired of status quo and mediocrity. If we fail to do so, history will tell and judge but more than any thing else, God will judge us also.

However there cannot be moral and courageous leadership without a well-defined set of core values that will shape the lives and especially those who are called to lead. Core values are constant and passionate beliefs that drive people lives, business decisions or nation's priorities. Core values determine and shape daily actions of people, business or government leaders. They are hidden motivations that dictate every decision and determine life's priorities. Vision, passion and purpose are driven by core values. Without core values or code of conduct, people, families, businesses or even nations will have a broken focus? Dr. Mike Murdock, one of the greatest wisdom teachers of our contemporary time said, "The passion of our daily routine is the hidden secret for our success, people fail because of broken focus." Daily routines are core values or value systems that drive and determine life's success. Daily routines determine and shape our daily actions.

The same is true of a nation. Core values ask the question, why do I do what I do? Developing national core values and the passion for why we as a nation do what we do will be the secret to our nations success. Well-defined strong national core values will not only contribute to our nation's success but also will also inspire people to reach their fullest potential, embrace good change, communicate what is important and enhance credible leadership. Core values are not only applicable to individuals or business organizations, families or churches, but also to nations, states and cities. Without a strong national value system no individual, family, church ministry, business enterprise or even a nation cannot be very successful.

### 7. Restore Tolerance of our Multi Religious, Spiritual, and Moral Difference

Religious intolerance, conflicts, spiritual bankruptcy and moral decay are also major challenges to our nation building. The diversity of cultural norms, religious beliefs and language barriers has created enormous problems for nation building. In fact religious challenges pose great threat to Africa's development. Muslims declare Africa the indigenous home of Islam and insist its sufferings result from white man's religions being forced on it. The realities that the Christian world in Africa faces: Africa is a battleground between Islam and Christianity as well as between African traditional religions and Christianity. In urban areas, the secularism versus Christianity conflict appears. Hindus, Mormons, Jehovah's Witness and Buddhists are active. Add the traditional hurling of the biblical based barbs by various Christian groups at each other, and you have an ideal environment for spiritual confusion which is the preferred working space of Satan, the Father of lies. Christians kill each other in Rwanda and Burundi and steal each other's churches and members elsewhere. Muslims kill Christians in Somalia and Sudan. Fetish priests put pythons in houses where Christian parents have had a new baby. African politicians and religious leaders must work together to ensure that Christians,

Moslems and paganisms become partners in this 21<sup>st</sup> century rather than enemies.

When will our religious leaders work together to educate these ignorant followers about tolerance and peaceful cohabitation? As human beings we do not grow in isolation rather we grow, develop and mature as people in the context of love, relationship and fellowship. And until we learn the cardinal principle of Islam and Christianity, which is forgivingness and reconciliation, we will never live in peace. Without genuine forgiveness and reconciliation, there cannot be unity and peace. Another cardinal truth of Christianity and Islam is love and without love, we cannot have genuine relationship. Relationship is the most vital aspect of life. Relationship is in fact the greatest human asset not oil or money, and business. Character, courage, love and relationship are the greatest assets of any faith and our Moslem brothers lack them in abundance.

8. **Restore and empower all Nigerians no matter their ethnic, tribal or religious beliefs who have the integrity, character, and capacity for Visionary Leadership**

The Bible says that, "when the righteous rule, the people rejoice; but when the wicked rule, the people groan (Proverbs 29:2). God established government to bring about peace and order as well as to provide opportunities for His human creation to discover and fulfill their God given desires and dreams through those who are placed in

392

position of authority. Rather people who occupy leadership positions today in government, business entities, families and even our churches and mosques seem not to comprehend the divine obligations of leadership. They appear to forget that the greatest task of the leader is to inspire, motivate and to help those under their power and influence to become all they can be. They do not understand that the primary goal of leadership must be to inspire people to live rightly and to enable them to accomplish their God-given purpose and mission on earth.

Nigerians must resist men and women who are intoxicated with power, wealth, fame and authority. We must reject visionless leaders. We must search out for Nigerians who are humble and ready to serve the people with love and compassion. We need people with wisdom, courage, and strength. We need men and women who show consistent credibility and godly integrity. Dr. Myles Munro, the guru of leadership development writes in his book Insights for the Frontline Leader, "True leadership cannot be divorced from the basic qualities that produce good sound character. The character of a leader should be one that commands respect from all, even his enemies. Leadership is born out of character and determination." Character is perhaps the greatest ingredient of pure leadership. Character is not about outward technique but of inner reality. We need men and women with such qualities: Character, courage, compassion, integrity but more than anything else the fear of God.

### 9. Restore Equitable and Fair Allocation of the Nations Natural and Human Resources Revenue

Today, we are witnesses of the renewed fight, revival and formation of new militant groups calling for peaceful separation because of unfair and unjust allocation of the Nations Natural and Human Resources Revenue. This similar call, demand and secessionist movement was made by former Major General Emeka Odumegwu Ojukwu in 1969 by is even louder today. Chief Ralph Uwazuruike, the leader of the revived movement for the actualization of the Sovereign State of Biafra (MASSOB) is strong, courageous and passionate about the movement he leads despite threats, imprisonment and killings of his followers by the federal government. Also Alhaji Mujaheeden Dokubo Asari, the fearless and outspoken leader of the militant Ijaw youth is also in custody for threatening to blow up the Idama Flow stations being controlled by the Chevron Nigeria Limited. He has persistently and passionately called for an independent state of Ijaw people and a peaceful separation of Ijaw people from Nigeria. The military dictator Abacha was able to silence the people of Ogoni after the brutal killing of Saro Wiwa, a man of high intellectual ability.

The Ogoni's were persecuted which led to the United States and Canadian government to grant them political asylum and refugee status into their countries. Today, Mr. Ledum Mitee is the leader of the Movement for the Survival of Ogoni people and he is very active and fighting hard for his people. The reason for all the anger, frustrations and fighting is because economic, political and social injustice is meted against the zones that are producing the wealth of the nation. President Obasanjo and his government have not done much to deal with leaders of these kinds of civil rights activists and freedom fighters like Alhaji Dokubo, Chief Uwazuruike and Mr. Ledum Mitee. A comprehensive economic, social, civil and judicial reform that will bolster job for the youth while providing path to economic prosperity must be pursued.

### 10. Restore Social, Economic and HealthCare System of our Nation through investment and development of basic infrastructure

Nigeria is a country where healthcare is epileptic. The basic necessities of life lack in abundance not to mention of sound medical care. Medical and sex education are practically at zero. The rampancy of HIV and AIDS cases in Nigeria today is as a result of an uncontrollable ring of organized prostitution of young Nigerian girls brought to Italy and other European countries in the early 1980's. Our government absolutely did nothing to stop them. Today, the society is reaping the severe consequences of such a sinful and greedy lifestyle.

### 11. Restore Freedom and Empower Nigerians to be Patriotic Citizens

There has to be patriotic decisions and passionate actions that determine and drive our nation's priorities. Leo Buscaglia 1924-1988, American Expert on love, lecturer and author said, "If we wish to free ourselves from enslavement, we must choose freedom and the responsibility it entails." The bible teaches that there are two kinds of freedom, Societal and Spiritual. The societal freedom is false, where man is free to do what he likes; the spiritual is the true where mankind is free to do what he ought" according to Charles Kingsley. Personally, I believe that neither freedom nor power will be granted without major struggle and sacrifice.

In 1950's Nigeria fought for independence from Britain. In 1960 Nigeria became independent and gained freedom to govern herself. Nigeria's independence did not come easy even though it was without bloodshed. It was granted due to the activities of eminent leaders like late Dr. Nnamdi Azikiwe, Chief Obafemi Awolowo, Alhaji Abubakar Tafawa Belewa, Alhaji Ahmadu Bello, Ernest Ikoli, H. O. Davis, Chief S. L. Akintola, Dr. M. I. Okpara, Solanke and Eyo Ita among many others. Since Nigeria gained societal freedom, she has not been able to enjoy national prosperity despite abundant natural and human resources. She has had many kinds of government – Unitary, Parliamentary, Military and democratic and yet without success. Despite her enormous human potential and abundant natural resources, the promises of these various governments have been a dismal failure. They have not kept their promises but floundered and left the Nigerian masses worse than when they were slaves under the colonial rule.

The root reason for the current situation in Nigerians is because we have not accepted and embraced the spiritual freedom that comes from God through Christ Jesus. The Bible teaches in Galatians 5:1, "It is for freedom that Christ has set us free. Stand firm, then, and do not let yourselves be burdened again by the yoke of slavery. We have been set free form the sin and have become slaves to righteousness. We have been freed from the bondage of sin, self, and Satan (Col. 1:13; Gal. 5:18-21; Acts 26:18). The Apostle Paul writes, "Now the Lord is the spirit, and where the Spirit of the Lord is, there is freedom (2

Corinthians 3:17). I think it is time to challenge and encourage Nigerians to embrace spiritual freedom and empower them to fight for the economic and political prosperity that have eluded them for so long now. I think it is time to form a national coherent core values that will give sense of patriotism and empower Nigerians everywhere to believe in themselves and their freedom in Christ. I think it is time for Nigerians to genuinely forgive one another before God or Allah or any other Supreme Being out there and bury our tumultuous and fractured history in order to restore our image again. Without genuine forgiveness and reconciliation, there cannot be unity and peace.

Human kind does not grow, develop and mature without relationship, fellowship and love. Relationship is the most vital aspect of life. It is the greatest human asset more than properties ands material things. Nigerian must seek genuine relationship with each other. Unity of purpose in doing things must be pursued. Unity produces treasured memories and enduring relationships. Both of them are needed for us to build sustained success. We must get rid of those who cause disunity among us no matter how talented and resourceful they may be. Jesus said that a house divided against it couldn't stand. Relationship and unity are essential to restore Nigerian image to its dignity and glory among the comity of nations.

Freedom is the true essence of living. It is in its true sense the quality of God, just as love, beauty, harmony, joy, abundance and peace are all extricable qualities of God. Freedom is the very nature of who we are. Like Nelson

Mandela said, "our path is to recognize freedom as a state of consciousness, not as a condition or circumstances. Nigerians must find that true freedom because it is in that freedom that we release our potential and fulfill our purpose on planet earth.

**FINAL WORDS**

The quest to reform, re-engineer and restore Nigeria image is possible and achievable if the leadership is committed to solid. Restoring Nigerian image and the reality of a new Nigerian can only come through energizing vision and dedicated act of wisdom, prayer and courageous leadership. For Nigeria to restore her dignity and glory among comity of nations, it must change its systems thinking, discoverer and energize her purpose. Nigerians must reject dubious, corrupt, greedy and ruthless leaders with dubious personal and professional life. We must hold them accountable, verify and validate their personal, professional and public life before elevating them to public service.

What we need are Nigerians who epitomize the true essence of leadership. Those who are wiling to sacrifice their life for the betterment of those they led. Remarkable, genuine, true, pure, moral, courageous, supernatural would not enough words to encapsulate such people. We need people who are willing to serve Nigerians in order to make it a better place and in the process made history and left a lasting legacy. This is my long life call and cry for Nigeria – a call and a cry for supernatural leaders - God led and Spirit empowered leadership.

The situation in Africa demands for leadership with

integrity and character and divinely called and appointed by God to deliver its people from the current satanic and demonic leadership oppression all over the continent. To achieve this goal, good African leaders must work together as one people of faith. They must be a people who understand the issues and how to build godly and strong value system and develop a continental passion that will inspire others to action. By so doing, they will salvage our generation that is being marginalized and wasted and then motivate people to embrace good change, to live their fullest potential, and thereby create and enhance credible future leadership reservoir.

Our true restoration must come from a genuine relationship with God and love for Him and for one another. However, we must understand that God's mercy, love and compassion always precede His justice. There can be no healing without justice and justice requires punishment. Even though not all of us are responsible yet all of are guilty.

I thank all of you for listening. God bless each and every one of you

In Love and Leadership,


*C. K.*
*Ekeke|* **Ph.D.**
**Leadership Wisdom Institute, Inc.**
**2 Chronicles 1:10-12**

# NOTES

1.  Donald C. Stamps and others.  The Full Life Study Bible – New International Version.  Zondervan Publishing House: Grand Rapids, Michigan, 1992.

2.  Chinua Achebe. The Trouble with Nigeria. Forth Dimension Publishers: Enugu, Nigeria, 1983.

3.  Joseph Nanven Garba.  Fractured History – Elite Shifts and Policy Changes in Nigeria. A Sungai Book: Princeton, N.J., 1995.

4.  Federal Government of Nigeria.  A Special Independence Issue of Nigeria Magazine October 1960 – Federal Government of Nigeria, 1960.

5.  http://www.nigeriaworld.com/

6.  http://www.onlinenigeria.com/

7.  http://www.motherlandnigeria.com/

8.  Annis A. Shorrosh.  Islam Revealed – A Christian Arab's View of Islam.  Thompson Nelson Publishers: Nashville, Tennessee, 1998.

9.  John MacArthur.  Terrorism, Jihad, and the Bible. W Publishing Group – A Division of Thomas Nelson Inc., USA, 2001.

10. Ibid. The Book on Leadership. Thomas Nelson Publishers: USA 2004.

11. Myles Munroe. Becoming a Leader – Everyone Can Do It. Pneuma Life Publishing: Lanham, MD, 1993.

12. Ibid. The Spirit of Leadership. Whitaker House: New Kensington, PA, 2005.

13. Henry and Richard Blackaby. Spiritual Leadership – Moving people on to God's Agenda. Broadman & Holman Publishers, Nashville, TN, 2001.

14. Mike Murdock. The Leadership Secrets of Jesus. Published by Wisdom International Inc., Dallas, Texas, 1996.

# ABOUT THE AUTHOR

Kingston Ekeke was born at Akwete, near oil rich city of Port Harcourt, Nigeria. He left for Italy in the late eighties at a very young age to study Accounting & Finance. After one year of graduate studies in Business and Economics at the University of Rome – "La Sapienza.", he worked for the Embassy of Nigeria of Nigeria.

In 1993, He came to United States to study for an MBA degree, but later received a call to ministry and began his seminary vocation at Luther Rice Seminary & University, where he obtained B. A. in Biblical and Theological Studies, M.A. in Ministry and Master of Divinity degree (M. Div.). He also holds a doctorate degree in Leadership.

Dr. Ekeke has served as Pastor and Associate Minister of Education and Leadership in various community Churches in Metro Atlanta area. He is multi-tasked - a theologian, technologist, thinker, and a passionate, motivational speaker and gifted writer. He is the founder of Leadership Wisdom Institute for training and mentoring young people for godly leadership. He is also an information technology consultant specializing in database and business intelligence technologies. He is the founder and president of Mcking Consulting and Technology Services, an e-business and database technology services company based in Douglasville, Georgia. He is an Oracle certified database professional.

He is an engaging minister and has a deep passion for moral, courageous and compassionate leadership. The central theme of his message is godly leadership. He is well known for his passionate biblical preaching and advocacy for godly leadership. He travels around the world ministering the power of God's empowered leadership. His writings are insightful, inspirational and prophetic that addresses the religious, social, economic and political issues facing mankind and especially the continent of Africa. Rev. Dr. Ekeke writes for Nigeriaworld and several other online magazines and a weekly contributor on Nigeria This Week with Black Television Network.

Dr. Ekeke is also listed in numerous biographical publications including Who's Who in America Universities and Colleges. He was the first black and foreign student to be elected student council president of Luther Rice Seminary & University, Lithonia, Georgia and was also the founding editor of Advisor, LRU magazine for student life. Rev. Dr. Ekeke presently serves as Rector at All Saints Anglican Church, Atlanta and spiritual adviser and consultant to emerging young leaders. He also serves on several boards including the Board of African Ministers Charter. He was the former president of Akwete National Association, USA Incorporated (ANA, USA Inc.), and serves as publicity secretary of Ndoki Association in North America (NANA, INC).

Kingston Ekeke is an ordained minister and an ambassador in the Kingdom of God. He is married to Nena, an Evangelist and prayer warrior. He is a husband and devoted father of two children – Chiedozie, a senior and Chisom, an 8$^{th}$ grader.

## ABOUT THE BOOK

Leadership Liability - A Clarion Call to Courageous, Compassionate and Wise leadership   is a collection of insightful, inspirational and prophetic essays, articles, and interviews being published in book form to commemorate Nigeria's Golden Jubilee independence anniversary.

Leadership Liability deals with the divine duty that leaders owe to their people and special insights and inspiration for leading wisely, morally, courageously and compassionately.  Leadership Liability seek to explain the responsibility of those elected, appointed or selected to lead and their divine duty and moral obligations to the people that chose or elected them.

Leadership Liability addresses the religious, moral, social and leadership challenges impacting not just Nigeria but also its indirect impact on other African and Western nations.  Leadership Liability is a call for moral and godly leadership.  It teaches the secrets for godly leadership.  The greatest need of this century is developing authentic, courageous, compassionate and wise leaders. Genuine Leadership is the greatest need of our time.  It will be perhaps the most important need of the 21st century. God kind of leadership is the only leadership that can lead our societies into a real and genuine change.

The reader will learn the biblical principles and wisdom for godly living and leadership. Leadership liability would be a timeless tool in your hand as a leader.

C. Kingston Ekeke, Ph.D.

NIGERIA'S GOLDEN JUBILEE INDEPENDENCE
ANNIVERSARY

LEADERSHIP LIABILITY

A Clarion Call to Courageous, Compassionate, and Wise
Leadership

SELECTED WRITINGS TO COMMEMORATE
NIGERIA'S 50th INDEPENDENCE

Author House, MN, USA

Rev. Dr. C. K. Ekeke - Selected Writings to Commemorate
Nigeria's 50th (Golden Jubilee)

Independence Anniversary

Book cover designed by Evangeline Agbogu